Zoltán Horváth (Ed.)

Central European Functional Programming School

First Summer School, CEFP 2005
Budapest, Hungary, July 4-15, 2005
Revised Selected Lectures

 Springer

Volume Editor

Zoltán Horváth
University Eötvös Loránd
Faculty of Informatics
Dept. of Programming Languages and Compilers
1117 Budapest, Pázmány P. s. 1/c, Hungary
E-mail: hz@inf.elte.hu

Library of Congress Control Number: 2006933759

CR Subject Classification (1998): D.1.1, D.1, D.3, F.3, D.2

LNCS Sublibrary: SL 1 – Theoretical Computer Science and General Issues

ISSN   0302-9743
ISBN-10   3-540-46843-9 Springer Berlin Heidelberg New York
ISBN-13   978-3-540-46843-1 Springer Berlin Heidelberg New York

Springer is a part of Springer Science+Business Media

springer.com

© Springer-Verlag Berlin Heidelberg 2006
Printed in Germany

Typesetting: Camera-ready by author, data conversion by Scientific Publishing Services, Chennai, India
Printed on acid-free paper   SPIN: 11894100   06/3142   5 4 3 2 1 0

Lecture Notes in Computer Science 4164

Commenced Publication in 1973
Founding and Former Series Editors:
Gerhard Goos, Juris Hartmanis, and Jan van Leeuwen

Editorial Board

David Hutchison
Lancaster University, UK
Takeo Kanade
Carnegie Mellon University, Pittsburgh, PA, USA
Josef Kittler
University of Surrey, Guildford, UK
Jon M. Kleinberg
Cornell University, Ithaca, NY, USA
Friedemann Mattern
ETH Zurich, Switzerland
John C. Mitchell
Stanford University, CA, USA
Moni Naor
Weizmann Institute of Science, Rehovot, Israel
Oscar Nierstrasz
University of Bern, Switzerland
C. Pandu Rangan
Indian Institute of Technology, Madras, India
Bernhard Steffen
University of Dortmund, Germany
Madhu Sudan
Massachusetts Institute of Technology, MA, USA
Demetri Terzopoulos
University of California, Los Angeles, CA, USA
Doug Tygar
University of California, Berkeley, CA, USA
Moshe Y. Vardi
Rice University, Houston, TX, USA
Gerhard Weikum
Max-Planck Institute of Computer Science, Saarbruecken, Germany

Preface

This volume presents the revised texts of lecture notes of selected lectures given at the First Central European Functional Programming School, CEFP 2005, held July 4-15, 2005 at Eötvös Loránd University, Budapest, Hungary.

The summer school was organized according to the traditions of the advanced functional programming schools. CEFP focuses on participants in Central Europe to involve more and more students, researchers and teachers from central/eastern European countries in functional programming. We were glad to welcome the invited lecturers and the participants: 20 professors and 48 students from 15 different universities and staff members of Ericsson Hungary. The intensive programme offered a very good environment and opportunity to present and exchange ideas in new topics in the field of functional programming.

The lectures covered a wide range of topics: new programming language concepts for subtyping, distributed computing, resource bounded computations, refactoring, verification, testing, generic programming of Web applications, the essence of dataflow programming, patterns, as well as industrial applications in Erlang.

We are very grateful to the lecturers, all excellent researchers in functional programming, for the time and effort they devoted to their lectures and writing the revised notes. The revised notes were each carefully checked by readers selected from among the most qualified available and then revised once more by the lecturers.

The Programme Committee members Rinus Plasmeijer and Kevin Hammond provided invaluable support in selecting the invited lecturers and referees, compiling the program and editing the proceedings.

Special thanks to Viktória Zsók, who did an excellent work in preparation and implementation of the summer school and managed the successful Erasmus IP application and reports. We would like to thank the work of all the members of the Organizing Commitee and the student volunteers.

The Web page for the summer school can be found at http://plc.inf.elte.hu/cefp/.

July 2006

Zoltán Horváth
Program Chair
CEFP 2005

Organization

CEFP 2005 was organized by the Department of Programming Languages and Compilers, Faculty of Informatics, University Eötvös Loránd, Budapest, Hungary.

Executive Committee

Program Chair	Zoltán Horváth
	(Eötvös L. University, Hungary)
Organizing Chairs	Zoltán Horváth and Viktória Zsók
	(Eötvös L. University, Hungary)
Organizing Committee	Zoltán Csörnyei
	Gergely Dévai
	Gáspár Erdélyi
	Hajnalka Hegedűs
	Róbert Kitlei
	Tamás Kozsik
	Ildikó László
	László Lövei
	Mónika Mészáros
	Gabriella Nádas
	Adrienn Olajos
	Zoltán Prokoláb
	Katalin Réti
	Csaba Seres
	(Eötvös L. University, Hungary)

Program Committee

Kevin Hammond	(University of St. Andrews, UK)
Zoltán Horváth	(Eötvös L. University, Hungary)
Rinus Plasmeijer	(Radboud University, The Netherlands)

Sponsoring Institutions

The summer school was supported by the European Commission's (Directorate-General for Education and Culture) SOCRATES/ERASMUS Intensive Programme (Grant no.: 45677-IC-1-2003-1-HU-ERASMUS-IPUC-2), the Hungarian National CEEPUS Office (via CEEPUS H81 Network) and by the Faculty of Informatics, University Eötvös Loránd, Budapest.

Table of Contents

Generic Editors for the World Wide Web

Rinus Plasmeijer and Peter Achten

Software Technology, Nijmegen Institute for Computing and Information Sciences,
Radboud University Nijmegen
{rinus, P.Achten}@cs.ru.nl

Abstract. In these lecture notes we present a novel toolkit to program web applications that have dynamic, complex behavior based on inter-connect forms. This toolkit is the iData Toolkit. We demonstrate that it allows programmers to create web applications on a level of abstraction that is comparable with 'ordinary' functional style programs. By this we mean that programmers can develop data structures and functions in the usual way. From the data structures the iData Toolkit is able to generate forms that can be used in a web application. It does this by making use of advanced programming concepts such as generic programming. The programmer need not be aware of this.

1 Introduction

The World Wide Web has become an important infrastructure for institutions such as universities, government, industry, and individuals to provide and obtain information from a wide variety of sources. The complexity of web sites range from simple static collections of HTML pages to advanced interactive sites with many interconnections and user feedback. In these notes we show a novel approach to program web applications that consist of an arbitrary number of forms with arbitrarily complex relations. As a typical example, we have constructed a *web shop* application for selling CDs. Fig. 1 contains a screen shot of this application. It displays a number of interconnected form elements, some of which are: *application browsing buttons* labelled *Home, Shop, Basket, OrderInfo* and the page to be displayed; *search fields* and the number of found and displayed items, as well as the range of selection browser buttons; *fill shopping cart* button, and *overview* of the most recently added item. In addition, it shows that there are also elements that are not related with forms, but rather with layout and make up. We consider these elements to be purely functionally dependent on the actual state of the forms.

In these lecture notes, we study web applications from the perspective of the functional programming paradigm. Key aspects that we pay attention to are the functional nature of a web application, exploitation of the expressiveness and richness of the type system, and the power of abstraction and composition. The iData Toolkit provides web application programmers with a means to express themselves on a high level of abstraction, without compromising the complexity of the applications. In contrast with the internal realization, the API of the iData

Z. Horváth (Ed.): CEFP 2005, LNCS 4164, pp. 1–34, 2006.

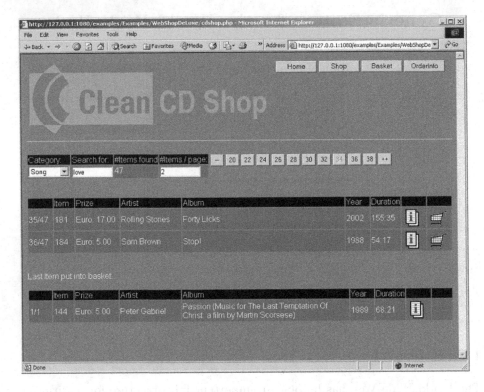

Fig. 1. A Web shop application, programmed with the iData Toolkit

Toolkit contains no advanced functional programming concepts: we deliberately have kept it as simple as possible. The most important advanced functional programming technique that is used to create the toolkit is *generic programming* [12,13]. We do not discuss the implementation, but focus on the application programmer instead. We have collected a number of examples and exercises so that the reader can obtain practical knowledge and insight of the toolkit.

We use the functional programming language Clean [19,20], version 2.1.1. Clean is a pure, lazy, functional programming language based on term graph rewriting. It has an expressive type system with support for *generic programming* [2], *dynamic types, uniqueness types, strictness types*, and more. The Clean compiler efficiently generates efficient code. For over a decade it supports desktop GUI programming with the Object I/O library. With this library its own IDE has been implemented, as well as the proof assistant Sparkle [8]. The Clean compiler has been written in Clean itself. We assume that the reader is already familiar with Clean and functional programming. The Clean programming environment can be downloaded for free from http://www.cs.ru.nl/~clean/.

These notes are structured as follows. In Sect. 2 we analyze the challenges that a web application programmer is confronted with. This analysis is independent of any programming paradigm. In Sect. 3 we provide one of the many possible answers in the context of the programming paradigm of lazy, strongly typed, functional programming languages. Having motivated our design decisions, we work out our solution with a number of case studies of increasing complexity and completeness of functionality in Sect. 4. Every case ends with a set of exercises that allow the student to practice his skills and understanding. Related work is discussed in Sect. 5. Finally, we come to conclusions in Sect. 6.

2   The Challenge...

When the World Wide Web was conceived by Tim Berners-Lee around 1990, it was intended to be a uniform portal for people to find information around the world [5]. Fig. 2 illustrates the 'classic' architecture with a simple *Message Sequence Chart*. A browser application (B) allows users to communicate with a web server (S). The web server retrieves the requested information that is stored somewhere on the server side. This information is encoded in HTML, which is interpreted and displayed by the browser.

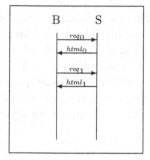
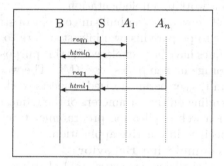

Fig. 2. 'Classic' W^3 **Fig. 3.** 'Contemporary' W^3

   The need for web sites with dynamic content soon arose after this simple scheme. One of the standards that emerged was the *Common Gateway Interface* (CGI). The key idea is that instead of the web server retrieving static web pages itself, it communicates with a bunch of applications that it executes that provide the requested information. In this way, the web server acts as an intermediary between the browser program and the CGI programs. This is depicted in Fig. 3. The collection of applications are labelled A_1 upto A_n. The dashed lines indicate that these applications are *executed on request*, and *terminate* after having produced the desired result. To the server, it is irrelevant in what system or programming language these applications are written. They can be generated by a wide variety of tools and techniques, such as general purpose programming languages, dedicated *scripting languages* such as php, Perl, or in a functional style, such as WASH/CGI. Complex web applications often consist of several dynamic applications, or separate scripts. This makes reasoning about their behavior and correctness difficult.

The architecture of the web leads to a number of *challenges* for web application developers:

1. **Cause and Effect**
   The specification of every interactive application must clearly and unambiguously prescribe the behavior of the application in case of particular user actions. It should be obvious that this behavior depends on the state of the application, as pressing the mouse button in an enabled button has an entirely different meaning than pressing it in a scroll bar.

   In traditional desktop GUI programming, both concepts of application state and user actions (*events*) have been well-defined. The state is partially determined by the underlying system (e.g. *widgets*, rendering environments, resources, customizable widgets), and partially by the application (think of data structures, variables with scope rules). The set of events is fixed by the underlying system (keyboard and mouse events, rendering requests, message passing events for customization purposes, and so on). This implies that it is clear (but not necessarily easy) how to map the specification of an application to a working implementation.

   The web has no built-in concept of state. This means that a programmer has to prepare his own infrastructure to realize a suitable state. Many techniques have been explored for this purpose: *cookies*, server side *database*, data storage in web pages, use XML. The web has a weak notion of event: forms can trigger parameterized requests to the web server to fetch new pages, depending on the parameters of the request. As a consequence, it is a challenge for a web application programmer to create a correct implementation of a specified interactive application.

2. **Accumulating Behavior**
   This challenge is related to 1. During execution, applications gather data. This data determines the future behavior of the application. Clearly, this requires state that is preserved during the run-time of the application. The web application programmer needs to make sure his data persists between invocations of his application.

3. **User Behavior**
   The web deliberately allows users great freedom in browsing through information that is available all over the world. Users bookmark links and visit them arbitrarily many times later. This implies that web applications can not assume that pages are always reached via a well-defined route. Users simply stop browsing by closing their browser program. This means that web applications are not closed-down gracefully as is the case with desktop GUI applications. These can decide what data should be stored persistently, and what should be garbage collected.

4. **(Dependent) Forms**
   The interactive parts of a web application are defined by *forms*. A form is a collection of primitive interactive elements such as edit boxes, check boxes, radio buttons, and so on. This is fairly similar to desktop GUIs. However, in a desktop GUI these elements can be considered to be objects that can

be manipulated by the application during run-time. Because the web lacks a built-in state concept, this can not be done with web applications. Instead, they need to be recreated every time a new page needs to be displayed. This becomes even more complicated when forms *depend* on each other, i.e. data entered in one form influences its own state, or also the existence or state of other forms.

5. **Separation of Model and View**
   Designing an attractive web application that is functionally complete is a difficult task. The maintenance of a web application may require either a change of its presentation, a change of functional requirements, or both. A good separation of presentation and application logic is important to reduce the maintenance effort. Changing the presentation of an application should cause at worst only minor changes in the application logic, and vice versa. Of course, this is not specific for web applications, but also applies to desktop GUI applications.

3 . . . A Functional Style Answer

In this section we rise to the challenges that have been presented in Sect. 2. Of course many people have already provided answers to these challenges in many different and excellent ways. We review related work in Sect. 5. In these notes we give an answer from the perspective of the functional programming paradigm. We first introduce the leading functions and types in Sect. 3.1. Having been exposed to the main elements of the iData Toolkit, we show how these elements provide answers to the challenges in Sect. 3.2.

3.1   Introducing the Leading Figures

In this section we introduce the leading figures of the iData Toolkit in a top-down style. Recall the way the contemporary web works (Fig. 3). A web application A may consist of several smaller scripts, i.e. $A = \{A_1 \ldots A_n\}$. Our view of the structure of a web application is depicted in Fig. 4. In our opinion, a web application A should be a single application. Of course, its *code* may consist of several modules, but the program as a whole is considered to be a single unit that is addressed by the web server as a single executable. In the functional paradigm, a program is a function. This is depicted as f in the diagram. Clearly, this f is in dire need of parameters if it is not to produce the same page at every invocation.

What is the type of f? Every interactive Clean program is a function of type *World → *World. Here, the type constructor World acts as an explicit parameter that represents the external environment of the Clean program. The *uniqueness attribute* * in front of it tells us that this environment can not be duplicated or shared: it is passed along in a single-threaded manner. This standard Clean style of passing along the environment explicitly is known as *explicit multiple environment passing*, and also as the *world-as-value* paradigm. However, this is

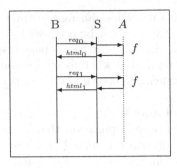

Fig. 4. The iData Toolkit W^3

not a very precise type. We need a type that expresses more clearly what the *purpose* is of a web application. In our view, the purpose of a web application is to provide the user with the illusion of an application that does not terminate between user actions, but instead can be regarded as a collection of objects that respond to his actions as if it were a regular desktop GUI application. Put differently, if it had a previous state of type HSt, then it must produce a new state of that type as well as a rendering in HTML of that state. This leads to the following type of f:

$$*HSt \rightarrow (Html, *HSt)$$

This type is connected with the type of an interactive Clean program with the following library wrapper function:

doHtml :: (*HSt → (Html,*HSt)) → *World → *World

The *arguments* of f come from the command-line. At every execution, the command-line contains a *serialized* representation of the current *state* of the application, as well as the *event* that has occurred. We show that in our view an event is a *change of the value of the state*. Put in other words, the user has *edited* the state. We have set up the system in such a way that edit operations always result in a new value of the same *type*. This is a powerful means of abstraction that helps programmers to reduce the implementation effort.

We show that the function body of f typically consists of two steps: updating the *forms* of the web application, and updating the HTML page, using the updated forms. To the programmer a *form* is an object that has a certain *model value* that is rendered according to a *view value*. The model value is of concern to the application programmer, the view value is of concern to the application user. They are both specified by means of custom data types. Their relative mapping is of course specified using functions between these data domains. These have to be provided by the application programmer. The iData Toolkit has one pivot function that implements a complete form for any given model value of type m, view value of type v, and model-view relationship of type (HBimap m v):

mkViewForm :: FormId m (HBimap m v) *HSt → (Form m,*HSt) | gHtml{|*|} v

The generic class gHtml is the silent witness of the fact that the iData Toolkit makes extensive use of generic programming. Its definition encompasses as much as four generic functions:

```
class gHtml t | gForm, gUpd, gPrint, gParse t
```

(As a technical aside: at this stage Clean does not allow the definition of generic classes. In this writing we will use it as a shorthand notation. In the true libraries you will see the expanded list of generic functions.)

In the remainder of this sequel the exact meaning of mkViewForm will be explained. Here we suffice with a rather informal specification based on its type signature: FormId identifies the form elements and their main attributes in a web application's page, m is the initial model value, and (HBimap m v) is the collection of relational functions between model and view. The result is a new form (Form m) that contains a model value, an HTML implementation, and a flag that tells whether the user has changed the form.

One important form attribute is the *life span* of the form's state. The programmer has fine grained control over this state. He can decide to make it fully persistent, or persistent only during the session of the application, or make it live only during the page itself.

Because of its generality, mkViewForm is not always easy to use. Therefore it has a couple of friends that capture a number of frequently occurring model-view patterns. The simplest one of these friends is mkEditForm:

```
mkEditForm :: FormId m *HSt → (Form m,*HSt) | gHtml{|*|} m
```

Given the identification of a form id, an initial model value m, (mkEditForm id m) creates a form that renders m and allows the user to manipulate this value.

3.2   The Challenges

We now have introduced the key elements of the iData Toolkit. It is about time to demonstrate how they will aid us in tackling the challenges that have presented in Sect. 2.

Cause and Effect: The account above demonstrates that we have built a standard framework for building web applications that contain objects with typed state. Also, a very clear notion of events has been introduced: the edit action of a user that changes the current state of an object into another.

Accumulating Behavior: The state of objects can be arbitrarily complex. The programmer also has fine grained control over the life span of these objects. States may be fully persistent, only during a session, or only during on page. This is expressed as an attribute of the form object.

User Behavior: In the iData Toolkit, the programmer can clearly identify the 'dangerous' parts of his web application. If all form states have a page based life span, then this means that the full state of the web application is in its pages. In that case, the application is certain to be correct with respect to arbitrary user behavior. Things get more complicated in case of (session) persistent state. These states are made explicit, and require special attention.

(Dependent) Forms: A web application is a single function that updates its
form always in the same specified order. This means that the programmer
imposes a functional relationship between updated forms and their values.
In this way, complicated connections can be realized in a functional style. In
addition, forms can be constructed that behave like memory storages, and
that can be manipulated as such. This increases their flexibility.

Separation of Model and View: From the start, the iData Toolkit merges
the *model-view* paradigm with the concept of forms. A form is always defined
in terms of a visualization of some model data. This is embodied with the
powerful function mkViewForm. For simpler situations, wrapper functions are
provided that give easier access to this scheme.

4   Case Studies

In this section we construct a number of case studies, each of which focusses
on one particular aspect of web programming with the iData Toolkit. As a brief
overview, we go through the following steps: we start with programming HTML
directly in sections 4.1 through 4.3. Once we know how to play with HTML, we
can concentrate on programming forms, in sections 4.4 through 4.6. Finally, we
give one larger example in Sect. 4.7.

4.1   Programming HTML

In Sect. 3.1 we have shown that an iData Toolkit web application programmer
really creates a function of type (*HSt → (Html,*HSt)). Such a function f is turned
into an interactive application by (doHtml f) :: *World → *World. The abstract
type HSt collects all the form information during the construction of a HTML
page. We defer its discussion until Sect. 4.4. Html is the root type of a collection
of algebraic data types (ADT) that capture the official HTML standard.

```
:: Html    = Html Head Rest
:: Head    = Head      [HeadAttr]      [HeadTag]
:: Rest    = Body      [BodyAttr]      [BodyTag]
           | Frameset  [FramesetAttr]  [Frame]
:: Frame   = Frame     [FrameAttr]
           | NoFrames  [Std_Attr]      [BodyTag]
:: BodyTag = A         [A_Attr]        [BodyTag]

             ⋮

           | Var       [Std_Attr]      String

           | STable    [Table_Attr]  [[BodyTag]]
           | BodyTag   [BodyTag]
           | EmptyBody
```

BodyTag contains the familiar HTML tags, starting with *anchors* and ending
with *variables* (in total there are 76 HTML tags). The latter three alternatives
are for easy HTML generation: STable generates a 2-dimensional table of data,

BodyTag collects data, and EmptyBody can be used as a zero element. Attributes are encoded as FooAttr data types.

As an example, the value hello :: Html defined by

```
hello = Html (Head ['Hd_Std [Std_Title "Hello World Example"]] [])
             (Body [] [Txt "Hello World!"])
```

corresponds with the following HTML code:

```
<html>
<head title = Hello World Example></head>
<body>Hello World!</body>
</html>
```

In order to get rid of some standard overhead HTML code, the following two functions prove to be useful:

```
mkHtml :: String [BodyTag] *HSt → (Html, *HSt)
mkHtml s tags hSt = (simpleHtml s tags,hSt)

simpleHtml:: String [BodyTag] → Html
simpleHtml s tags = Html (header s) (body tags)
where header s    = Head ['Hd_Std [Std_Title s]] []
      body tags   = Body [] tags
```

With these functions, the above example can be shortened to:

```
hello = mkHtml "Hello World Example" [Txt "Hello World!"]
```

The Html value is transformed to HTML code and written to file. This is one of the tasks of doHtml. The complete code for this example then is:

module fragments

```
import StdEnv    // import the standard Clean modules import
StdHtml          // import the iData Toolkit modules

Start world = doHtml hello world
where hello = mkHtml "Hello World Example" [Txt "Hello World!"]
```

The collection of data types shows that HTML can be encoded straightforwardly into a set of ADTs. There are some minor complications. In Clean, as well as in Haskell [18], all data constructors have to be different. In HTML, the same attribute names can appear in different tags. Furthermore, certain attributes, such as the standard attributes, can be used by many tags. We do not want to repeat all these attributes for every tag, but group them in a convenient way. To overcome these issues, we use the following naming conventions:

- The data constructor name represents the corresponding HTML language element.
- Data constructors need to start with an uppercase character and may contain other uppercase characters, but the corresponding HTML name is printed in lower-case format.

- To obtain unique names, every data constructor name is prefixed in a consistent way with Foo_. When the name is printed we skip this prefix.
- A constructor name is prefixed with ' in case its name has to be completely ignored when printed.

We have defined one generic printing function gHpr that implements the naming conventions that have been discussed above, and prints the correct HTML code. Its definition is not relevant here.

Our approach has the following advantages:

- One obtains a grammar for HTML which is convenient for the programmer.
- The type system eliminates type and typing errors that can occur when working in plain HTML.
- We can define a type driven generic function for generating HTML code.
- Future changes of HTML are likely to change the ADT only.
- Because the HTML is embedded in our programming language as a set of ADTs, we can use the language to create complex HTML.

4.2   Deriving HTML from Types

In the previous section we have demonstrated how one can construct HTML pages in a typed style. Although the use of a typed language eliminates many errors, it is not convenient to program web pages in this way. Instead, we like to *generate* HTML for data of arbitrary type automatically. This reduces the effort of creating web pages, reduces the risk of making errors, and increases consistency. Because this transformation is intended to work for every type, it has to be a generic function:

```
toHtml :: a → BodyTag | gForm{|*|} a
```

It uses the generic function gForm. This function is introduced in Sect. 4.4. One of its purposes is to generate HTML for any data value. It is this aspect that is used by toHtml.

Let's start with simple stuff, and move towards more complicated types. Table 5 shows what the generated HTML looks like in a web browser for the basic types Bool, Int, Real, and String. These are obtained by replacing *expr* in:

```
Start world = doHtml (mkHtml "Example" [toHtml expr]) world
```

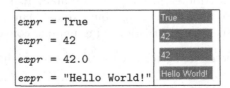

expr = True	True
expr = 42	42
expr = 42.0	42
expr = "Hello World!"	Hello World!

Fig. 5. HTML generated by toHtml for several basic types

Next we proceed with types that have been composed by the standard type constructors of Clean. Filling in *expr*= ("Nfib "<$40<$" = ",Nfib 40), which has type (String,Int) yields the following HTML output:

Nfib 40 =	331160281

The operator <$ is a useful abbreviation for the frequently occurring case of concatening a String value with something that can be turned into a String:

```
(<$) infixl :: !String !a → String | toString a
(<$) str x = str +++ toString x
```

The *strictness annotation* ! just in front of the type constructors states that <$ is strict in both arguments.

Within the Clean compiler, the internal representation of lists is

```
:: [a] = _Cons a [a] | _Nil
```

This algebraic structure is clearly visible in case of *expr*= [1..6], which has type [Int]:

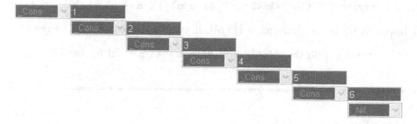

Note that the iData Toolkit derives and defines instances of the generic function gForm for the basic types and {2,3,4}-tuples, but not for lists. For this reason, you need to include the following in your code:

derive gForm []

In order to demonstrate the compositional character of the mechanism, let's create a list of pairs of strings and integers, i.e.: it has type [(String,Int)]. An example value is *expr*= [("Nfib "<$n<$" = ",Nfib n) \\ n ← [0,5..30]]:

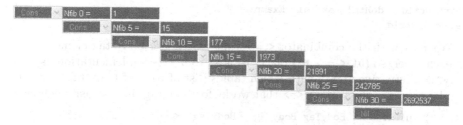

In Clean, records are algebraic data types that have exactly one (invisible) data constructor, and labelled fields. The iData Toolkit displays the field names, together with the field values, in the same recursive way. Consider for instance the following record type for a simplistic personnel administration, and two values of that type:

```
:: Person = { name::String, address::String, city::String } derive
gForm Person
```

```
peter = {name="Achten",    address="Abersland", city="Wijchen"}
rinus = {name="Plasmeijer",address="Knollenberg",city="Mook"}
```

Then the value *expr*= peter is displayed as:

Exercises

1. *Lists, differently*

The example of a list of NFib numbers was created with:

$$expr= [(\text{"Nfib "}\text{"<\$n<\$"} = \text{" "},\text{Nfib n}) \ \backslash\backslash \ n \leftarrow [0,5..30]].$$

What happens with the generated HTML if you replace [toHtml *expr*] with

$$[\text{toHtml } (\text{"Nfib "}\text{"<\$n<\$"} = \text{" "},\text{Nfib n}) \ \backslash\backslash \ n \leftarrow [0,5..30]]?$$

4.3   More Fun with HTML

The previous section has demonstrated that the iData Toolkit is able to derive a HTML representation for any conceivable data type T as long as you include a **derive gForm** T. It also demonstrates that the resulting HTML representations are not always attractive. In this section we introduce a few *body tag* combinators that give you more control over the layout of the elements of a HTML page.

The main program that we use in this section is slightly different from the previous one:

```
Start world = doHtml (mkHtml "Example"
[expr]) world
```

We start with the combinator <.=.> that places two body tag elements next to each other, so (b1 <.=.> b2) places b2 next to b1. Its implementation uses the BodyTag alternative STable with which tables (list of rows of body tag elements) can be created. The variant <=> that works for bodytag lists is easily defined:

```
(<.=.>) infixl 5 :: BodyTag BodyTag → BodyTag (<.=.>) b1 b2 =
STable [ Tbl_CellPadding (Pixels 0)
                , Tbl_CellSpacing (Pixels 0)
                ] [[b1,b2]]
```

```
(<=>) infixl 5 :: [BodyTag] [BodyTag] → BodyTag
(<=>) b1 b2 = (BodyTag b1) <.=.> (BodyTag b2)
```

With these combinators, we can easily place two values next to each other. Consider for instance *expr*= toHtml peter <.=.> toHtml rinus. This yields the following HTML:

Name:	Achten	Name:	Plasmeijer
Address:	Abersland	Address:	Knollenberg
City:	Wijchen	City:	Mook

This suggests that if you have a list of items that you want to display in a single row, it is sufficient to turn them into HTML elements first (using map toHtml), and then replacing every *cons* by <.=.> (by folding <.=.> over the resulting list). This is done with the iData Toolkit function mkRowForm, defined concisely as:

```
mkRowForm :: [BodyTag] → BodyTag
mkRowForm xs = foldr (<.=.>) EmptyBody xs
```

As an example, to produce a horizontal list of integer elements, one can define *expr*= mkRowForm (map toHtml [1..7]), and get:

In exactly analogous ways, we can do this for *vertical* layout, and introduce:

```
(<.||.>) infixl 4 :: BodyTag BodyTag → BodyTag
(<.||.>) b1 b2 = STable [ Tbl_CellPadding (Pixels 0)
                        , Tbl_CellSpacing (Pixels 0)
                        ] [[b1],[b2]]

(<||>) infixl 4 :: [BodyTag] [BodyTag] → BodyTag
(<||>) b1 b2 = (BodyTag b1) <.||.> (BodyTag b2)

mkColForm :: [BodyTag] → BodyTag
mkColForm xs = foldr (<.||.>) EmptyBody xs
```

With this combinator, we can create a more appealing representation of the list of *nfib* numbers that was given earlier. We define:

expr= mkColForm (map toHtml [("Nfib "<$n," = ",Nfib n) \\ n ← [0..10]]).

This yields:

Nfib 0	=	1
Nfib 1	=	1
Nfib 2	=	3
Nfib 3	=	5
Nfib 4	=	9
Nfib 5	=	15
Nfib 6	=	25
Nfib 7	=	41
Nfib 8	=	67
Nfib 9	=	109
Nfib 10	=	177

Finally, elements can be arranged in a table, using the function mkSTable:

```
mkSTable :: [[BodyTag]] → BodyTag
mkSTable table = Table [] (mktable table)
where mktable table = [Tr [] (mkrow rows) \\ rows ← table]
      mkrow   rows = [Td [ Td_VAlign Alo_Top
                         , Td_Width (Pixels defpixel)
                         ] [row]             \\ row ← rows]
```

The exercises below use this function.

Exercises

2. *Table headers*

The function mkSTable displays a table of elements, arranged as a list of rows. Write a function (augmentTable h v t) that augments a table t (a value of type [[BodyTag]]) with a horizontal header h (of the proper length) and a vertical header v (of the proper length).

```
augmentTable :: [BodyTag] [BodyTag] [[BodyTag]] → [[BodyTag]]
```

3. *The* Ackermann *function*
Write an application that uses the function augmentTable to show the *Ackermann* i j values with i ∈ {0...3} and j ∈ {0..7}. The *Ackermann* function is defined as follows:

```
Acker :: Int Int → Int
Acker 0 j = j + 1
Acker i 0 = Acker (i -1) 1
Acker i j = Acker (i - 1) (Acker i (j - 1))
```

The *Ackermann* function is well-known in theoretical computer science, because it was presented as a counter example of the thesis that every computable function could be expressed as a primitive recursive function. The *Ackermann* function is well-defined, computable, but not primitive recursive.

The application should look something like:

	j=0	j=1	j=2	j=3	j=4	j=5	j=6	j=7
i=0	1	2	3	4	5	6	7	8
i=1	2	3	4	5	6	7	8	9
i=2	3	5	7	9	11	13	15	17
i=3	5	13	29	61	125	253	509	1021

4.4   Programming Direct Forms

In the previous sections we have had experience with programming HTML pages that consist of *explicit* HTML as encoded by the Html type and friends, and *generated* HTML using the generic function toHtml. It is time now to do *form* programming. In web terminology, a form is a collection of interactive elements such as buttons, check boxes, radio buttons, edit text fields, and so on. The user can manipulate these elements. Depending on the application (for instance by pressing the *submit* button), at some point in time the results of these manipulations are sent to the web server which starts the web application and provides it with this information. The application processes the information and responds with a new page that is presented to the application user. In this way, interaction has been achieved between a user and a web application.

The key idea of the iData Toolkit is that a page is represented by a *value* of some *type*. Therefor, a form is also represented by a value of some type. User manipulations are really *edit* operations that modify the value into another value *of the same type*. Hence, a form is an editor of values of some type. This definition is reflected in the type signature of the function mkEditForm:

```
mkEditForm :: FormId d *HSt → (Form d,*HSt) | gHTML{|*|} d
```

Recall from Sect. 3.1 that the class gHtml is really a (syntactically illegal) shorthand for a collection of four generic functions, one of which is gForm. This is a generic function of signature:

```
generic gForm d :: FormId d *HSt → (Form d,*HSt)
```

(gForm id dv hSt) creates a form (an editor) that is *identified* with id, and that has *initial value* dv. With an identification value of type FormId, the application programmer sets a number of mandatory attributes of each form. The following types are involved:

```
:: FormId   = { id        :: String
             , lifespan  :: Lifespan
             , mode      :: Mode    }
:: Lifespan = Persistent | Session | Page
:: Mode     = Display    | Edit
```

The first mandatory attribute is an *identification tag* (id::String). This tag must unambiguously identify the form in the collection of forms used by the web application. This is the responsibility of the programmer. The second mandatory attribute is the *life span* (lifespan::Lifespan) of the form. The life span states how long the current value of the form (its state) lives: Persistent values live 'forever' and reside on disk, Session values live during a session, and Page values live only during the life span of the page that they are part of. Finally, the third mandatory attribute is the *mode* (mode::Mode) of the form. All of the examples above *displayed* values: the user is not able to manipulate them. This is in fact set by the toHtml function that calls gForm. For a form it makes more sense to allow user manipulations, and set the mode to Edit instead.

The iData Toolkit provides a few constructor functions to easily create FormId values:

```
nFormId  :: String → FormId  // Page         + Edit
sFormId  :: String → FormId  // Session      + Edit
pFormId  :: String → FormId  // Persistent   + Edit

ndFormId :: String → FormId  // Page              + Display
```

```
sdFormId :: String → FormId   // Session   + Display
pdFormId :: String → FormId   // Persistent + Display
```

The form that is returned by gForm is a small record type:

```
:: Form d = { changed :: Bool
            , value   :: d
            , form    :: [BodyTag] }
```

A form may have been edited by the user. This is set in the changed field of the form. Forms always have a value of the type that is associated with them. This is set in the value field. Finally, a form needs an HTML rendering. This is set in the form field. In fact, the [BodyTag]s that we have used in the examples above come from this field. Except for the HSt parameter, we can now explain the function toHtml:

```
toHtml :: a → BodyTag | gForm{|*|} a toHtml a
    ♯ ({form},_) = gForm{|*|} {id="__toHtml",lifespan=Page,mode=Display} a ...
    = BodyTag form
```

In all examples that have been presented so far, it is OK to replace toHtml with form versions, using mkEditForm, and plug in their HTML renderings using the form fields of these forms.

As a first example of a web application with a direct form, we create a (Form Person) (Person and rinus were defined at the end of Sect. 4.2). For completeness, we give the full code:

```
module fragments

import StdEnv
import StdHtml

Start world = doHtml personPage world
where personPage hSt
            ♯ (person,hSt) = mkEditForm (nFormId "person") rinus hSt
            = mkHtml "Person" [ H1 [] "Person"
                              , BodyTag person.form
                              ] hSt

:: Person = // Person definition here
derive gForm  Person
derive gUpd   Person
derive gPrint Person
derive gParse Person
```

The example shows that the HTML rendering of a form f can be used at any arbitrary location, just by taking the f.form field of that form. Because mkEditForm relies on a collection of generic functions, we also need to derive instances for these functions for Person. This should become standard idiom when defining new types for forms.

Because we have created an *editable* form, the behavior of this program is quite different from the one that only displays a person. This is what it looks like initially:

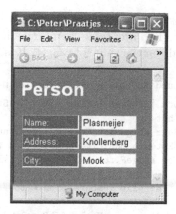

This application allows the user to edit any of the fields of a person record. An edit operation is finished as soon as the user 'confirms' editing by leaving the input focus of the edit box, and not during every keystroke or copy-paste action).

Despite its size, this example shows the general structure of web applications with forms. The function of type *HSt → (Html,*HSt), personPage in the example, that defines the page first needs to update its forms, and then updates the HTML that corresponds with the new forms.

```
myPage :: *HSt → (Html,*HSt)
myPage hSt
  # (forms,hSt) = updateForms hSt
  = updatePage forms hSt
```

In the remainder of this sequel, we adopt this scheme and modify the updateForms and updatePage functions. In the example, updateForms is simply

$$(\text{mkEditForm (nFormId "person") rinus})$$

and updatePage is

$$(\lambda\text{person hSt} \rightarrow \text{mkHtml ... hSt}).$$

Here is an example of a slightly more interactive web application. We extend the *nfib* table example from Sect. 4.3 with an integer form in which the application user can enter a number n. As a result, the application shows all *nfib* numbers from 0 to n. For this also a form is used. Let's first construct the two forms:

```
updateForms :: *HSt → ((Form Int,Form [(String,String,Int)]),*HSt)
updateForms hSt
  # (rangeF,hSt) = mkEditForm (nFormId "range") 10 hSt
  # (nfibF, hSt) = mkEditForm (ndFormId "nfib") [ ("Nfib "<$ n," = ",Nfib n)
                                                 \\ n←[0..rangeF.value]
                                               ] hSt
  = ((rangeF,nfibF),hSt)

derive gForm []; derive gUpd []
```

The integer form `rangeF` is straightforward. Its initial value is 10, and it is identified with tag `"range"`. The *nfib* table form `nfibF` is more interesting, as its construction clearly depends on the value of `rangeF`. It is identified by tag `"nfib"`, and is not editable.

Given these two forms, `updatePage` needs to create the proper web page:

```
updatePage :: (Form Int,Form [(String,String,Int)]) *HSt → (Html,*HSt)
updatePage (rangeF,nfibF) hSt
  = mkHtml "NFib" [ H1 [Hnum_Align Aln_Center] "NFib numbers"
                  , Txt "Enter a positive number (not too large please)."
                  , BodyTag rangeF.form
                  , Br
                  , Txt ("The Nfib numbers from 0 to "<$rangeF.value<$" are:")
                  , Br
                  , mkColForm (map toHtml nfibF.value)
                  ] hSt
```

The interesting bits are the fact that from `rangeF` we use both its `form` and `value`, and from the `nfibF` only its `value`. Note the arbitrary order in which these elements are mixed with static HTML code.

The initial look of this application is given below, together with its look after the user has edited the integer form into the value 15.

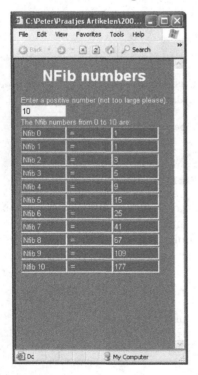 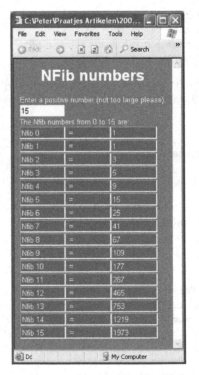

In the beginning of this section we have defined forms to be collections of interactive elements such as buttons, check boxes, radio buttons, and so on. We introduce these elements right now. As you may gather by now, we have no intention in programming these kinds of elements directly in HTML (which is perfectly possible because we have full HTML at our disposal), but rather program them by means of values of types that provide a higher level of abstraction.

Let's start with push buttons. A push button either has a text label label and a certain width width, and is defined as (LButton width label), or it uses an image file located at path and with dimensions dim and is defined by (PButton dim path). When the user presses the button, it enters the Pressed state. After processing by the iData Toolkit, it returns to its previous state. This gives the following, compact definition of a button:

```
:: Button = Pressed | LButton Int String | PButton (Int,Int) String
```

Fig. 6 gives the result of the following definitions (assuming that the local files "rinus.jpg" and "peter.jpg" exist and contain sensible material):

```
updateForms :: *HSt → ([Form Button],*HSt) updateForms hSt
  ♯ (rP,hSt) = mkEditForm (nFormId "rinusB") (PButton dim "rinus.jpg")   hSt
  ♯ (pP,hSt) = mkEditForm (nFormId "peterB") (PButton dim "peter.jpg")   hSt
  ♯ (rL,hSt) = mkEditForm (nFormId "rinusL") (LButton (snd dim) "Rinus") hSt
  ♯ (pL,hSt) = mkEditForm (nFormId "peterL") (LButton (snd dim) "Peter") hSt
  = ([rP,pP,rL,pL],hSt)
where dim      = (60,80)

updatePage :: [Form Button] *HSt → (Html,*HSt) updatePage
[rP,pP,rL,pL] hSt
  ♯ [rP,pP,rL,pL:_] = map (λf → BodyTag f.form) [rP,pP,rL,pL]
  = mkHtml "Buttons" [ H1 [] "Buttons!!", mkSTable [[rP,pP],[rL,pL]] ] hSt
```

Fig. 6. Several examples of Buttons

The next form elements are the 'twin" definitions for *check boxes* and *radio buttons*. Both only offer a choice between being checked or not. Radio buttons usually are grouped together to provide the application user with a single choice out of a limited collection of alternatives. Check boxes usually do the same, but allow several or no choices.

```
:: CheckBox    = CBChecked String | CBNotChecked String
:: RadioButton = RBChecked String | RBNotChecked String
```

Another way of providing the application user with a single choice from a limited collection is to use a *pull down menu*. A pull down menu defined by (PullDown (nrVisible,width) (index,items)) displays nrVisible elements, has width width, and a collection of items out of which element index is selected.

```
:: PullDownMenu = PullDown (Int,Int) (Int,[String])
```

Finally, for completeness, there exist *text input* boxes, defined by:

```
:: TextInput = TI Int Int | TR Int Real | TS Int String
```

The first argument of these data constructor set the width of the elements, the second the initial value.

We have now discussed all elements of direct form programming. The applications that we can construct now may consist of several forms that are really editors of arbitrary values. These forms, and their values, can already depend on each other in arbitrarily complex ways. The layout of the page is done by direct HTML programming.

As a final example, we extend the *nfib* table example given earlier in this section with a check for illegal input. We do not change the updateForms function, but only the updatePage function:

```
updatePage :: (Form Int,Form [(String,String,Int)]) *HSt →(Html,*HSt)    1.
updatePage (rangeF,nfibF) hSt                                             2.
| rangeF.value < 0 || rangeF.value > 40                                  3.
    # (backF,hSt) = mkEditForm (nFormId "button") (LButton 80 "Back") hSt 4.
    = mkHtml "Wrong Input"                                                5.
        [ H1 [Hnum_Align Aln_Center] "NFib numbers"                       6.
        , Txt "I am truly sorry. This input is beyond my capacity."       7.
        , Br                                                              8.
        , BodyTag backF.form                                             9.
        ] hSt                                                           10.
| otherwise
                                                                        11.
    = /* as previously */
```

The guard at line 3 tests for incorrect input values. If this is not the case, we proceed as previously. If the input value is illegal, then we create a different page in which the application user is politely informed about the incorrect input. This is done in lines 4–10. In order to allow the user to go back and give it another try, a *local* button is created, especially for this page. This is possible because the updatePage function has access to the HSt environment. Fig. 7 shows the result after the user has entered incorrect data.

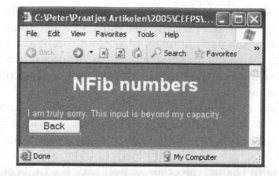

Fig. 7. Handling different pages within one application

It is sometimes convenient to be able to introduce a form locally within a BodyTag context. In such a context, one does not have access to a HSt environment. For this purpose, the function toHtmlForm can be used:

toHtmlForm :: (*HSt → (Form d,*HSt)) → [BodyTag] | gHTML{|*|} d

Using this function, we could have defined the above exceptional case to the same effect in the following way:

```
updatePage (rangeF,nfibF) hSt
| rangeF.value < 0 || rangeF.value > 40
   = mkHtml "Wrong Input"
          [ H1 [Hnum_Align Aln_Center] "NFib numbers"
          , Txt "I am truly sorry. This input is beyond my capacity."
          , Br
          , BodyTag backF.form
          ] hSt
   with backF = toHtmlForm (mkEditForm (nFormId "button") (LButton 80 "Back"))
| otherwise
   = /* as previously */
```

Exercises

4. *Correct input for the* Nfib *table*

Above we have discussed how the application can check for illegal input in the case of the *nfib* table. Implement a version using a *pull down menu* in which the user can only choose between legal values. Legal values are element of {0..40}.

4.5   Programming Model-View Forms

In the previous section we have introduced the mkEditForm function that creates a form with which users can edit values for some data domain. Although this is a powerful abstraction mechanism, it has two shortcomings:

1. The form allows users to change values into arbitrary other values of the data domain. This means that the full range of inhabitants of the domain can be entered by the user. In many cases, forms impose restrictions on the set of admissible values. These restrictions are expressed in a natural way by means of functions, and their expressiveness goes well beyond the capacity of the type system.
2. The form is derived generically from a data domain, and one of its values. This implies that the *presentation* and the *functionality* of the form are strongly coupled. Such a strict coupling of concerns leads to software in which one can not change either the presentation or functionality of a form without having to change the other as well with the same effort.

Based on earlier work, we know that both aspects can be dealt with by means of *abstraction* [1]. With abstraction, the application works with forms that are modelled by means of values of type m, but that are *visualized* by means of values of type v. This is a variant of the well-known model-(controller-)view paradigm [15]. What is special about it in this context, is that views are also defined by means of a data model, and hence can be handled generically in exactly the same way as other data models. This is a powerful concept, and we have used it successfully in the past for desktop GUI programming. It turns out that it can be integrated smoothly in the iData Toolkit.

The relation between a model domain m and its view domain v is given by the following collection of functions (FormBimap m v):

```
:: FormBimap m v
   = { toForm     :: m → Maybe v → v
     , updForm    :: Changed → v → v
     , fromForm   :: Changed → v → m
     , resetForm  :: Maybe (v → v)   }
:: Changed
   = { isChanged  :: Bool
     , changedId  :: String          }
```

Model domain values are transformed to view domain values with toForm. It can use the previous view domain value if necessary. The local behavior of the form that corresponds with the view data model is given by updForm. The Changed parameter indicates whether the value of this form was edited by the user. This record has the same role and value in the function fromForm which transforms the view domain value back to the model domain value. Finally, resetForm is an optional separate normalization *after* the local behavior function updForm has been applied.

Abstraction is incorporated in the iData Toolkit by a more general function than mkEditForm, viz. mkViewForm. Its type is:

```
mkViewForm :: FormId m (FormBimap m v) *HSt → (Form m, *HSt) | gHTML{|*|} v
```

Note that its signature is almost identical to that of mkEditForm. It has an additional argument of type (FormBimap m v), and it assumes that all the generic machinery is available for the view type v instead of the model type m.

The function mkEditForm is a special case of mkViewForm. It is defined as follows:

```
mkEditForm formId data hSt
  = mkViewForm formId data
        { toForm   = toFormid
        , updForm  = case formId.mode of
                        Edit    = λ_ v → v
                        Display = λ_ _ → data
        , fromForm = λ_ v → v
        , resetForm= Nothing
        } hSt
```

```
toFormid :: d (Maybe d) → d
toFormid m Nothing  = m
toFormid m (Just v) = v
```

(toFormid is a useful function that always takes the previous view value, unless there was none.)

Let's construct a slightly more elaborate model-view form. This form should have a simple integer *model* but a *view* in which the user can edit integer values by means of a text box or a spin button. We have :: Model := Int. We first design the View type. The view consists of an integer edit box and a spin button. The integer edit box is modelled by the Int type. For the spin button we use two labelled buttons, hence two Button types suffice. Therefore the view type is :: View := (Int,Button,Button). Next, we define the relationship between the model type and the view type, which is expressed as a value of type (FormBimap Model View). We define the four functions:

toForm :: Model (Maybe View) → View
    This function transforms the model into the view. The integer component is simply copied. The two buttons, down and up, are labelled with "-" and "+" respectively. This amounts to:

```
toForm = λn → toFormid (n,down,up)
down   = LButton (defpixel/6) "-"
up     = LButton (defpixel/6) "+"
```

(defpixel is globally used in the iData Toolkit to serve as the default width of elements.)

updForm :: Changed View → View
    This function defines the local behavior of the form. Edit operations on the integer edit box are always legal, due the type safeness of the iData Toolkit. Edit operations on the down (up) button can only be the value Pressed. In case of that operation, the integer value is decreased (increased). We have:

```
updForm = λ_ view → case view of
                (n,Pressed,_) → (n-1,down,up)
                (n,_,Pressed) → (n+1,down,up)
                int_edited    → int_edited
```

fromForm :: Changed View → Model

This function transforms the view back to the model. In this case, the integer component is returned:

```
fromForm = λ_ (n,_,_) = n
```

resetForm :: Maybe (View → View)

Finally, this function allows the programmer to reset the view after the new model value has been returned. In this case, this is not necessary, hence Nothing can be returned.

```
resetForm = Nothing
```

For completeness, we show the full implementation here:

```
counterForm :: FormId Int *HSt → (Form Int,*HSt)
counterForm name i hSt = mkViewForm name i counterView hSt
where counterView = { toForm    = λn → toFormid (n,down,up)
                    , updForm   = λ_ view → case view of
                                        (n,Pressed,_) = (n-1,down,up)
                                        (n,_,Pressed) = (n+1,down,up)
                                        int_edited    = int_edited
                    , fromForm  = λ_ (n,_,_) → n
                    , resetForm = Nothing
                    }
      where down = LButton (defpixel / 6) "-"
            up   = LButton (defpixel / 6) "+"
```

We can now use this model-view form of type (Form Int) and mix it with other forms of that type. Consider an application that takes a number of forms of this type, and presents them below each other, along with a display of the sum of their values. Fig. 8 shows what this application looks like. The updatePage function for such an application is rather straightforward:

```
updatePage :: [Form Int] *HSt → (Html,*HSt)
updatePage intFs hSt
    = mkHtml "Integer Forms"
          ([ H1 [] "Integer Forms" ] ++ bodies ++ [ toHtml (sum values)]) hSt
where
    (bodies,values) = unzip [(BodyTag form,value) \\ {form,value}←intFs]
```

This function generates the proper page, regardless of the actual content of the list of integer forms. For the screen shot in Fig. 8 we have used the following updateForms function:

```
updateForms :: *HSt → ([Form Int],*HSt)
updateForms hSt
    # (intF1,hSt) = mkEditForm  (nFormId "simple_int")  1 hSt
    # (intF2,hSt) = counterForm' (nFormId "counter_int") 2 hSt
    = ([intF1,intF2],hSt)
```

Fig. 8. Mixing various (Form Int)s

It should be clear that the order of integer forms as well as their number is quite irrelevant. This example illustrates that model-view forms allow for local behavior, and separation of model and view.

Exercises

5. *A boolean model-view form*

Create, in an analogous way as done above for the counterForm, the following function:

boolForm :: FormId Bool *HSt → (Form Bool,*HSt)

This should generate a model-view form with a boolean model type, and as view an unlabelled *check box* that is checked in case of *true* values (☑), and unchecked in case of *false* values (☐).

6. *Self correcting forms*
In module htmlFormlib of the iData Toolkit you can find a number of predefined specializations of mkViewForm. Two of these functions are mkSelfForm and mkSelf2Form. Explain the difference between these model-view forms and give an example that illustrates their difference.

7. *Storage forms*
In module htmlFormlib of the iData Toolkit you can find a number of predefined specializations of mkViewForm. One of these functions is mkStoreForm. Explain what it does and give an example that illustrates its use.

4.6   More Fun with Model-View Forms

In the previous section we have created a number of model-view forms by defining a Model and View type, and suitable relation functions as (FormBimap Model View).

In this section we show that you can also create new model-view forms on the level of forms themselves.

As a first example, consider a function that creates a list of direct forms from a list of values. It has type:

```
listForm :: FormId [a] *HSt → (Form [a],*HSt) | gHTML{|*|} a
```

If the value list is empty, no visualization (form field) is required. The value is clearly the empty list, and the user can't have changed it:

```
listForm _ [] hSt
  = ({ changed=False, value=[], form=[] },hSt)
```

For a non-empty list [x:xs], listForm proceeds recursively over xs, producing xsF and creates the direct form xF for x. The new form is a rather straightforward composition of these elements. The form is changed if either forms are changed (changed = xF.changed || xsF.changed); the value assembles the values in a list (value = [xF.value:xsF.value]); the form is the sequential composition of both forms (form = [BodyTag xF.form:xsF.form]). The identification values of the intermediate forms are derived from the argument identification value by appending it with their reversed position in the list (nformid). This gives:

```
listForm formid [x:xs] hSt
  # (xsF,hSt) = listForm    formid xs hSt
  # (xF, hSt) = mkEditForm nformid x hSt
  = ({ changed = xF.changed || xsF.changed
     , value   = [xF.value:xsF.value]
     , form    = [BodyTag xF.form:xsF.form]
     },hSt)
where nformid = {formid & id = formid.id<$length xs}
```

A closer inspection at this function shows that it has room for generalization:

- the sequential combination of the forms can be generalized to any specific layout;
- there is no real need to create direct forms, any form creation function should do.

Based on these observations, we create a more general function, layoutListForm that is parameterized with a form layout combinator function (of type [BodyTag] [BodyTag] → [BodyTag]), and a form creation function (of type FormId a *HSt → (Form a,*HSt)). Its definition follows in a trivial way from listForm above:

```
layoutListForm :: ([BodyTag] [BodyTag] → [BodyTag])
                  (FormId a *HSt → (Form a,*HSt))
                  FormId [a] *HSt → (Form [a],*HSt) | gHTML{|*|} a
layoutListForm _ _ _ [] hSt
  = ({changed=False, value=[], form=[]}, hSt)
layoutListForm layoutF formF formid [x:xs] hSt
  # (xsF,hSt) = layoutListForm layoutF formF formid xs hSt
  # (xF, hSt) = formF nformid x hSt
  = ({changed = xF.changed || xsF.changed
```

```
      ,value   = [xF.value:xsF.value]
      ,form    = layoutF xF.form xsF.form
      },hSt)
where nformid = {formid & id = formid.id <$ length xs}
```

listForm can now be expressed concisely as a special case of this function, as well as a range of other useful functions:

```
listForm       = layoutListForm (λf1 f2 → [BodyTag f1:f2]) mkEditForm
horlistForm    = layoutListForm (λf1 f2 → [f1 <=> f2])     mkEditForm
vertlistForm   = layoutListForm (λf1 f2 → [f1 <||> f2])    mkEditForm
table_hv_Form  = layoutListForm (λf1 f2 → [f1 <||> f2])    horlistForm
```

The layoutListForm function is useful for combining form creation functions which view types are assembled lists. We now discuss a more general combinator function that abstracts also from this aspect. It's signature is:

```
layoutIndexForm :: ([BodyTag] [BodyTag] → [BodyTag])
                    (Int Bool FormId x *HSt → (Form y,*HSt))
                    y (y y → y)
                    Int Bool FormId [x] *HSt → (Form y,*HSt)
```

The first two arguments serve the same purposes as with layoutListForm: the first arguments combines the layout of forms, the second argument creates forms. These forms have a view type y, and therefore we need to have a value of type y in case of the empty list of data, as well as a combinator function of type y y → y. These are the third and fourth argument of layoutIndexForm. The integer argument is required for generating fresh identification values from the given identification value. The boolean argument indicates whether the elements are going to be initialized.

The implementation of layoutIndexForm is analogous to layoutListForm. In case of an empty list of data from which forms need to be generated, a form is returned with the given 'neutral' value:

```
layoutIndexForm _ _ r _ _ _ _ [] hSt
  = ({changed=False, value=r, form=[]},hSt)
```

In case of a non-empty list [x:xs], layoutIndexForm proceeds recursively over xs producing xsF, and applies the form creation function to x, yielding xF. The new form is assembled from these two forms. Its changed and form values are computed in an identical way as by layoutListForm. Its value is computed by the value combinator function combineF.

```
layoutIndexForm layoutF formF r combineF n b formid [x:xs] hSt
  ♯ (xsF,hSt) = layoutIndexForm layoutF formF r combineF (n+1) b formid xs hSt
  ♯ (xF, hSt) = formF n b formid x hSt
  = ({changed = xF.changed || xsF.changed
     ,value   = combineF xsF.value xF.value
     ,form    = layoutF xF.form xsF.form
     },hSt)
```

With this general function we can assemble a form which view is defined by a list of buttons, and which model is an associated *callback function*. This function has signature:

```
ListFuncBut :: (Bool FormId [(Button, a → a)] *HSt → (Form (a → a),*HSt))
```

The most important argument is the third one: this argument associates callback functions with buttons. The intention is that for a list of button-callback function pairs $[(b_0, f_0) \ldots (b_n, f_n)]$ a form is created that has value f_i whenever the application user has pressed button b_i and the identity function otherwise. This function can be implemented using the general layoutIndexForm given above:

```
ListFuncBut = layoutIndexForm (λf1 f2 → [BodyTag f1:f2]) FuncBut id (o) 0
```

The lower level function FuncBut creates a (Form (a → a)) with a Button view. It uses the boolean and the integer to generate a fresh identification value for that element. Function composition is used to combine the callback functions from all button elements.

In a similar way, we can define a form that displays *table* of buttons, and that returns the callback function of the associated button that has been pressed:

```
TableFuncBut :: (FormId [[(Button,a → a)]] *HSt → (Form (a →
a),*HSt)) TableFuncBut
    = layoutIndexForm
        (λf1 f2 → [f1 <||> f2])
        (layoutIndexForm (λf1 f2 → [BodyTag f1:f2]) FuncBut id (o))
        id (o) 0 False
```

We conclude this section with an example that creates a simple integer based *calculator* (see Fig. 9). The calculator uses a number of buttons to enter integer values and do basic arithmetic. Clearly, we intend to use the TableFuncBut that we have constructed above as the view, and program with callback functions as the model. The callback functions have type CalcSt → CalcSt with :: CalcSt :== (Int,Int).

We arrange the buttons as:

```
buttons = [ [btn "7" (set 7),   btn "8" (set 8),   btn "9" (set 9)   ]
          , [btn "4" (set 4),   btn "5" (set 5),   btn "6" (set 6)   ]
          , [btn "1" (set 1),   btn "2" (set 2),   btn "3" (set 3)   ]
          , [btn "0" (set 0),   btn "C"  clear                       ]
          , [btn "+" (app (+)), btn "-" (app (-)), btn "*" (app (*))]
          ]
where set   i (t,b) = (t       , b*10 + i)
      clear   (t,b) = (t       , 0)
      app fun (t,b) = (fun t b, 0)

      btn lbl cbf  = (LButton (defpixel / 3) lbl,cbf)
```

The calculator consists of two forms: one that displays the current value and entered value (displayF) and one that shows the buttons of the calculator (buttonsF). These forms are, as usual, created by the updateForms function:

Fig. 9. A simple integer based calculator

```
updateForms :: *HSt → ((Form (CalcSt → CalcSt),Form CalcSt),*HSt)
updateForms hSt
  ♯ (buttonsF,hSt) = TableFuncBut (nFormId "calcbut") buttons hSt
  ♯ (displayF,hSt) = mkStoreForm (ndFormId "display") (0,0) buttonsF.value hSt
  = ((buttonsF,displayF),hSt)
```

With these forms the definition of the page is easily constructed:

```
updatePage :: (Form (CalcSt → CalcSt),Form CalcSt) *HSt →
(Html,*HSt) updatePage (buttonsF,displayF) hSt
  = mkHtml "Calculator" [ H1 [] "Calculator"
                        , toHtml t <.||.> toHtml b
                        : buttonsF.form
                        ] hSt
where (t,b) = displayF.value
```

4.7 Login Form

We conclude this survey of the iData Toolkit with a larger example (50 *loc*) that implements a frequently occurring component of web applications, viz. a *login form*. With such a form applications protect themselves from access by unregistered users. A screen shot of the login page that we develop is given in Fig. 10.

Logins are kept in a record of type Login in which the login name and password are stored. Both a generic and overloaded equality operator on Login values are defined.

```
:: Login = { loginName::String, password::String }
derive gForm Login; derive gUpd Login; derive gPrint Login; derive gParse Login
derive gEq   Login
instance == Login where (==) login1 login2 = login1 == login2
```

Fig. 10. The initial login page

```
mkLogin :: String String → Login
mkLogin name pwd = {loginName=name, password=pwd }
```

By now, the standard overhead of an iData Toolkit program should be familiar:

module loginAdmin

import StdEnv, StdHtml, GenEq

Start world = doHtml MyPage world

The function MyPage is the function that does the 'real' work. The application basically switches between two pages: a *login page* in which a name and password need to be entered, and a *member page* that should be reached only if a valid member has logged in. Because this exercise is not about the actual member page, we keep it rather minimal, and only display a welcome message:

```
memberPage :: (Form Login) → (*HSt → ([BodyTag],*HSt))
memberPage loginF = return [Txt ("Welcome "<$ loginF.value.loginName )]
```

The login page uses a *login store* to keep track of all valid username/password combinations. For this purpose, a *persistent* form of type (Form [Login]) is useful. This form is identified by the tag "loginDB". In order to ensure that exactly this form is used throughout the application, it is a good discipline to use a single function that associates a form with its tag:

```
loginStore :: ([Login] → [Login]) *HSt → (Form [Login],*HSt)
loginStore = mkStoreForm (pFormId "loginDB") []
```

The application first needs to determine in what stage of its session it actually is. This depends on the current content of the login form and the database. If the user has entered valid data, the member page should be presented, and otherwise the login page should be presented:

```
MyPage :: *HSt → (Html,*HSt) MyPage hSt
    ♯ (loginF,  hSt) = mkEditForm (sFormId "login") (mkLogin "" "") hSt
```

```
♯ (loginDBF,hSt) = loginStore id hSt
♯ (page,      hSt) = if (isMember loginF.value loginDBF.value)
                        (memberPage loginF hSt)
                        (loginPage  loginF hSt)
    = mkHtml "Login" [BodyTag page] hSt
```

The login page allows the user to add his username and password to the database. For this purpose an additional button form is created, making use of the callback scheme that is offered by the ListFuncBut function that was discussed in Sect. 4.6. Of course, if no information was entered (both Login fields are "") then this should not be possible. In that case, the button is in display mode:

```
addLoginButton :: Login *HSt → (Form (Bool → Bool),*HSt)
addLoginButton value = ListFuncBut False (formid "addlogin") pagebuttons
where pagebuttons    = [ (LButton defpixel "addLogin", const True) ]
      formid         = if (value ≠ mkLogin "" "")
                          nFormId
                          ndFormId
```

If the user has pushed this button (the .changed field is true), then his username/password combination should be added to the persistent database, and the member page should be displayed. If the user did not push the button, then the login page should be displayed again.

```
loginPage :: (Form Login) *HSt → ([BodyTag],*HSt)
loginPage loginF hSt
    ♯ (addloginF,hSt) = addLoginButton loginF.value hSt
    ♯ (loginDBF, hSt) = loginStore (addLogin loginF.value addloginF.changed) hSt
    | isMember loginF.value loginDBF.value
                     = memberPage loginF hSt
    | otherwise      = ( [ Txt "Please log in ..."
                         , Br, Br
                         , BodyTag loginF.form
                         , Br
                         , BodyTag addloginF.form
                         ] , hSt)
where
    addLogin :: Login Bool [Login] → [Login]
    addLogin newname added loginDB
        | added && newname ≠ mkLogin "" "" && not (isMember newname loginDB)
                 = [newname:loginDB]
        | otherwise = loginDB
```

The application that we have created enforces a user to either enter a valid username/password combination or add a new, non-existing, combination. Only in these cases, the user reaches the member page.

5   Related Work

Lifting low-level Web programming has triggered a lot of research. Many authors have worked on turning the generation and manipulation of HTML (XML) pages into a typed discipline. Early work is by Wallace and Runciman [24] on XML transformers in Haskell. The Haskell CGI library by Meijer [16] frees the programmer from dealing with CGI printing and parsing. Hanus uses similar types [11] in Curry. Thiemann constructs typed encodings of HTML in extended Haskell in an increasing level of precision for *valid* documents [22,23]. XML transforming programs with GenericH∀skell has been investigated in UUXML [3]. Elsman and Larsen [9] have worked on typed representations of XML in ML [17]. Our use of ADTs can be placed between the single, generic type used by Meijer and Hanus, and the collection of types used by Thiemann. It allows the HTML definition to be done completely with separate data types for separate HTML elements.

iData components are form abstractions. A pioneer project to experiment with form-based services is Mawl [4]. It has been improved upon by means of Powerforms [6], used in the <bigwig> project [7]. These projects provide *templates* which, roughly speaking, are HTML pages with *holes* in which scalar data as well as lists can be plugged in (Mawl), but also other *templates* (<bigwig>). They advocate compile-time systems, because this allows one to use type systems and other static analysis. Powerforms reside on the client-side of a web application. The type system is used to filter out illegal user input. The use of the type system is what they have in common with our approach. Because iData are encoded by ADTs, we get higher-order forms/pages for free.

Web applications can be structured with *continuations*. This has been done by Hughes, with his arrow framework [14]. Queinnec states that "A browser is a device that can invoke continuations multiply/simultaneously" [21]. Graunke *et al* [10] have explored continuations as (one of three) functional compilation technique(s) to transform sequential interactive programs to CGI programs. Our approach is simpler because for every page we have a complete (set of) model value(s) that can be stored and retrieved generically in a page. An application is resurrected simply by recovering its previous state.

6   Conclusions

In these lecture notes we have described the iData Toolkit. With this toolkit, the programmer can create dynamic web applications that use interconnected forms. Programming these applications can be very hard due to the complex interactions between these forms, and the form programming itself. We have shown how a functional style approach can help reduce the complexity of this problem. The following key ideas have been crucial:

- A web application should be a single function.
- A form should be a type-directed editor.
- Forms should be regarded as objects.
- Web interfaces should be generated from typed specifications.
- There should be a strict separation between model and view.

The result is a toolkit that gives the programmer the freedom to shape the data structures that he really needs for his problem domain, instead of being forced to squeeze his problem domain in terms of API predetermined data struc-tures. This essentially relies on the generative power of generic programming. Although the implementation of the iData Toolkit relies on generic program-ming, this is not necessary for the application programmer. We have spent a lot of effort to keep the API of the iData Toolkit as simple as possible.

We hope you have enjoyed this tutorial and the exercises.

Acknowledgements

Javier Pomer Tendillo visited our department during his Erasmus project. He has helped in setting up the iData Toolkit, and in finding out the nitty-gritty details of HTML programming. The authors like to thank the anonymous referee for improving the presentation of this document.

References

1. P. Achten, M. van Eekelen, and R. Plasmeijer. Compositional Model-Views with Generic Graphical User Interfaces. In *Practical Aspects of Declarative Program-ming, PADL04*, volume 3057 of *LNCS*, pages 39–55. Springer, 2004.
2. A. Alimarine and R. Plasmeijer. A Generic Programming Extension for Clean. In T. Arts and M. Mohnen, editors, *The 13th International workshop on the Im-plementation of Functional Languages, IFL'01, Selected Papers*, volume 2312 of *LNCS*, pages 168–186. Älvsjö, Sweden, Springer, Sept. 2002.
3. F. Atanassow, D. Clarke, and J. Jeuring. UUXML: A Type-Preserving XML Schema-Haskell Data Binding. In *International Symposium on Practical Aspects of Declarative Languages (PADL'04)*, volume 3057 of *LNCS*, pages 71–85. Springer-Verlag, June 2004.
4. D. Atkins, T. Ball, M. Benedikt, G. Bruns, K. Cox, P. Mataga, and K. Rehor. Experience with a Domain Specific Language for Form-based Services. In *Usenix Conference on Domain Specific Languages*, Oct. 1997.
5. T. Berners-Lee. World wide web seminar. http://www.w3.org/Talks/General.html, 1991.
6. C. Brabrand, A. Møller, M. Ricky, and M. Schwartzbach. Powerforms: Declarative client-side form field validation. *World Wide Web Journal*, 3(4):205–314, 2000.
7. C. Brabrand, A. Møller, and M. Schwartzbach. The <bigwig> Project. In *ACM Transactions on Internet Technology (TOIT)*, 2002.
8. M. de Mol, M. van Eekelen, and R. Plasmeijer. Theorem proving for functional programmers - Sparkle: A functional theorem prover. In T. Arts and M. Mohnen, editors, *The 13th International Workshop on Implementation of Functional Lan-guages, IFL 2001, Selected Papers*, volume 2312 of *LNCS*, pages 55–72, Stockholm, Sweden, 2002. Springer.
9. M. Elsman and K. F. Larsen. Typing XHTML Web applications in ML. In *In-ternational Symposium on Practical Aspects of Declarative Languages (PADL'04)*, volume 3057 of *LNCS*, pages 224–238. Springer-Verlag, June 2004.
10. P. Graunke, S. Krishnamurthi, R. Bruce Findler, and M. Felleisen. Automatically Restructuring Programs for the Web. In M. Feather and M. Goedicke, editors, *Pro-ceedings 16th IEEE International Conference on Automated Software Engineering (ASE'01)*. IEEE CS Press, Sept. 2001.

11. M. Hanus. High-Level Server Side Web Scripting in Curry. In *Proc. of the Third International Symposium on Practical Aspects of Declarative Languages (PADL'01)*, pages 76–92. Springer LNCS 1990, 2001.
12. R. Hinze. A new approach to generic functional programming. In *The 27th Annual ACM SIGPLAN-SIGACT Symposium on Principles of Programming Languages*, pages 119–132. Boston, Massachusetts, January 2000.
13. R. Hinze and S. Peyton Jones. Derivable Type Classes. In G. Hutton, editor, *2000 ACM SIGPLAN Haskell Workshop*, volume 41(1) of *ENTCS*. Montreal, Canada, Elsevier Science, 2001.
14. J. Hughes. Generalising Monads to Arrows. *Science of Computer Programming*, 37:67–111, May 2000.
15. G. Krasner and S. Pope. A cookbook for using the Model-View-Controller user interface paradigm in Smalltalk-80. *Journal of Object-Oriented Programming*, 1(3):26–49, August 1988.
16. E. Meijer. Server Side Web Scripting in Haskell. *Journal of Functional Programming*, 10(1):1–18, 2000.
17. R. Milner, M. Tofte, R. Harper, and D. MacQueen. *The Definition of Standard ML (Revised)*. MIT Press, 1997.
18. S. Peyton Jones and Hughes J. et al. *Report on the programming language Haskell 98*. University of Yale, 1999. http://www.haskell.org/definition/.
19. R. Plasmeijer and M. van Eekelen. *Functional Programming and Parallel Graph Rewriting*. Addison-Wesley Publishing Company, 1993. ISBN 0-201-41663-8.
20. R. Plasmeijer and M. van Eekelen. *Concurrent CLEAN Language Report (version 2.0)*, December 2001. http://www.cs.ru.nl/~clean/.
21. C. Queinnec. The influence of browsers on evaluators or, continuations to program web servers. In *Proceedings Fifth International Conference on Functional Programming (ICFP'00)*, Sept. 2000.
22. P. Thiemann. WASH/CGI: Server-side Web Scripting with Sessions and Typed, Compositional Forms. In S. Krishnamurthi and C. Ramakrishnan, editors, *Practical Aspects of Declarative Languages: 4th International Symposium, PADL 2002*, volume 2257 of *LNCS*, pages 192–208, Portland, OR, USA, January 19-20 2002. Springer-Verlag.
23. P. Thiemann. A Typed Representation for HTML and XML Documents in Haskell. *Journal of Functional Programming*, 2005. Under consideration for publication.
24. M. Wallace and C. Runciman. Haskell and XML: Generic combinators or type-based translation? In *Proc. of the Fourth ACM SIGPLAN Intnl. Conference on Functional Programming (ICFP'99)*, volume 34-9, pages 148–159, N.Y., 1999. ACM.

Fully Automatic Testing with Functions as Specifications

Pieter Koopman and Rinus Plasmeijer

Institute for Computing and Information Science,
Radboud University Nijmegen, The Netherlands
{pieter, rinus}@cs.ru.nl

Abstract. Although computer systems penetrate all facets of society, the software running those systems may contain many errors. Producing high quality software appears to be difficult and very expensive. Even determining the quality of software is not easy. Testing is by far the most used way to estimate the quality of software. Testing itself is not easy and time consuming.

In order to reduce the costs and increase the quality and speed of testing, testing should be automated itself. An automatical specification based test tool generates test data, executes the associated tests, and makes a fully automatically verdict based on a formal specification. Advantages of this approach are that one specifies properties instead of instances of these properties, test data are derived automatically instead of manually, the tests performed are always up to date with the current specification, and automatic testing is fast and accurate.

We will show that functions in a functional programming language can be used very well to model properties. One branch of the automatic test system GAST handles logical properties relating function arguments and results of a single function call. The other branch of GAST handles specifications of systems with an internal state.

1 Introduction

Testing is still by far the most used method to judge the quality of software. Human testing of software is error-prone, dull, and expensive. Systems are becoming larger and more complex, and hence harder to test. Moreover, the time to market should be reduced, which limits the time for testing. Hence, many approaches to automatic software testing are proposed and used.

Most test systems execute a fixed number of human specified tests. These specified tests are specified either in code, as in JUnit [1], or by a capture and playback tool. We focus on automatic test systems that generate test cases based on a formal specification, e.g. [2]. Instead of specifying a fixed number of fixed values and the expected response, one specifies a relation between input and output that holds for all arguments. Apart from generating the test cases, the test system also executes the tests, and makes a verdict based on the test results.

Advantages of generating test cases from the specification are that a change of specification do not invalidate the test script: it is generated from the updated

Z. Horváth (Ed.): CEFP 2005, LNCS 4164, pp. 35–61, 2006.

specification. Increasing the number of tests in order to improve the confidence just requires the change of a parameter.

In [3,4,5,6] it is shown that a functional programming language, as used by the test tool GAST, is an excellent carrier for the formal specifications needed. GAST is able to handle two kind of specifications: logical properties about (a combination of) functions, and specifications of reactive systems by Extended State Machines, ESMs. The reactive systems are specified by a, potentially infinite and nondeterministic, state transition function. Those specifications can be partial.

The quality of the test is dependent on the quality of the specification. Obviously, aspects that are not specified cannot be tested by a system that generates tests based on the specification. Experience shows that writing formal specifications is a very useful activity on its own. Most inaccuracies and misconceptions in the requirements are discovered during the construction of the specification.

Nevertheless, experience shows that a significant number of issues raised during testing is caused by inaccuracies in the specification. A better specification increases the speed of testing the product and improves the value of the test results. One can validate the specification to see if it captures the informal requirements correctly. This is a human activity that can be supported by tools. On the other hand one can also verify the consistency of the formal specification. This is usually done by inspections, or by verifying properties of the formal specification using a model checker or theorem prover. Especially for specifications that are heavily data dependent, model checkers have troubles with automatic verification.

In this paper we show that consistency properties of ESM-specifications can also be tested fully automatically using the logical branch of our test tool GAST. Advantages of this lightweight and effective method to improve the quality of specifications are that it do not require the transformation of specifications, errors are reported in terms of the original model, and last-but-not-least it works also very well for models that are strongly dependent on sophisticated data types. The limitation is that the test results are usually weaker than the results of a complete formal verification (if it is possible).

The testing of individual functions is discussed in section 2. The specification and testing of reactive systems in the next section. The testing of specifications in order to verify their quality, is discussed in section 4. Finally, we will discuss related work and draw conclusions.

2   Testing Functions with First Order Logic

The relation between input and output of a single function can be conveniently specified in predicate logic. As an example we consider a function that takes a string and a character as argument and yields a sorted list of the indices for all occurrences of the given character in the string, e.g. $indices("A\ test",'t')$ should yield the list $[2,5]$. We can specify the result of this function in at least two ways: we can give a reference implementation (perhaps very inefficient, but obviously correct), or we can state a property about the resulting list on indices.

Specification. The declarative specification gives a property of all indices in the sequence yielded by *indices*:

$$s \in String, \ c \in Char, \ i \in 0..\#s - 1 \bullet isMember(i, indices(s, c)) \Leftrightarrow s[i] = c$$

The function *isMember* checks if the element occurs in a list, and $\#s$ is the length of the string s. The characters are numbered from 0 to $\#s - 1$ in $s[i]$ which indicates string subscription.

This property states that an index i is part of the result of $indices(s, c)$ if and only if $s[i] = c$. The universal quantifiers over c and s are often omitted, as is usual in logic.

Every logical property is transformed to a function. The name of the function is used as reference to the property. The function arguments are interpreted as universal quantifiers. GAST provides a complete set of logical operators including $\forall$, $\exists$, $\vee$, $\wedge$, $\neg$, $\Rightarrow$ and $\Leftrightarrow$. The property state above is expressed in CLEAN as:

```
propIndices :: String Char → Property
propIndices s c = p For [0..size s-1]
where p i = isMember i (indices s c) ⟺ (s.[i] == c)
```

The operators **For** and $\Longleftrightarrow$ in this function definition is provided by the GAST-library. In this situation it is safe to replace $\Longleftrightarrow$ by the equality $==$. For implementation reasons the result of a specifying function is **Property** instead of **Bool**, if the specification contains a test operator like $\Longleftrightarrow$.

Note that this specification does not specify that the resulting list ought to be sorted, e.a. a function that yields $[5, 2]$ as result to $indices("A \ test", 't')$ also obeys this property (and hence passes the test). This is not a fundamental problem, in fact it is a feature: in practice we usually work with partial specifications, rather than complete specifications. Specifying that the indices should be increasing can look like:

```
propIncreasing :: String Char → Bool
propIncreasing s c = increasing (indices s c)

increasing [x,y:r] = x < y && increasing [y:r]
increasing other   = True
```

Reference Implementation. Using a reference implementation the function *indices* can be specified in CLEAN as:

```
propIndices2 :: String Char → Bool
propIndices2 s c = indices s c == [i \\ i ← [0..size s-1] | s.[i] == c]
```

In this function the reference implementation is stated as the list comprehension $[i \backslash\backslash i \leftarrow [0..\text{size } s-1] | s.[i] == c]$, this are all numbers i between 0 and size s-1 where element i of string s is equal to the given character c.

Invoking Tests. The first property can be tested by evaluating the expression `test propIndices`, e.g.:

```
Start = test propIndices
```

This will cause the evaluation of the function `propIndices` for at most 1000 (the standard number of tests) values. In this test the function `indices` is the Implementation Under Test, IUT, all other parts of the language are expected to work correctly.

Partial Functions. Many functions used in programming are partial functions, they work correctly for a part of the input domain. For example the square root function works only for non-negative real numbers and the factorial function works only for non-negative integer values. From the outside it is not visible that these functions are partial functions, hence the test system is not able to limit the test data automatically to the part of the input type where the function is defined.

GAST provides two ways to cope with partial functions. In logic properties of partial functions usually include an implication operator restricting the actual property to input values that should behave as requested, e.g. $\forall x \in R.x \geq 0 \Rightarrow (\sqrt{x})^2 = x$. In GAST we can directly express this:

```
propSqrt :: Real → Bool
propSqrt x = x ≥ 0 ⟹ let y = sqrt x in y*y = x
```

As an experienced programmer may expect, GAST finds counterexamples very quickly due to rounding errors. A better specification states that the difference $(\sqrt{x})^2$ and x should be less than some small number δ:

```
propSqrt2 :: Real → Property
propSqrt2 x = x ≥0.0 ⟹ let y = sqrt x in y*y - x < delta
where delta = 1E-10
```

The other way to cope with partial functions is to limit the test data explicitly to allowed inputs. For our square root example this can be:

```
propSqrt3 :: Real → Bool
propSqrt3 x = let y = sqrt x in y*y - x < delta
where delta = 1E-10

Start = test (propSqrt3 For [0.0, 0.123456789 .. ])
```

Of course limiting the test data to allowed inputs is more efficient in terms of actual tests done. For the actual testing rejecting test data (and generating them) is a waste of time.

2.1   The Test Algorithm

The IUT passes the test if the property holds for all generated arguments, i.e. it evaluates to `True`. The property does not hold if a counterexample is found.

For a property *prop* with one universal quantified variable, that is a function with one argument, the test algorithm is given by *testLogical*. The function takes the list of all possible test data and the number of test to be done as arguments. If the number of tests to be done is 0, the property passes the test. Otherwise, the property is evaluated for the first test value t. If this test succeeds, evaluates to True, testing continues with the rest of the test values. Otherwise a counterexample is found, and the test yields fail. The actual implementation shows also the test value that is the counterexample.

$$testLogical\,([t:ts],n) = \textbf{if } n = 0$$
$$\textbf{then } \textsf{pass}$$
$$\textbf{else if } prop(t)$$
$$\textbf{then } testLogical\,(ts, n-1)$$
$$\textbf{else } \textsf{fail}$$
$$testLogical\,([\,],n) = \textsf{proof}$$

The list of test values is provided by the operator **For**, or generated by the function **ggen** discussed below. For properties with more than one universal quantified variable the test algorithm tries every combination in a fair order: Instead of combining the first value of the first argument with all possible values for the second argument before looking at the second value for the first argument, the values are combined in an interleaved way. For a 2-argument function f, the system generates two sequences of arguments, call them $[a, b, c, ..]$ and $[u, v, w, ..]$ respectively. The desired order of tests is $f\,a\,u, f\,a\,v, f\,b\,u, f\,a\,w, f\,b\,v, f\,c\,u, ..$ rather than $f\,a\,u, f\,a\,v, f\,a\,w, .., f\,b\,u, f\,b\,v, f\,b\,w, ...$

2.2   Implementation of the Test System

The properties to be tested are functions with a variable number of arguments, the universal quantified variables. The result is either a Boolean or an element of the type **Prop** introduced above. We introduce the class **Testable** in order to create a function that eats all kinds of everything as an argument.

```
class Testable a where evaluate :: a RandomStream Admin → [Admin]
```

The random stream is a list of pseudo random numbers used in the selection of test data. The type **Admin** is used to record information of the current test. In theory it would be sufficient to yield a Boolean result indicating if the test was successful or not. In practice we also want to record some information about the tests done. For instance, we do not only want to know that there exists a counterexample, but also the value of the universal quantified variables for this counterexample. This information is stored in the record **Admin**. The list of admin's that is the result of the function **evaluate** contains one record for each test performed. An additional function is used to combine the results of the first N tests.

The instance of **evaluate** for Booleans is very easy. There is only one element in the list of results. If the Boolean is True the property holds (**OK**), otherwise a counterexample (**CE**) is found.

```
instance Testable Bool
where
    evaluate b rs admin
      = [{admin & res = if b OK CE, args = reverse result.args}]
```

A function a→b as argument of evaluate implies that we have to test a logical expression containing a universal quantified variable of type a. We can test this expression if a is a valid test argument, and we can test things of type b. A type a is a valid test argument if elements of this type can be transformed to strings by genShow {|*|}, and generated by ggen {|*|}.

```
class TestArg a | genShow {|*|} , ggen {|*|} a
```

```
instance Testable (a→b) | Testable b & TestArg a
where
    evaluate f rs result
    ♯ (rs,rs2) = split rs
    = forAll f (generateAll rs) rs2 result
```

For the implementation of logical operators it is a little inconvenient that the class Testable eats almost each function. The type Property is merely used to stop the class Testable from evaluating a function as a logical expression. In order to be able to continue the evaluation of such an expression we just have to remove the constructor Prop.

```
:: Property = Prop (RandomStream Admin → [Admin])
```

```
instance Testable Property
where evaluate (Prop p) rs result = p rs result
```

The operator **For** that can be used to supply a list of test data that is to be used instead of the test data generated by GAST is defined as:

```
(For) infixl 0 :: !(x→p) ![x] → Property | Testable p & TestArg x
(For) p list = Prop (forAll p list)
```

The logical implication operator, ⇐, is used for argument selection. If its left-hand argument evaluates to False, this test case is rejected: it is neither a success nor a counterexample.

```
class (⟹) infixr 1 b :: b p → Property | Testable p
```

```
instance ⟹ Bool
where
    (⟹) c p
    | c = Prop (evaluate p)
        = Prop (\rs r = [{r & res = Rej}])
```

A similar instance of ⟹ exists for Property.

2.3 Generating Test Data

Test data are generated by the *generic*[1] [13] function ggen. GAST contains instances of the function ggen for all basic types. By deriving an instance for a user

---

[1] To avoid confusion with generic programming in object oriented languages this is also called *polytypical* programming. Generic programming in the OO-spirit is called polymorphic programming in functional programming.

defined type, all instances of this type are enumerated in a pseudo random order
with a very strong small to large bias. The basic idea is that generic programming provides an universal tree representation of arbitrary data types. The test
data are obtained by a breadth-first traversal of the tree of all possible instances
of the type.

For an individual test it is possible to deviate from the arguments by **ggen**.
For instance, if we want to test the function *indices* only for the strings
"Hello world!" and "A test", we evaluate the expression:

```
test  (propIndices  For ["Hello World!","A test"])
```

Using the given strings in all situations where GAST needs to quantify over
strings is obtained by defining an instance of **ggen** for the type **String** like:

```
ggen {|String|} x y = ["Hello World!","A test"]
```

The arguments x and y can be used to vary the order of the generated elements.

The generic function **ggen** and the operator **For** yield powerful and flexible
generation of test data. The ability to combine logical operators with the concise
high level computations of a functional language and the flexible automatic test
data generation, makes GAST a very powerful tool for testing functions over
complex data types.

Generic Test Data Generation. One of the distinguishing features of GAST
is that it is able to generate test data in a systematic way [12]. This guarantees
that test are never repeated, which is useless in a referential transparent language like CLEAN. For finite data types it is even possible to prove properties
using a test system: a properties is proven if it holds for all elements of the finite
data type.

The generic function **gen** generates the lazy list of all values of a type by
generating all relevant generic representations [13] of the members of that type.

```
generic gen a :: [a]
```

For the type UINT there is only one posibility: the constructor UNIT.

```
gen {|UNIT|} = [UNIT]
```

For a PAIR we combine the lists of values generated by f and g in all possible
ways. We use the library function diag2 rather than a list-comprehension like
[Pair a b \\ a←f, b←g] in order to obtain the required fair order. The function
diag2 from the StdEnv combines elements for the given lists in a diagonal way.
For instance diag2 ['a'..] [1..] yields a list that begins like: [('a',1), ('b',1),
('a',2), ('c',1), ('b',2), ('a',3), ('d',1), ('c',2), ('b',3), ('a',4),...

```
gen {|PAIR|} f g = map (λ(a,b)⇒PAIR a b) (diag2 f g)
```

For the choice in the type EITHER we use an additional Boolean argument to merge
the elements in a nice interleaved way. The definition of the function **merge** is
somewhat tricky in order to avoid that it becomes strict in its list elements.

```
gen {|EITHER|}  f g = merge True f g
where
    merge :: !Bool [a] [b]  → [EITHER a b]
    merge left as bs
    | left
       = case as of
           [] = map RIGHT bs
           [a:as] = [LEFT a: merge (not left) as bs]
       = case bs of
           [] = map LEFT as
           [b:bs] = [RIGHT b: merge (not left) as bs]
```

In order to let this merge algorithm terminate for recursive data types we assume that the non recursive case (like Nil for lists, Leaf for trees) is listed first in the type definition. Using some insight knowledge of the generic representation of algebraic data types allow us to make the right initial choice in gen {|EITHER|} . In principle the generic representation contains sufficient information to find the terminating constructor dynamically, but this is more expensive and that does not add any additional power.

Finally we have to provide instances of gen for the basic types of CLEAN. Some examples are:

```
gen {|Int|}   = [0: [i \\ n←[1..maxint], i←[n,~n]]]
gen {|Bool|}  = [False,True]
gen {|Char|}  = map toChar [32..126] ++ ['\t\n\r']
gen {|String|} = map toString lists
where
    lists :: [[Char]]
    lists = gen {|*|}
```

The actual algorithm used in GAST is slightly more complicated. It uses a stream of pseudo random numbers to make small perturbations to the order of elements generated. Basically the choice between Left and Right in ggen {|Either|} becomes a pseudo random one instead of strict alternating one.

Pseudo Random Order of Test Arguments. Many testers believe that for good test results the order of test should be (pseudo) random. There is hardly any evidence that this general claim is correct, but it is easy to satisfy these testers. We want to keep the systematic generation of test values in order to avoid needless repetitions of identical tests and to produce proofs by exhaustive testing. The order of elements in the test suite can be changed a little without effecting the quality of the tests. We still want to have border values near the beginning of the test suite and other values later.

The actual implementation of GAST use a generic function ggen rather than gen. The difference is that ggen has a pseudo random perturbation of the elements in the list of test values. In the resulted list is looks like elements are moved back and forth a bit in a pseudo random order. The actual algorithm used by ggen is a bit more cleaver, only the values really needed in the list are generated. See [12] for details about this algorithm. The only real difference is in the instance for

EITHER. In order to avoid a complicated analysis of the generic representation of a data type we assume that the nonrecursive constructors in a type, like Nil and Tip, are defined first. The argument n is there for technical reasons, it controls the change between choosing between LEFT and RIGHT in the instance ggen {|EITHER|} . If merge goes deeper in the recursion, the change of selecting LEFT increases. This cause termination for any shape of the type that has the nonrecursive constructors defined first. The other additional argument is a list of pseudo random numbers controlling the choice between LEFT and RIGHT.

```
ggen {|EITHER|} f g n rnd
        ♯ (r1,rnd) = split rnd
          (r2,rnd) = split rnd
        = merge n rnd (f n r1) (g (n+1) r2)
where
    merge :: Int RandomStream [a] [b] → [EITHER a b]
    merge n [i:r] as bs
    | (i rem n) ≠ 0
        = case as of
            [] = map RIGHT bs
            [a:as] = [LEFT a: merge n r as bs]
        = case bs of
            [] = map LEFT as
            [b:bs] = [RIGHT b: merge n r as bs]
```

Also the generation of elements of basic types is pseudo random. For instance for integers we make sure that the common border values occur very soon and we continue with the list of pseudo random numbers rnd.

```
ggen {|Int|} n rnd = randomize [0,1,-1,maxint,minint] rnd 5 id
```

Having the border values in front of the test set guarantees that the error in a property like

```
propAbs :: Int → Bool
propAbs n = abs n ≥ 0
```

is found quickly. The result of executing Start = test propAbs is: *Counterexample 1 found after 1 tests: -2147483648(minint)*. The exact number of tests needed is dependent of the seed used in the generation of pseudo random numbers. Any experienced computer scientist knows that the inverse of minint in 2-complement notation is minint itself. This implies that the absolute value of any integer but minint is positive.

2.4   Controlling Input Values

GAST provides a rich palette of tools to control the actual values used as test argument. In this section we will give an overview and some examples of their use. This should make it easier to chose the most appropriate approach for a particular test.

Generic generation should be the default choice for generating values of a data type. The algorithm outlined above generates a list of values from small to large with some pseudo random perturbation of the order. Especially for recursive and parameterized data types this is very useful.

Consider the type `Tree` as an example.

```
:: Tree a = Empty | Node (Tree a) a (Tree a)
```

For this tree we define a function `swap` that recursively swaps the left and right subtree in a given tree.

```
swap :: (Tree a) → Tree a
swap Empty = Empty
swap (Node l n r) = Node (swap r) n (swap l)
```

A desirable property for each tree is that swapping it twice yields the original tree: `twice swap t == t`. In order to prevent that we have to define equality for trees, we use the generic equality `==`. The desired instance is derived by writing **derive gEq Tree**. Also the generation of trees, **ggen**, and the printing of trees, **genShow**, is derived.

In order to execute the test CLEANneeds a fixed type for the trees to be generated: the overloading in `propSwap` should be solved. We should chose a type of trees to be generated and tested. Usually it is a good strategy to use a finite and small type, like `Char` or `Bool`, in the actual tests. Swapping trees with the same structure, but different constants in de nodes does not yield more information. Here we have chosen to test trees of Booleans by giving `propSwap` the type `(Tree Bool)` → `Bool` rather than the more general `(Tree a)` → `Bool | < a`.

```
derive ggen Tree
derive gEq Tree
derive genShow Tree

propSwap :: (Tree Bool) → Bool
propSwap t = twice swap t == t

Start = test propSwap
```

As you might expect, this property passes any number of tests.

User defined generation of elements of a type can be very useful if only a small fraction of the domain has to be used in the tests. The generic function **ggen** yields a list of all elements to be used as test value: the *test suite*.

Suppose that for one reason of another we want to test only with trees that have only empty left subtrees. Instead of deriving the generation of trees, we can define:

```
ggen {|Tree|} elems n r = l
where l = [Empty: [ Node Empty e t \\ (e,t) ← diag2 (elems n r) l]]
```

In order to make a pseudo random perturbation of the order of these elements we can use the function `randomize` from the GAST-library. Apart from the list of values to be randomized, the function randomize has a list of pseudo random numbers as argument, a number controlling the amount of perturbation, and a function that given a list of pseudo random integers yields the rest of the numbers to be generated. We can randomize our trees with empty left subtrees by:

```
ggen {|Tree|}  elems n r = randomize l r 2 (λ_→[])
where l = [Empty: [ Node Empty e t \\ (e,t) ← diag2 (elems n r) l]]
```

Usually user defined instance of ggen are not used for recursive types, but for small sets of constants. The function holidays produces the number of days off per year given an age between 18 and 65. Suppose that we want to test whether the number of days per year is between 20 and 30. A straight forward definition of this property seems:

```
propHolidays a = 20 ≤ h && h ≤ 30 where h = holidays a
```

Testing this property with Start = test propHolidays shows immediately strange answers for the default arguments like 0, maxint and minint. A more accurate property is:

```
propHolidays1 a = 18 ≤ a && a ≤ 65 ⟹ 20 ≤ h && h≤ 30 where h = holidays a
```

But the test results of Start = test propHolydays1 are disappointing: none of the first 5000 generated integers appears to be a valid age. This implies that nothing is tested about holidays. This is not strange if we consider that only 48 of the 2^{32} integers are valid test arguments. Changing the general generation of integers is clearly undesirable.

There are at least three ways to tackle this problem. First we can transform an arbitrary integer to a valid age in an ad-hoc way:

```
propHolidays2 a = propHolidays1 (18+abs (a rem (65-18+1)))
```

This works, but has as disadvantages that it is rather ad-hoc, that it does more tests than needed (testing the same age multiple times), and does not give maximal information (a proof by exhaustive testing is possible for this small number of arguments.

The second way to solve the testing problem does not suffer from these disadvantages. We specify the arguments that should be used in the actual test by the For combinator: Start = test (propHolydays1 For [18..65]). This yields the proof we had hoped.

When we want to test more properties with this age the third way to solve the problem becomes more appropriate. We can define a special type for age and define the instances by hand instead of deriving them:

```
:: Age = Age Int
ggen {|Age|} n r = map Age [18..65]
derive genShow Age
```

This has as additional advantage that the values get tagged by their type. This can be very handy for properties over many variables over similar types. The property can be stated as:

```
propHolidays3 (Age a) = 20≤h && h≤30 where h = holidays a
```

As you night expect testing this property also yields a proof.

For properties over many variables proofs of properties over ages might become too much work. In those situation it is worthwhile to randomize the test values with the function `randomize` from the GAST library. According to good testing practise we take care of testing the boundary values 18 and 65 quickly:

```
ggen {|Age|} n r = map Age ([18,65] ++ randomize [19..64] r 46 λ_→[])
```

The choice between a property with the operator **For** and a special type with a dedicated instance of `ggen` depends on the taste of the test architect and the expected use. When the values are needed at several places we do encourage the use of a special type. Data types involved in this kind of properties are usual not recursive, hence writing a handcrafted instance of `ggen` is usually pretty easy.

Abstract and restricted data types require their own approach in testing. Suppose that we want to test a particular implementation of a binary search tree. The interface of this type (given in a `.dcl`-file) is:

```
:: SearchTree a

empty :: (SearchTree a)
addElement :: a (SearchTree a) → SearchTree a | < a
isElement :: a (SearchTree a) → Bool | < a
```

How can we test this abstract data type, ADT? Here we cannot derive instances of `SearchTree` for two reasons. (**1**) For the user of this library the search trees are an ADT. This also implies that the generic system has no knowledge about the internal structure of the ADT. Hence, it is impossible to derive an instance of `ggen` for search trees. (**2**) Since search trees are restricted data types, (all elements smaller that the value of a node should be in the left subtree, ..) deriving instance of such a restricted data type do not produce only correct instances: the generic system only knows the types and nothing about the additional restrictions. In addition what property can we specify over an instance of an ADT with unknown content and structure?

Nevertheless, we can test this ADT. The key step is to fill a tree with a list of known elements. A simple property is that a search tree should contain a value if and only if it is inserted in the tree:

```
propSearchTree :: Char [Char] → Property
propSearchTree c list = isMember c list ⟺ isElement c (toSearchTree list)

toSearchTree list = foldr addElement empty list
```

For a proper implementation of `SearchTree` this property passes any number of tests, but it does not guarantee that the ADT is really constructed using search trees.

In order to test whether the trees are really subtrees we add an instance of
toList to the interface of search trees that yields the values in the tree according
to an inorder tree walk:

```
instance toList SearchTree
where toList l = inorder l []
      where inorder Empty c = c
            inorder (Node l n r) c = inorder l [n:inorder r c]
```

For a proper search tree this list of values should be sorted. We can test this
with a property like:

```
propIsSearchTree :: ([Char] → Bool)
propIsSearchTree = increasing o toList o toSearchTree
```

Using increasing from section 2. Our implementation of search trees passes any
number of tests initiated by Start = test propIsSearchTree. Together with the
results of testing propSearchTree this greatly increases our confidence in the
correctness of the implementation of SearchTree.

This shows that it is also possible to test abstract and restricted data types
with GAST. In general the ability to derive the generation of instances of arbitrary types from the generic algorithm is a great pleasure. In this section we
have shown that there can be reasons to define a list of test values explicitly and
how this can be done.

3   Testing Reactive Systems

A reactive system has an internal state that can be changed by inputs and is
preserved between the inputs. This implies that the reaction on the current input
can depend on previous inputs. E.g. the system gets numbers as input and the
response is the number of inputs seen. The reactive systems that are discussed
here can be nondeterministic. During the tests we look only at the inputs and
responses of the reactive system, the internal state is not known. This is called
Black Box Testing, BBT.

The reactive system tested is the Implementation Under Test, IUT. Since
the state of the IUT is hidden, stating properties relating input, output and
state is not feasible. To circumvent this problem we specify reactive systems by
an extended state machine and require that the observed behavior of the IUT
conforms to this specification.

From Finite State Machines, FSMs, we inherit the synchronous behavior of
systems. Each input yields a, possibly empty, sequence of outputs. After producing this sequence of outputs the system becomes quiescent; it waits for a new
input. Among other advantages this yields a convenient notion of no output: the
empty sequence. We extend the FSM model in several directions:

– The state, input and output can be of any (recursive) data type. This includes
  also infinite data types and parameterized data types. Hence, we have a state
  machine rather than a *finite* state machine. A machine specification having
  parameterized data types is also known as an *extended* state machine.

– It is not required that the specification or implementation of the state machine is deterministic.

3.1   Extended State Machines

An Extended State Machine, ESM, as used by GAST consists of states with labelled transitions between them. A transition is of the form $s \xrightarrow{i/o} t$, where s, t are states, i is an input which triggers the transition, and o is a, possibly empty, list of outputs. A transition $s \xrightarrow{i/o} t$ is formalized as a tuple (s, i, t, o). A relation based specification δ_r is a set of these tuples: $\delta_r \subseteq S \times I \times S \times [O]$. Where S is the type of states, I is the type of inputs, and O is the type of outputs. We use $[O]$ in the transitions to indicate a sequence of elements of type O. It is not required that all these types are different. Specifications can be *partial*: not for every $s \in S$ and $i \in I$ there must be a tuple in δ_r specifying the new state and the output. A specification is *total* if it is not partial. If a specification is *nondeterministic* there are $s \in S$ and $i \in I$ with more than one tuple in δ_r.

In practice it is usually more convenient to have a specifying function instead of a transition relation. The transition function takes the current state and input as argument and produces the set of all specified tuples of target state and output sequence. The transition function is defined by $\delta_f(s, i) = \{(t, o) | (s, i, t, o) \in \delta_r\}$. The type of this function is: *State* $\times$ *Input* $\rightarrow \mathbb{P}(\textit{State} \times [\textit{Output}])$. Here we used $\mathbb{P}(X)$ as notation for a set of elements of type X. Transition $s \xrightarrow{i/o} t$ is equivalent to $(t, o) \in \delta_f(s, i)$. A specification is *partial* if for some state s and input i, $\delta_f(s, i) = \emptyset$. A specification is *deterministic* if for all states and inputs the size of the set of targets contains at most one element: $\# \delta_f(s, i) \leq 1$.

A trace σ is a sequence of inputs and associated outputs from the given state. A trace is defined inductively: the empty trace connects a state to itself: $s \xrightarrow{\epsilon} s$. We can combine a trace $s \xrightarrow{\sigma} t$ and a transition $t \xrightarrow{i/o} u$, to the trace $s \xrightarrow{\sigma;i/o} u$. An *input trace* contains only the input elements of a trace.

We define $s \xrightarrow{i/o} \equiv \exists t.s \xrightarrow{i/o} t$ and $s \xrightarrow{\sigma} \equiv \exists t.s \xrightarrow{\sigma} t$. All traces from a given state are defined as: $\textit{traces}(s) \equiv \{\sigma | s \xrightarrow{\sigma} \}$.

The inputs allowed in some state are given by $\textit{init}(s) \equiv \{i | \exists o.s \xrightarrow{i/o} \}$. The states after applying trace σ in state s are given by $s \textbf{ after } \sigma \equiv \{t | s \xrightarrow{\sigma} t\}$. We overload *traces*, *init*, and **after** for sets of states instead of a single state by taking the union of the notion for the members of the set. When the transition function, δ_f, to be used is not clear from the context, we will add it as subscript.

We will often identify a machine with its transition function. However, a complete description also determines the initial state s_0.

Examples. As illustration we show some state machines modelling coffee vending machines in figure 1. In section 4 we will test some properties of these specifications. The global specification of these coffee vending machines is that it can deliver coffee after insertion of coins with a value of 10 cent, and pressing the coffee button. An input is either a nickel, a 5-cent coin, a dime, a 10-cent coin, or pressing the coffee button. The output is either the return of a coin, or coffee. For simplicity we will use the same type IO for input and output, we take care that the *Coffee* is never an input and *Button* is never an output. The state of the

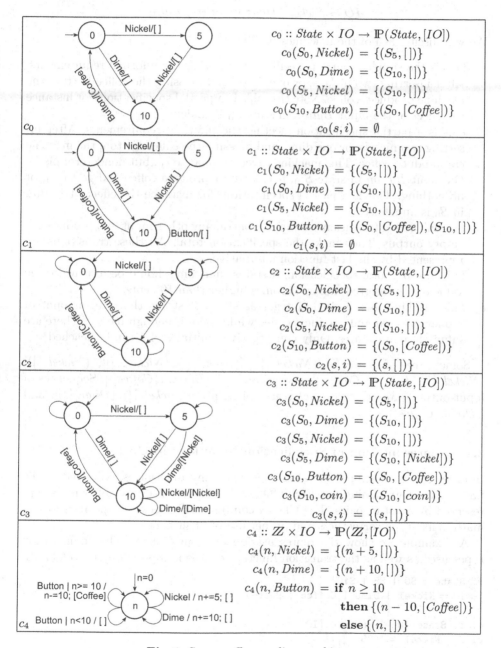

$$c_0 :: State \times IO \to \mathbb{P}(State, [IO])$$
$$c_0(S_0, Nickel) = \{(S_5, [])\}$$
$$c_0(S_0, Dime) = \{(S_{10}, [])\}$$
$$c_0(S_5, Nickel) = \{(S_{10}, [])\}$$
$$c_0(S_{10}, Button) = \{(S_0, [Coffee])\}$$
$$c_0(s, i) = \emptyset$$

$$c_1 :: State \times IO \to \mathbb{P}(State, [IO])$$
$$c_1(S_0, Nickel) = \{(S_5, [])\}$$
$$c_1(S_0, Dime) = \{(S_{10}, [])\}$$
$$c_1(S_5, Nickel) = \{(S_{10}, [])\}$$
$$c_1(S_{10}, Button) = \{(S_0, [Coffee]), (S_{10}, [])\}$$
$$c_1(s, i) = \emptyset$$

$$c_2 :: State \times IO \to \mathbb{P}(State, [IO])$$
$$c_2(S_0, Nickel) = \{(S_5, [])\}$$
$$c_2(S_0, Dime) = \{(S_{10}, [])\}$$
$$c_2(S_5, Nickel) = \{(S_{10}, [])\}$$
$$c_2(S_{10}, Button) = \{(S_0, [Coffee])\}$$
$$c_2(s, i) = \{(s, [])\}$$

$$c_3 :: State \times IO \to \mathbb{P}(State, [IO])$$
$$c_3(S_0, Nickel) = \{(S_5, [])\}$$
$$c_3(S_0, Dime) = \{(S_{10}, [])\}$$
$$c_3(S_5, Nickel) = \{(S_{10}, [])\}$$
$$c_3(S_5, Dime) = \{(S_{10}, [Nickel])\}$$
$$c_3(S_{10}, Button) = \{(S_0, [Coffee])\}$$
$$c_3(S_{10}, coin) = \{(S_{10}, [coin])\}$$
$$c_3(s, i) = \{(s, [])\}$$

$$c_4 :: \mathbb{Z} \times IO \to \mathbb{P}(\mathbb{Z}, [IO])$$
$$c_4(n, Nickel) = \{(n + 5, [])\}$$
$$c_4(n, Dime) = \{(n + 10, [])\}$$
$$c_4(n, Button) = \textbf{if } n \geq 10$$
$$\textbf{then } \{(n - 10, [Coffee])\}$$
$$\textbf{else } \{(n, [])\}$$

Fig. 1. Some coffee vending machines

first three machines is the algebraic data type *State*, it just records the amount of money inserted. The last machine uses a number as state. The types *State* and *IO* are enumeration types defined as:

$$State = S_0 \mid S_5 \mid S_{10}$$
$$IO = Nickel \mid Dime \mid Coffee \mid Button$$

We will discus each of the machines briefly:

c_0 This is the simplest partial specification meeting the informal requirements. After inserting two nickels, or one dime, and pressing the coffee button, the machine produces coffee. Note that this is a partial specification, for instance the effect of the input *Button* in state S_0 is undefined.

c_1 This is a partial specification meeting the informal requirements. After inserting two nickels, or one dime, and pressing the coffee button, the machine can produce coffee. This machine is very similar to c_0, but nondeterministic. On input *Button* in state S_{10}, it can either produce coffee and go to S_0, or do nothing. This is a partial specification, for instance the effect of *Button* in S_0 is undefined.

c_2 The unlabelled transitions are applicable on any other input and produce the empty output. They make the specification total. All these transitions are represented by the last function alternative.

c_3 This is also a total specification. It states that coins should be returned if the value of the inserted money becomes higher than 10 cents.

c_4 This machine uses a single integer as state. It stores the total amount of money inserted and produces coffee while there is enough money. There are infinitely many states. Only non-negative multiples of 5 can be reached.

Some traces of c_2 are: $[]$, $[(Nickel,[])]$, $[(Nickel,[]),(Nickel,[])]$, $[(Nickel,[]), (Nickel,[]),(Button,[Coffee])]$, and $[(Dime,[]),(Button,[Coffee])]$. Sequences of input-output pairs that are *not* traces of c_2 are: $[(Nickel,[]),(Dime,[])]$, and $[(Dime,[Coffee])]$.

3.2   Representation of Specification Functions in Gast

In order to test machines in GAST, the specifying function is expressed in the functional programming language CLEAN [7]. The resulting set of pairs is represented by a list of pairs. The CLEAN compiler will check the specification on matters like type correctness and proper use of identifiers.

As example we show the representation of c_1 in CLEAN. The enumeration types used as well as the transition function can be mapped directly to CLEAN.

```
:: State = S0 | S5 | S10
:: IO = Nickel | Dime | Coffee | Button

c1 :: State IO → [(State,[IO])]
c1 S0   Nickel = [(S5 ,[])]
c1 S0   Dime   = [(S10,[])]
```

```
c1 S5   Nickel = [(S10,[]) ]
c1 S10  Button = [(S0  ,[Coffee ]), (S10,[])]
c1 s    i      = []
```

Function arguments starting with a capital are constants that must be matched to the actual arguments in order to make this alternative applicable. Lowercase arguments match any actual argument. Alternatives are tried in textual order, the first one that matches is applied.

Using higher order functions, specifications can be manipulated. As a very simple example we list the function enableInput, that enables input in any state. This function takes a machine specification m as argument, and yields an input enabled version of m. If no transition is specified for some state and input, it adds the transition to the same state with an empty output sequence. Since this is a polymorphic function, it will work for any specification using arbitrary types for state s, input i and output o.

```
enableInput :: (s i → [(s,[o])]) → s i → [(s,[o])]
enableInput m = m'
where m' s i = case m s i of
                 [] = [(s,[])]
                 r  = r
```

Applying this function to c_0 yields a specification that is equivalent to c_2. Applying it to c_2, c_3, or c_4 does not change these specifications. Note that enableInput c1 is not equivalent to c_2, the first specification still contains the transition $S_{10} \xrightarrow{Button/[]} S_{10}$, which is not present in c_2.

3.3   Implementations Under Test

The assumption is that also the implementation under test is an extended state machine. Since the IUT is a black box, its state is invisible. Even if the IUT is nondeterministic, it will choose exactly one transition on each input.

In contrast to the specification, the implementation should be *input enabled*: the result of any input in any reachable state should be specified. In terms of the transition function this is $\forall s \in State.\forall i \in Input.\delta_f(s,i) \neq \emptyset$. The motivation for this requirement is that an IUT cannot prevent that inputs are applied. It is perfectly accaptable if some inputs in specific states brings the implementation in an error state. For our tests it is sufficient if the IUT accepts each input that is allowed by the specification. The broader input enabledness requirements prevents complicated analysis or runtime problems.

In the examples above, a coffee vending machine cannot prevent that a user presses the button or inserts a coin in any state. This implies that c_1 cannot be a correct implementation. or instance the effect of applying the input *Button*, pressing the coffee button, in state S_0 is undefined. The machines c_2, c_3 and c_4 are input enabled, and hence can be used as IUT.

The implementation can be in any programming language or even in hardware, for testing it is only required that GAST can provide an input to the IUT and observe the associated output.

3.4 Conformance

Intuitively an IUT is conform to a specification if the observed transitions are part of the specification, or the specification does not specify anything for this state and input: $\delta_f(s, i) = \emptyset$. Formally, conformance of the iut to the specification spec is defined as:

$$\text{iut } conf \text{ spec} \equiv \forall \sigma \in traces_{\text{spec}}(s_0).\forall i \in init(s_0 \text{ after}_{\text{spec}} \sigma)\forall o \in [O].$$

$$(t_0 \text{ after}_{\text{iut}} \sigma) \xrightarrow{i/o} \Rightarrow (s_0 \text{ after}_{\text{spec}} \sigma) \xrightarrow{i/o}$$

If the specification allows input i after trace σ, the observed output of the IUT should be allowed by the specification.

This notion of conformance is very similar to the *ioco* relation of [8] for Labelled Transition Systems, LTSs. In an LTS each input and output is modelled by a separate transition. In our approach an input and all induced outputs up to *quiescence* are modelled by a single transition with a sequence of outputs. The conformance relation for (timed) EFSMs in [9] is similar, our systems have a sequences of output. If there is no other information we use quiescence to determine the end of the sequence of outputs of the IUT. In [9] there is no notion of quiescence, and the EFSMs have only a single output.

Examples. Since both the specification and the IUT are given as an ESM, an ESM can be used as specification *and* as IUT. We have seen that c_1 in figure 1 cannot be a correct implementation since it is not input enabled. The machines c_2, c_3 and c_4 are correct implementations of c_1. Although the response $[]$ to the input *Button* in S_{10} will never occur. According to the conformance relation this is not necessary. It is sufficient that the behavior for some specified input after a trace is allowed by the specification. Note that c_3 and c_4 have behavior that is not covered by the specification. This is allowed according to the conformance relation because nothing is specified for that combination of state and input.

Machine c_3 is not a correct implementation of c_2. After the inputs [*Dime*, *Dime*] the machine c_2 only allows the output $[]$, while c_3 produces [*Dime*]. The same input trace shows that c_2 is not a correct implementation of c_3.

Although c_4 behaves correctly to c_2 as specification for the input sequence [*Dime*, *Dime*], it is not a correct implementation. This is shown for instance by the input sequence [*Dime*, *Dime*, *Button*, *Button*]. For this input c_4 produces a second cup of coffee, while c_2 only allows an empty output.

Finally, c_4 is not a correct implementation of c_3, nor is c_3 an implementation of c_4. This is shown for instance by the input sequence [*Dime*, *Dime*].

Testing Conformance. The testing algorithm takes a sequence of inputs as argument. The specification and implementation start in their initial state. As long as the specification specifies transitions for the current state and input, $spec(s, i) \neq \emptyset$, the next input is applied to the IUT. If the response is conform to the specified behavior, testing continues with the next input element and the new state of the specification, otherwise an error is found. If nothing is specified for the current state and input, testing of this input sequence is terminated. The associated test result is pass. If the end of the input sequence is reached the implementation has been successfully tested with this input sequence.

The function $testConformance$ takes the sequence of inputs, the observed trace and the number of steps to go as argument and produces a test verdict.

$$testConformance\ ([i:is], \sigma, n) = \textbf{if}\ n \neq 0 \wedge i \in init(s_0\ \textsf{after}_{\textsf{spec}}\ \sigma)$$
$$\textbf{then let}\ o = iut.apply(i)\ \textbf{in}$$
$$\textbf{if}\ (s_0\ \textsf{after}_{\textsf{spec}}\ \sigma) \xrightarrow{i/o}$$
$$\textbf{then}\ testConformance\ (is, \sigma; i/o, n-1)$$
$$\textbf{else fail}$$
$$\textbf{else pass}$$
$$testConformance\ ([], \sigma, n)\ = \textsf{proof}$$

The first condition checks if there are still inputs to be tested, $n \neq 0$, and if the specification states something for the next input after the observed trace, $i \in init(s_0\ \textsf{after}_{\textsf{spec}}\ \sigma)$. The innermost condition verifies whether the observed transition is allowed by the specification in the current state. For a more efficient implementation we keep track of the states allowed after the current trace. For deterministic specifications there is at most one state allowed at any moment. If the transition is allowed, testing continues with the rest of the inputs. An IUT passes the test of an input sequence, if the sequence becomes empty. During one test run, GAST can test several input sequences. The IUT and the specification are reset before each new input sequence.

Test Data Generation. In order to test conformance, GAST needs a collection of input sequences. GAST has several algorithms for input generation, e.g.:

- Systematic generation of sequences based on the input type by the same algorithm that is used for logical properties.
- Sequences that cover all transitions in a *finite* state machine. Under the assumption that the IUT has more states than the specification, this can prove the conformance of the IUT [10].
- Pseudo random walk through the transitions of a specification. This generates long test sequences that can penetrate deep in the state space. It appears to be very effective for machines with a large or infinite number of transitions
- User defined sequences for specific purposes.

Due to the lazy evaluation of CLEAN, only those inputs are generated than are actually needed by the test algorithm. This allows us to work with potentially infinite lists of inputs. This is known as *on-the-fly* generation of test data.

The machines given in figure 1 are so small that each of these algorithms indicated the errors very soon if the implementation is incorrect. The FSM-based algorithm can be used to prove that c_3 is correct implementations of c_2, it cannot be used for c_4 as specification since it has infinitely many states.

In section 4 we will use the part of GAST introduced in the next section to test properties of these ESM-specifications.

4   Quality of Specifications

Apart from the number of tests, the quality of testing is determined by the quality of the properties stated. Obviously, aspects of a system that are not specified cannot be tested. The CLEAN-compiler used by GAST checks many aspects, like proper use of identifiers and type-correctness, of the specification before it can be used. Semantical errors cannot be caught by the compiler. Incorrect specifications can cause strange test results. If the specification and the IUT contain the same error, it will pass unnoticed. In practice many issues spotted during testing are due to incorrect specifications.

In an incremental software process this is not a serious problem. The specification and the implementation are improved at the same time. Testing shows the differences in behavior of the implementation and the specification. In this way the quality of the specification and the implementation increases. This approach is only feasible when testing is fast and automatic, GAST was found to be very useful [5].

For software processes that creates the software in one go, like the waterfall-model or the V-model, incorrect specifications can seriously delay the delivery of the system. It is desirable to verify and improve the quality of specifications before they are used to test the actual implementation.

4.1   Testing Specifications

In every situation it is desirable to check properties of the specifications used. This can be done by a model checker, like FDR or SPIN, but also by testing. Formal verification by a model checker requires a transformation of the model to a suitable input language, like CSP or Promela. Testing can be done with the given specifications and appears to be fast and effective. For specifications of small finite systems[2], a number of properties cannot only be tested, but the property can even be proven correct or falsified by a counterexample. The specifications of reactive systems introduced in section 3 are ordinary functions in CLEAN, hence they can be tested like any function as shown in section 2. In this section we will show how, general or domain specific, properties of ESM specifications can be tested.

General properties like determinism and completeness can be checked for any ESM specification. A specification is deterministic is for every state and input there is at most one transition defined:

$$\forall\, s \in S, i \in I \bullet \# \delta_f(s,i) \leq 1$$

To make this property applicable to any specification in GAST we parameterize it with the machine specification m:

---

[2] A system is finite if the number of states, inputs and outputs is finite.

```
propDeterministic :: (Spec s i o) s i → Bool
propDeterministic m s i = length (m s i) ≤ 1
```

Where `Spec s i o` is an abbreviation for `s i →` $[(s,[o])]$. Specification `c1` introduced above can be tested by evaluating `test (propDeterministic c1)`. GAST spots the counterexample for state S_{10} and input *Button* in a split second. Due to the limited number of states and inputs GAST will prove that specifications `c2` and `c3` are deterministic. For `c4` there are infinitely many states, so a proof by exhaustive testing is not possible. Testing yields **pass**.

In the same spirit we can test whether a specification is total:

$$\forall s \in S, i \in I \bullet \delta_f(s,i) \neq \emptyset$$

This can also be specified directly in GAST:

```
propTotal :: (Spec s i o) s i → Bool
propTotal m s i = not (isEmpty (m s i))
```

As we might expect, GAST find counterexamples for `c1`, proves the property for `c2` and `c3` and machine `c4` passes any number of tests. These general properties can be applied to any ESM-specification and are part of the library GAST.

Note that all properties in this section are tested at a specification, and not at an implementation of that model. These tests can be done before an implementation exists.

Domain Specific Properties. As example of a domain specific property we require that coffee machines "do not lose money": the value of a state and the input should be equal to the value of the target state and the associated output for any transition specified. In logic this property reads:

$$\forall s \in S, i \in I, (t,o) \in \delta_f(s,i) \bullet value(s) + value(i) = value(t) + value(o)$$

This can be directly transformed to GAST. First, we construct a class *value* that yields the value of states, inputs and outputs. The value of a state is the amount of money inserted, the value of a coin is its value, the value of *Coffee* is 10, and the value of *Button* is 0. In order to test various machines easily, we make the specification to check an argument, m, of the property.

```
propFair m s i = p For m s i
where p (t,o) = value s + value i == value t + value o
```

GAST proves this property for c_1, and c_3. The property does not hold for c_2, one of the counterexamples found by the test system is inserting a *Dime* in state S_5. The property holds also for c_4. Since this machine has infinitely many states, the property passes the test, but a proof for all states is impossible. The states can be limited to multiples of 5 between 0 and 100 by evaluating `test (propFair m5 For [0,5..100])`. Now the property is proven by GAST.

This property shows also that making a specification input enabled by adding transitions to the same state without output, as done by `enableInput`, is not

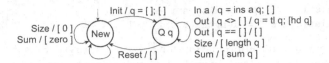

Fig. 2. The priority queue as state chart

an harmless operation. Property `propFair` does not hold for the input enabled version of machine c1, `enableInput` c1.

Finally, we can require that the value of a target state is nonnegative if the value of the source state is nonnegative: $s \xrightarrow{i/o} t \bullet value(s) \geq 0 \Rightarrow value(t) \geq 0$.

`propNonNeg m s i = p For m s i`
`where p (t,o) = value s ` $\geq 0 \implies$ ` value t ` ≥ 0

This property is proven for the states $[0,5..100]$ of m5, but testing it for all states yields counterexamples due to integer overflow. GAST proves this property for the other specifications.

4.2 A Priority Queue

As a more sophisticated example we show a priority queue that always dequeues the smallest elements first. It is only able to enqueue and dequeue elements after the input *Init*. The input *Reset* brings it back to the state *New*. This system is specified by the state chart in figure 2, or the function *QSpec* in figure 3.

Using overloading, the function *QSpec* is defined to be very general, it works for any type for which the operators `<`, `+`, and a `zero` are defined. This implies that we can put for instance integers, doubles, or characters in such a priority queue.

Testing General Properties of the Specification. The quality of this specification can be investigated by testing some of its desired properties. The specification passes any number of tests for being deterministic. When testing it for being total, GAST almost immediately spots a counterexample for state Q [] and input *Init*. The fact that the specification is not total implies that not all behavior can be tested by GAST: according to the conformance relation, any behavior is allowed if the specification does not specify a transition for a given state and input.

Testing Specific Properties of Specifications. For this specification we can also state and test some specific properties like for all states s_1 that are reached after applying the input sequence $[In\ c]$ for any c starting in any state s, the size of the queue should be one bigger than it was before. The size of the queue is determined by applying the input *Size*.

$$\forall s \in (Qstate\ Char), \forall c \in Char, \forall (s_0, [Int\ n]) \in QSpec(s, Size),$$
$$\forall s_1 \in (s\ \text{after}_{QSpec}\ [In\ c]), \forall (s_2, [Int\ m]) \in QSpec(s_1, Size) \cdot m = n + 1$$

$$QSpec :: (Qstate\ a) \times (Qin\ a) \rightarrow [(Qstate\ a, [Qout\ a])] \mid <, +, zero\ a$$
$$QSpec\,(New, Init) = [(Q\ [\,], [\,])]$$
$$QSpec\,(New, Size) = [(New, [Int\ 0])]$$
$$QSpec\,(New, Sum) = [(New, [El\ zero])]$$
$$QSpec\,(New, any) = [(New, [\,])]$$
$$QSpec\,(Q\ q, In\ a) = [(Q(ins\ a\ q), [\,])]$$
$$QSpec\,(Q\ [a : q], Out) = [(Qq, [El\ a])]$$
$$QSpec\,(Q\ q, Size) = [(Qq, [Int\ (length\ q)])]$$
$$QSpec\,(Q\ q, Sum) = [(Qq, [El\ (sum\ q)])]$$
$$QSpec\,(state, Reset) = [(New, [\,])]$$
$$QSpec\,(state, Out) = [(state, [\,])]$$
$$QSpec\,(state, i) = [\,]$$

The additional function *ins* inserts an element at the appropriate place in an ordered list. It can be defined as:

$$ins\,(a, [\,]) = [a]$$
$$ins\,(a, [b : x]) \mid a < b = [a, b : x]$$
$$= [b : ins\ a\ x]$$

Fig. 3. The priority queue as function

We used list comprehensions in CLEAN to mimic set notation. The operator **after** implements the after operation introduced in section 3.1.

```
propQsize :: (Qstate Char) Char → Bool
propQsize s c = and [ m == n+1  \\ (s0,[Int n]) ← QSpec s Size
                    ,  s1 ← ([s] after QSpec) [In c]
                    ,  (s2,[Int m]) ← QSpec s1 Size ]
```

After 6 tests, GAST tells us that this property does not hold for the state *New* and input $'d'$, in fact it does not hold for any input in state *New*.

Since the priority queue works for any type with operator < and +, and a **zero**, we can choose the type used in testing. If it works for one type, it will work for every type, provided that the operators are implemented correctly. Usually, a small type gives the best test results. For that reason we will use characters here, although a small special type like :: T = A | B | C is even more effective.

In the same way we can test whether the sum of the elements increases if we insert a positive element. Even if we rule out the problems with the state *New*, GAST finds counterexamples caused by overflow. This indicates that the specification does not handle the limitations of finite representations of elements.

$$\forall s \in (Qstate\ Char), \forall c \in Char, \forall(s_0, [El\ v]) \in QSpec(s, Sum),$$
$$\forall s_1 \in (s\ \mathbf{after}_{QSpec}\ [In\ c]), \forall(s_2, [El\ w]) \in QSpec(s_1, Size) \cdot w > v$$

```
propQ4a s c = c > zero ⟹ and [ w>v \\ (s0,[El v]) ← QSpec s Sum
                              , s1 ← ([s] after QSpec) [In c]
                              , (s2,[El w]) ← QSpec s1 Sum ]
```

Since we have access to the states of the specification, we can use its internals in our tests. For instance, we can test whether the elements in the queue are ordered such that head of the list is smaller that or equal to any element in that list. With this test we verify the distinguishing feature of a *priority* queue. This property is not enforced by the type system, but by the manipulations allowed in *QSpec*. We test this for every state reached by applying any input sequence in the initial state *New*.

$$\forall i \in (Qin\ Char), \forall (Q\ q) \in (New\ \text{after}_{QSpec}\ i), \forall e \in q \cdot hd(q) \le e$$

For GAST this can be expressed as:

```
propPriority :: [Qin Char] → Bool
propPriority i = and [ hd q ≤ e \\ Q q ← ([New] after QSpec) i, e ← q ]
```

This property passes any number of tests, GAST tests 100,000 different input sequences in 40 seconds.

Usually, properties of specifications are verified with a model checker. Due to the data dependencies used in the properties it is in this case not simple to verify the shown properties with a model checker. Moreover, in order to use a model checker the given model specification has to be translated to the world of the model checker, and produces results in terms of its own model. Here the model specification in CLEAN is used by GAST to test its properties. Only the desired logical property has to be stated in CLEAN.

The successful tests shown here do not indicate that testing of specifications has the same power as a fully fledged model checker. Due to the sophisticated logic used in state-of-the-art model checkers, they have their own significant contribution. Nevertheless, testing specifications is an elegant, powerful and lightweight alternative approach to verify properties of specifications.

Testing Implementations. In order to verify the testing quality of GAST we made a correct implementation of this queue and ten mutants containing common (programming) errors like: an ordinary queue instead of a priority queue, a stack instead of a priority queue, a queue of at most 25 elements, various errors in the function *ins* for duplicated elements, return to the state *New* when the queue becomes empty by an *Out*, and an implicit *Init* on an input *In a* when the system is in the state *New*.

We tested with the standard generic generation of test data for a queue of characters. GAST generates, tests and evaluates about 50,000 individual inputs per second on an average PC. It found errors in all mutants. Errors were always spotted within 0.5 seconds, usually much faster. This depends on the order of inputs and hence on the seed used for the generation of pseudo random numbers.

5   Related Work

Many automatic test tools are developed in order to speedup testing and make (regression) more accurate. Most of these test tools are script based and execute a predefined sequence of actions. One of the best known examples is JUNIT [1] for JAVA-programs, it has been ported to a very large number of other programming languages.

Model based tools like GAST are more powerful since they generate the test data themselves. In this way it is possible to increase the quality of the test by generating more test data, instead by manually specifying more tests. Moreover, generating test data based on the current version of the specification guarantees that the tests done are always conform the current version of the specification.

For the testing of logical properties the test tool Quickcheck [6], is clearly the closest related tool. Distinguishing futures of GAST are the systematic generation of test data (instead of programmer controlled pseudo random generation), and hence the ability to proof properties. Also the set of logical operators in GAST is richer.

For the testing of reactive systems a number of model based test systems is available. The dominant approach is based on labelled transition systems and Torx [8] can be regarded as the godfather of tools using this approach. None of these tools uses a functional programming language to express the state transition function. We have shown that a fpl yields a very concise way to specify reactive systems.

Much work has been done to verify and improve the quality of specifications. Most notably is the work to prove properties of the specifications with proof tools or model checkers. In fact a number of the properties shown can be verified with CLEAN's own proof system called SPARKLE [14]. This would require a significant user guidance that looses its value after any tiny change of the specification.

Model checkers, like [15, 16], are usually geared to verify properties about the communication between processes, they have troubles with data intensive systems like the priority queue used in this paper. Model checkers require a translation of our specifications. Moreover, these systems require user guidance, and hence specific skills of the user. Testing properties provides a valuable and effective alternative within the framework used to write the specification.

The tools BLAST [17] and MOPS [18] verify properties of C-programs. Both model checkers are FSM based. They differ in model, programming language, purpose and techniques used from our approach.

There are a few reports on specification testing in the literature, e.g. [19, 20, 21, 22], usually based on Z, [11], VDM, or B specifications. It focuses on animation of specifications to validate the specification by humans, on the evaluation of given input-output combinations, or on the question if there are instances of the specified transitions. A number of significant consistency aspects is checked by the strong type system of the CLEAN-compiler. To the best of our knowledge, this is the first report on testing specifications fully automatically in a systematic way, by generating test values, executing the tests, and generating a test verdict.

6   Discussion

In specification based testing one states general properties instead of instances of these properties for specific arguments. Advantages of this approach are the higher level of abstraction, and the automatic generation of test data from the specification. Manual generation of test data is dull and error-prone. Moreover, the validity of generated test data has to be checked after every change of the underlaying specification.

Using functional programming languages as notation for specifications appears to be very effective. The obtained specifications are very concise, and well suited to be handled by a test system like GAST.

Having the ability to test logical properties and reactive systems united in a single tool, allows us to verify the quality of specifications by automatic testing. This is a unique property of GAST. The properties tested are consistency rules for the specification of reactive systems. The same specification is used to test implementation and properties of the specification itself. Testing consistency properties of ESMs is possible since GAST combines the ability to automatically test logic properties and reactive systems. The tested properties can be general properties of specifications as well as domain specific. Testing specifications increases the quality and confidence in those specifications, and hence the quality of tests of implementations done with these specifications. Testing these properties is a lightweight and effective alternative for model checking. It works also in data intensive situations that are often hard for model checkers. An other advantage is that no other formalisms, translations and tools are needed. The examples in this paper show that many "obvious" properties of specifications are falsified by testing.

By verifying logical properties through testing, an ESM-specification can be made consistent. Another important quality attribute of an ESM-specification is to validate that it correctly states what the user requires. This validation cannot be done by fully automatic testing, but requires human guidance. Due to the executable nature of our specifications, they are also very suited for validation by simulation. We will address this in another paper.

References

1. See www.junit.org
2. Bernot, G., Gaudel, M. C., and Marre, B. Software testing based on formal specifications: a theory and a tool, Software Engineering Journal, Nov. 1991, pp387–405.
3. P. Koopman, A. Alimarine, J. Tretmans and R. Plasmeijer. GAST: Generic Automated Software Testing. In R. Peña, *IFL 2002*, LNCS 2670, pp 84–100, 2002.
4. P. Koopman and R. Plasmeijer. Testing reactive systems with GAST. In S. Gilmore, *Trends in Functional Programming 4*, pp 111–129, 2004.
5. A. van Weelden et al: On-the-Fly Formal Testing of a Smart Card Applet. SEC 2005. Or technical report NIII-R0403, at www.cs.ru.nl/research/reports.
6. K. Claessen, J. Hughes. QuickCheck: A lightweight Tool for Random Testing of Haskell Programs. ICFP, ACM, pp 268–279, 2000. See also www.cs.chalmers.se/~rjmh/QuickCheck.

7. R. Plasmeijer, M van Eekelen. Clean language report version 2.1. www.cs.ru. nl/~clean.
8. J. Tretmans. Testing Concurrent Systems: A Formal Approach. In J. Baeten and S. Mauw, editors, *CONCUR'99* – 10th, LNCS 1664, pp 46–65, 1999.
9. M. Núñez, I. Roderíguez. Encoding PARM into (Timed) EFSMs. FORTE 2002, LNCS 2529, pp 1–16, 2002.
10. D. Lee and M. Yannakakis. Principles and methods of testing finite state machines – a survey. *Proc. IEEE*, 84(8):1090–1126, 1996.
11. ISO/IEC 13568:2002 standard. See also vl.zuser.org.
12. P. Koopman and R. Plasmeijer. Generic Generation of Elements of Types. In *Sixth Symposium on Trends in Functional Programming (TFP2005)*, Tallin, Estonia, Sep 23-24 2005.
13. A. Alimarine and R. Plasmeijer. A Generic Programming Extension for Clean. In: Arts, Th., Mohnen M.: IFL 2001, LNCS 2312, pp 168–185, 2002.
14. M. de Mol, M. van Eekelen, R. Plasmeijer. Theorem Proving for Functional Programmers. - SPARKLE: A Functional Theorem Prover. In: Arts, Th., Mohnen M.: IFL 2001, LNCS 2312, pp 55–71, 2002.
15. G. Holzmann. The SPIN Model Checker. ISBN 0-321-22862-6, 2004.
16. G. Behrmann, A. David, K. Larsen. A Tutorial on Uppaal LNCS 3185, 2004.
17. D. Beyer, A. Chlipala, T. Henzinger, R. Jhala, R. Majumdar. The Blast query language for software verification. LNCS 3148, pp 2–18, 2004
18. H. Chen, D. Dean, and D. Wagner. Model checking one million lines of C code. Proceedings 11th Annual NDSS, San Diego, CA, February 2004
19. Kazmierczak P. Dart, L. Stirling, M. Winikoff: Kazmierczak Dart, Stirling, Winikoff: Verifying requirements through mathematical modelling and animation. *Int. J. Softw. Eng. Know. Eng.*, 10(2), pp 251–273, 2000.
20. R. Kemmerer Testing formal specifications to detect design errors. *IEEE Tr. on Soft. Eng.*, 11(1), pp 32–43, 1985.
21. S. Liu Verifying consistency and validity of formal specifications by testing in J. Wing et al: FM'99, LNCS 1708, pp 896–914, 1999.
22. T. Miller and P. Strooper A framework and tool support for the systematic testing of model-based specifications *ACM Tr. Soft. Eng. and Meth.*, pp 409–439, 2003.

Functional Array Programming in SaC

Sven-Bodo Scholz

Dept of Computer Science, University of Hertfordshire, United Kingdom
S.Scholz@herts.ac.uk

Abstract. These notes present an introduction into array-based programming from a functional, i.e., side-effect-free perspective.

The first part focuses on promoting arrays as predominant, stateless data structure. This leads to a programming style that favors compositions of generic array operations that manipulate entire arrays over specifications that are made in an element-wise fashion. An algebraically consistent set of such operations is defined and several examples are given demonstrating the expressiveness of the proposed set of operations.

The second part shows how such a set of array operations can be defined within the first-order functional array language SaC. It does not only discuss the language design issues involved but it also tackles implementation issues that are crucial for achieving acceptable runtimes from such genericly specified array operations.

1 Introduction

Traditionally, binary lists and algebraic data types are the predominant data structures in functional programming languages. They fit nicely into the framework of recursive program specifications, lazy evaluation and demand driven garbage collection. Support for arrays in most languages is confined to a very resricted set of basic functionality similar to that found in imperative languages. Even if some languages do support more advanced specificational means such as array comprehensions, these usualy do not provide the same genericity as can be found in array programming languages such as APL, J, or NIAL.

Besides these specificational issues, typically, there is also a performance issue. Lazy evaluation and garbage collection pose a major challenge on an efficient implementation for arrays. A large body of work went into dealing with the performance issue [vG97, PW93, CK01]. Most of these approaches rely on explicit single-threading, either by using monads or by using uniqueness typing, as this allows all array modifications to be implemented destructively. The drawback of this approach is that it requires programmers to be aware of the states of the arrays they are dealing with. Arrays need to be allocated and copied whenever more than one versin of an array is needed. Although this copying to some extend can be hidden behind libraries, it does come for the price of potentially superfluous copying at the library interfaces [CK03].

In this paper, we present a radically different approach. We introduce a new functional programming language called SaC which is designed around the idea of runtime efficient support for high-level programming based on arrays

Z. Horváth (Ed.): CEFP 2005, LNCS 4164, pp. 62–99, 2006.

as predominant data structure. This facilitates an array-oriented programming style as it can be found in dedicated array programming languages such as APL [Int84], J [Bur96], or NIAL [JJ93]. In contrast to these languages, the absence of side-effects in SAC provides the ground for several advanced optimization techniques [Sch03] leading to runtimes competitive with those obtained from hand-optimized imperative programs [GS00, SSH+06].

The paper consists of two major parts. In the first part, an introduction to array-oriented programming is given. Starting from array essentials such as array representation, inspection, and creation in Section 2, Section 3 provides the core array operators. The set of high-level operators defined in this part are prototypical for the basic operations found in any other array programming language. Nevertheless, they reflect part of the functionality provided by the standard library of SAC. Section 4 describes a SAC-specific language feature called **Axis Control Notation** which, when used jointly with the basic operators, allows many array algorithms to be specified in a combinator style. Several examples to this effect round-off the first part of the paper.

The second part of this paper focuses on the language SAC itself. After a brief introduction to the basic design issues of SAC in Section 5, Section 6 gives a detailled desciption of the central language construct of SAC called WITH-**loop**. Several examples and exercises are given to demonstrate how the generic aray operations defined in the foirst part can be implemented in SAC itself. How such program specifications can be compiled into efficiently executable code is sketched in Section 7.

2   Array Basics

All arrays are represented by two vectors: a **data vector** which contains its elements, and a **shape vector** which defines its structure. Fig. 1 shows a few example arrays. As can be seen from the examples, the length of the shape vector corresponds to the dimensionality (also referred to as **rank**) of the array and the individual entities of it define the extent of the array with respect to the individual axes. The data vector enumerates all elements with increasing indices. For arrays with more than one axis, index increment proceeds with indices from right to left. From this relation between data and shape vector we obtain:

Lemma 1. *Let* $[d_0, \ldots, d_{q-1}]$ *denote the data vector of an array and let* $[s_0, \ldots, s_{n-1}]$ *denote its shape vector. Then we have* $q = \prod_{i=0}^{n-1} s_i$.

The bottom of Fig. 1 shows that scalar values can be considered 0-dimensional arrays with empty shape vector. Note here, that Lemma 1 for scalars still holds.

2.1   Specifying Arrays

Given the representation of n-dimensional arrays by two vectors, we use the following notation for arrays:

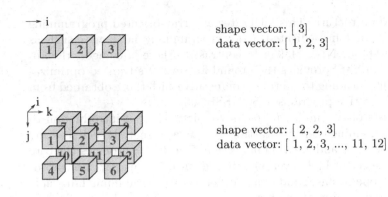

shape vector: [3]
data vector: [1, 2, 3]

shape vector: [2, 2, 3]
data vector: [1, 2, 3, ..., 11, 12]

shape vector: [ ]
data vector: [42]

Fig. 1. Array representations

$$\text{reshape}(\ [s_0, ..., s_{n-1}],\ [d_0, ..., d_{q-1}])$$

where $q = \prod_{i=0}^{n-1} s_i$. The special cases of scalars and vectors may be denoted as

$$s \equiv \text{reshape}([],\ [s]) \qquad\qquad , \text{and}$$
$$[v_0, ..., v_{n-1}] \equiv \text{reshape}([n],\ [v_0, ..., v_{n-1}]) \qquad .$$

This shortcut notation gives rise to considering **reshape** a built-in array operator which holds the following property:

$$\begin{aligned}\text{reshape}(\ \text{shp\_vec},\ \text{reshape}(\ \text{shp\_vec\_2},\ \text{data\_vec})) \\ == \text{reshape}(\ \text{shp\_vec},\ \text{data\_vec})\end{aligned} \tag{1}$$

provided that Lemma 1 holds for the resulting array.

2.2 Inspecting Arrays

Alongside the array constructing operator **reshape**, functions for extracting shape and data information are required. We introduce two operations for retrieving shape information:

shape returns an array's shape vector, and
dim returns an array's dimensionality

For example, we have:
```
  shape( 42) == []
  shape( [1, 2, 3]) == [3]
  shape( reshape( [2, 3], [1, 2, 3, 4, 5, 6])) == [2, 3]
```
Formally, **shape** is defined by

$$\text{shape}(\text{reshape}(\text{shp\_vec}, \text{data\_vec})) == \text{shp\_vec} \tag{2}$$

and dim is defined by

$$\text{dim}(\text{reshape}(\text{shp\_vec}, \text{data\_vec})) == \text{shape}(\text{shp\_vec})[0] \qquad (3)$$

where the square brackets denote element selection. Note here that the element selection is well defined as shp_vec denotes an n-element vector and, thus, shape(shp_vec) is a one element vector.

From these definitions, we can derive

$$\forall a : \text{dim}(a) == \text{shape}(\text{shape}(a))[0] \qquad (4)$$

as

dim(reshape(shp_vec, data_vec))

$\overset{(3)}{==}$shape(shp_vec)[0]

$\overset{(2)}{==}$shape(shape(reshape(shp_vec, data_vec)))[0]   □

So far, we have used square brackets to denote selection within vectors. However, we want to introduce a more versatile definition for array selections. It is supposed to work for n-dimensional arrays in general. As one index per axis is required, such a definition requires an n-element vector as index argument rather than n separate scalar index arguments. Hence, we define an operation

```
sel( idx_vect, array)
```

which selects that element of array that is located at the index position index_vect. For example:

```
sel( [1], [1, 2, 3]) == 2
sel( [1, 0], reshape( [2, 3], [1, 2, 3, 4, 5, 6])) == 4
```

As we can see from the examples, we always have shape(idx_vect)[0] == dim(array). This leads to the formal definition

$$\text{shape}(\text{sel}(\text{idx\_vec}, \text{reshape}(\text{shp\_vec}, \text{data\_vec}))) == 0$$
$$\text{provided that} \qquad \text{shape}(\text{idx\_vec}) == \text{shape}(\text{shp\_vec}) \qquad (5)$$

From it, we obtain for scalars s:

```
sel( [], s) == s
```

In order to extend this property to non-scalar arrays (5) is generalized into

$$\text{shape}(\text{sel}(\text{idx\_vec}, \text{reshape}(\text{shp\_vec}, \text{data\_vec})))$$
$$== \text{shape}(\text{shp\_vec}) - \text{shape}(\text{idx\_vec}) \qquad (6)$$
$$\text{provided that} \qquad \text{shape}(\text{idx\_vec}) <= \text{shape}(\text{shp\_vec})$$

This extension enables the selection of entire subarrays whenever the index vector is shorter than the rank of the array to be selected from. For example, we have

```
sel( [1, 0], reshape( [2, 3], [1, 2, 3, 4, 5, 6]))
   == 4

sel( [1], reshape( [2, 3], [1, 2, 3, 4, 5, 6]))
   == [4, 5, 6]

sel( [], reshape( [2, 3], [1, 2, 3, 4, 5, 6]))
   == reshape( [2, 3], [1, 2, 3, 4, 5, 6])
```

2.3   Modifying Arrays

Similar to the generalized form of array element selection, we introduce an array modification operation which is not restricted to modifications of individual elements but permits modifications of entire subarrays. It takes the general form

$$\texttt{modarray(array, idx\_vect, val)}$$

and results in an array which is identical to **array** but whose subarray at the index position **idx_vect** is changed into **val**. Hence, we have

$$\texttt{shape(modarray(reshape(shp\_vec, data\_vec), idx, val))} \\ \texttt{== shp\_vec} \tag{7}$$

and

$$\texttt{modarray(array, idx, val)[idx2]} == \begin{cases} \texttt{val} & \text{iff idx2} == \texttt{idx} \\ \texttt{sel(idx2, array)} & \text{otherwise} \end{cases} \tag{8}$$

It should be noted here that this "modification" conceptually requires the creation of a copy of the array. This is a consequence of the functional setting which requires the arguments of a function application to be unaffected by the evaluation of the application. However, static analysis often can determine that an array provided as argument is not referred to anywhere else. In these situations, **modarray** can be implemented in a destructive manner.

2.4   Generating Arrays

While an explicit specification of arrays is convenient for arrays with few elements only, large arrays require operator support. To this effect, we introduce an operation

$$\texttt{genarray(shape, val)}$$

which creates an array of shape **shape** with elements **val**. Similar to the operations introduced in the previous sections, **val** is not restricted to scalar values but can be an arbitrary array. For example, we have

```
genarray( [2], 42)
    == reshape( [2], [42, 42])

genarray( [2], [1, 2, 3])
    == reshape( [2, 3], [1, 2, 3, 1, 2, 3])

genarray( [2, 3], 1)
    == reshape( [2, 3], [1, 1, 1, 1, 1, 1])     .
```
Formally, we obtain for **genarray**

$$\texttt{shape(genarray(shp\_vec, reshape(shp\_vec2, data\_vec)))} \\ \texttt{== shp\_vec ++ shp\_vec2} \tag{9}$$

where **++** denotes vector concatenation and

$$\texttt{genarray(shp\_vec, a)[idx] == a} \\ \text{provided that} \quad \texttt{shape(shp\_vec) == shape(idx)} \tag{10}$$

2.5   Exercises

Exercise 1. Given the language constructs introduced so far, can you define the following array of shape [5,2,2]

```
[ [[ 0, 0 ], [ 0, 0 ]],
  [[ 1, 0 ], [ 0, 0 ]],
  [[ 0, 1 ], [ 0, 0 ]],
  [[ 0, 0 ], [ 1, 0 ]],
  [[ 0, 0 ], [ 0, 1 ]] ]
```

in a way so that the letter 1 is not used more than once?

Exercise 2. What are the results of the following expressions, if we assume a to be defined as [1,2,3,4], and b to be defined as [a,a]?

- modarray(modarray(a, [0], 0), [1], 0)
- modarray(b, [0], [0,0,0])
- modarray(b, [0], modarray(a, [0], 0))

3   Array Operations

The operations introduced in the previous section pertain to very basic functionality only: array creation, inspection, and element/subarray replacement.

In this section, we introduce operations that compute arrays from other arrays in a more elaborate manner. The design of these operations is inspired by those available in array languages such as APL, J, or NIAL. However, several aspects - in particular wrt. special case treatment - have been adjusted to allow for a more runtime favorable compilation. The operations can be divided into three different categories: structural operations, that predominantly change the shapes of the argument arrays or the placement of the individual elements within them; element-wise operations which are mappings of scalar operations such as +, -, <, etc. into the domain of arrays; and so-called reductions which by means of dyadic operations successively fold all elements of an array into a scalar value.

3.1   Structural Operations

Concatenation of vectors, denoted by ++, has been used in Section 2. Here, we provide a more generic definition of concatenation. The basic idea is to consider n-dimensional arrays vectors of $n-1$-dimensional subarrays. This leads to the following definitions

$$
\begin{aligned}
&\text{shape(reshape(shp\_vec, data\_vec)} \\
&\quad \text{++ reshape(shp\_vec2, data\_vec2)} \\
&== \text{modarray(shp\_vec, [0], shp\_vec[[0]] + shp\_vec2[[0]])} \\
&\text{provided that shape(shp\_vec) == shape(shp\_vec2) otherwise}
\end{aligned} \tag{11}
$$

and
$$\text{reshape(shp\_vec, data\_vec)}$$
$$\text{++ reshape(shp\_vec2, data\_vec2)} \tag{12}$$
$$\text{== reshape(shp\_res, data\_vec ++ data\_vec2)}$$

where shp_res is defined as specified in (11). This definition realizes concatenation wrt. the left-most axis. Thus, we have
$$\text{reshape([2,2], [1,2,3,4]) ++ reshape([2,2], [5,6,7,8])}$$
$$\text{== reshape([4,2], [1,2,3,4,5,6,7,8])} \qquad .$$
Besides concatenation, we introduce two operations for cutting off parts of an array:

take that selects a prespecified portion of an array, and
drop that cuts off a prespecified portion of an array.

In their simplest form we have for example
$$\text{take(2, [1,2,3,4,5]) == [1,2]}$$
$$\text{drop(2, [1,2,3,4,5]) == [3,4,5]} \qquad .$$
Formally, we define take by

$$\text{shape(take(n, reshape(shp\_vec, data\_vec)))}$$
$$\text{== modarray(shp\_vec, [0], n)} \tag{13}$$
$$\text{provided that} \quad n \geq 0$$

and
$$\text{take(n, reshape(shp\_vec, data\_vec))[idx]}$$
$$\text{== reshape(shp\_vec, data\_vec)[idx]} \tag{14}$$
$$\text{provided that} \quad n \geq 0$$

The symmetry between take and drop can be captured by defining drop through

$$\forall a : \text{drop}(n, a) == \text{take}(n - \text{shape}(a)[[0]], a) \tag{15}$$

and by extending take for negative arguments:

$$\text{shape(take(n, reshape(shp\_vec, data\_vec)))}$$
$$\text{== modarray(shp\_vec, [0], } |\, n\, | \text{)} \tag{16}$$

and
$$\text{take(n, reshape(shp\_vec, data\_vec))[idx]}$$
$$==\begin{cases} \text{reshape(shp\_vec, data\_vec)[idx]} & \text{iff } n \geq 0 \\ \text{reshape(shp\_vec, data\_vec)[idx2]} & \text{otherwise} \end{cases} \tag{17}$$
$$\text{where idx2 == modarray(idx, 0, idx[[0]] + offset)}$$
$$\text{where offset == shp\_vec[[0]] - } |\, n\, |$$

Applying the above definitions of take, we obtain
$$\text{take(-2, [1,2,3,4,5]) == [4,5]}$$
$$\text{take(-1, reshape([3,2], [1,2,3,4,5,6]))}$$
$$\text{== reshape([1,2], [5,6])} \qquad .$$
We also obtain

```
take( 0, [1,2,3,4,5]) == reshape( [0], [])
take( 0, reshape( [3,2], [1,2,3,4,5,6]))
    == reshape( [0,2], [])
```

From these examples, we can observe that our array calculus requires us to distinguish between infinitely many differently shaped empty arrays. As numbers in square brackets are used as a shortcut notation for vectors, [] in fact denotes the array reshape([0], []).

To further extend the expressiveness of take, we use vectors instead of scalars as first argument and map the vector's components to the individual axes of the second argument. For example, we have

```
take( [2,1], reshape( [3,2], [1,2,3,4,5,6]))
    == reshape( [2,1], [1,3])

take( [2], reshape( [3,2], [1,2,3,4,5,6]))
    == reshape( [2,2], [1,2,3,4])

take( [], reshape( [3,2], [1,2,3,4,5,6]))
    == reshape( [3,2], [1,2,3,4,5,6])
```

A formal definition of this extended version of take is left as an exercise.

Two further structural operations are useful when it comes to operating on arrays in a cyclic fashion: shift and rotate. Both move all array elements towards increasing or decreasing indices. They only differ in the way they handle the border elements. While shift ignores the element(s) that is(are) moved out of the array and inserts a pre-specified one on the other end of the index range, rotate reuses the moved-out elements. An extension to n-dimensional arrays yields:

```
shift( [1], 0, [1,2,3]) == [0,1,2]

shift( [-1], 0, [1,2,3]) == [2,3,0]

shift( [1,1], 0, reshape( [3,3], [1,2,...,9]))
    == shift( [1], reshape( [3,3], [0,1,2,0,4,5,0,7,8]))
    == reshape( [3,3], [0,0,0,0,1,2,0,4,5])

rotate( [1], [1,2,3]) == [3,1,2]

rotate( [-1], [1,2,3]) == [2,3,1]

rotate( [1,1], reshape( [3,3], [1,2,...,9]))
    == rotate( [1], reshape( [3,3], [3,1,2,6,4,5,9,7,8]))
    == reshape( [3,3], [9,7,8,3,1,2,6,4,5])
```

Again, formal definitions are left as an exercise.

3.2   Element-Wise Operations

Most of the operations that in non-array languages are provided for scalars can be easily extended for usage on entire arrays by mapping them on an element-wise basis. In the context of this lecture, we assume that all binary arithmetic, logic and relational operations of C can be applied to n-dimensional arrays. The only restriction we impose on these operations is shape conformity. More precisely, we demand that the shapes of the two argument arrays are either identical or at least one of them needs to be a scalar.

Here, a few examples:

```
[1,2,3] + [2,3,4] == [3,5,7]
reshape( [2,2], [1,2,3,4] ) * 2 == reshape( [2,2], [2,4,6,8] )
[1,2,3] < [0,4,5] == [false,true,true]
```

3.3 Reductions

Reduction operations fold the scalar elements of an array into a single one by folding the data vector according to a binary operation. Again, most of the standard C operators can be used to that effect. In the context of this lecture, we focus on the following 4:

sum derives from +;
prod derives from *;
all derives from &&;
any derives from ||;

A few example applications of the above reduction operations:

```
sum( [1,2,3]) == 6
prod( reshape( [2,2], [1,2,3,4] )) = 24
all( [1,2,3] < [0,4,5]) == all( [false,true,true]) == false
any( [1,2,3] < [0,4,5]) == any( [false,true,true]) == true
```

3.4 Examples

The operations introduced so far suffice to conveniently express many operations on arrays without being required to write explicit loops over index ranges. This section provides a few examples as they typically occur when writing numerical codes.

Our first example relates to situations where all boundary elements of an array need to be cut off, i.e., we create an array that contains only those elements of a given argument array a, whose indices are all neither zero nor maximal. This can be achieved by a combination of the generic versions of take and drop:

```
take( shape( a)-2, drop( shape( a)*0+1 , a))
```

The most challenging aspect in this expression is the subexpression shape (a)*0+1 which computes a vector of ones whose length matches the dimensionality of the array a.

In numerical methods, approximations are usually applied repetitively until a certain convergence criterion is met. Assuming approx to be an array that holds the current approximation and solution to be an identically shaped array of the solution to be approximated, the quality of the approximation can be computed by sum(abs(approx - solution))

This example shows how the array notation helps in denoting expressions in a rather abstract style close to a mathematical notation.

Another example for the similarity to mathematical notation is the scalar product of two vectors v1 and v2 which can be specified as

sum(v1 * v2)

Even more complex expressions lend themselves to a specification in terms of generic array operations. As an example, consider the kernel of Danielson-Lanczos's FFT algorithm. Essentially, it computes a vector v's fast furier transform by recursively applying FFT to subvectors which consist of those elements of v that are located at even or odd index positions, respectively. The results of the recursive calls are then combined into a single vector which constitutes the overall result. Assuming the availability of a function compress which allows us to extract every second element from a vector, this kernel can be specified as

fft(compress([2], v)) ++ fft(compress([2], drop([1], v)))

3.5   Exercises

Exercise 3. What results do you expect from the following expressions:

- reshape([3,0,5], [])[[]]?
- reshape([3,0,5], [])[[1]]?
- reshape([3,0,5], [])[[1,0]]?
- reshape([3,0,5], []) + reshape([3,0,5], [])?
- reshape([1,1], [1]) + reshape([1], [1])?

Exercise 4. Give a formal definition of the extended version of take. Derive the dual definition for drop from your definition for take and equation (15).

Exercise 5. Give a formal definition of the structural operations shift and rotate.

Exercise 6. Reformulate the following expressions in terms of take, ++, and the basic operations defined in the previous section. Try to sketch a correctness proof of your solution by using the formal definitions of the individual operations.

- drop(v, a)?
- shift([n], e, a)?
- shift([m,n], e, a)?
- rotate([n], a)?
- rotate([m,n], a)?

Can we define the general versions of shift and rotate as well?

Exercise 7. All operations introduced in this part apply to all elements of the array they are applied to. Given the array operations introduced so far, can you specify row-wise or column-wise summations for matrices? Try to specify these operations for a 2 by 3 matrix first.

3.6 Further Reading

There are several possible approaches for defining a consistent representation for n-dimensional arrays and the basic operations on them. The representation presented here, to a large extent, is based on that of APL as suggested in [Ive62]. Several variants have been proposed such as the Mathematics of Arrays [Mul88], APL2 [Bro85], or SHARP APL [Ass87]. An alternative approach is the Array Theory of T. Moore [JF99]. It is based on the idea of nested arrays and serves as basis for NIAL [JG89]. In [MJ91], this approach is contrasted to the Mathematics of Arrays. A more general discussion of the design space can be found in [JF99].

4   Axis Control Notation

As can be seen from the Exercise 7, without further language support, it is rather difficult to apply an array operation to certain axes of an array only. This section introduces two language constructs of SaC which, when taken together, can be used to that effect. While **Generalized Selections** are convenient for separating individual axes of an array, **Set Notations** allow to recombine such axes into a result array after applying arbitrary operations to them. However, as the two constructs in principle are orthogonal, we introduce them separately before showing how they can be combined into an instrument for **Axis Control**.

4.1 Generalized Selections

The selection operation introduced in Section 2.2 does not only allow scalar elements but entire subarrays of an array to be selected. However, the selection of (non-scalar) subarrays always assumes the given indices to refer to the leftmost axes, i.e., all elements wrt. the rightmost axes are actually selected. So far, a selection of arbitrary axes is not possible. As an example consider the selection of rows and columns of a matrix. While the former can be done easily, the latter requires the array to be transposed first.

To avoid clumsy notations, we introduce special syntactical support for selecting arbitrary subarrays called **Generalized Selections**. The basic idea is to indicate the axes whose elements are to be selected entirely by using dot-symbols instead of numerical values within the index vectors of a selection operation.

Note here, that vectors containing dot-symbols are not first class citizens of the language, i.e., they can exclusively be specified within selection operations directly!

There are two kinds of dot-symbols, single-dots which refer to a single axis and triple-dots which refer to as many axes as they are left unspecified within a selection. In order to avoid ambiguities, a maximum of one triple-dot symbol per selection expression is allowed.

Fig. 2 shows a few examples of generalized selections. The examples in the upper half demonstrate how arbitrary axes can be selected by using dot symbols in the selection vector. The lower examples feature the triple-dot notation. While in the left example the triple-dot refers to the two leftmost axes of the array A,

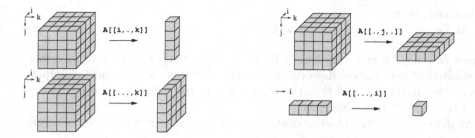

Fig. 2. Generalized Selections

the right example shows that in fact the triple-dot notation may refer to zero axes if the selection vector provides as many indices as the array to be selected from has axes.

4.2 Set Notation

The means for composing arrays that have been described so far are rather restricted. Apart from element-wise definitions all other operations treat all elements uniformly. As a consequence, it is difficult to define arrays whose elements differ depending on their position within the array. The so-called **set notation** facilitates such position dependent array definitions. Essentially, it consists of a mapping from index vectors to elements, taking the general form

$$\{ \text{ idx\_vect } \rightarrow \text{ expr } \}$$

where idx_vect either is a variable or a vector of variables and expr is an expression that refers to the index vector or its components and defines the individual array elements. The range of indices this mapping operation is applied to usually can be determined by the expression given and, thus, it is not specified explicitly. Fig. 3 provides a few examples. The first example constitutes an element-wise

```
{ idx_vec -> a[idx_vec] + 1 } == a + 1
{ [i,j] -> mat[[j,i]] }
{ [i,j] -> ( i == j ? mat[[i,j]] : 0) }
```

Fig. 3. Set Notation examples

increment of a matrix a, the second example implements the transposition of a matrix mat, and the last example replaces all elements that are not located on the main diagonal of a matrix mat by the value 0. In all these examples, the ranges for idx_vec, i, or j are inferred from the selection operations on the right hand side, or, more precisely, from the shapes of the arrays the selections are applied to. It should be mentioned here, that the requirement to be able to infer the index ranges restricts the range of legal set notations. Examples for non-legal set notations are

```
{ idx_vec -> 1 }
{ idx_vec -> a[[ foo( idx_vec)]] }
```

where **foo** may be any user defined function. This restriction may seem rather prohibitive at first glance. However, in practice, it turns out that most examples suffice this restriction and that the readability of the examples benefits vastly from the implicit range inference.

As the following examples demonstrate, range inference is not limited to single occurences of the index variables.

```
{ idx_vec -> a[[ foo( idx_vec)]] + b[[ idx_vec]]}
{ [i,j] -> a[[i]] + a[[j]] }
{ [i,j] -> a[[i]] + a[[j]] + [1][[j]] }
```

In case of more than one use within a selection operation, the element-wise minimum of all selection shapes is used. Furthermore, the index variables may occur in non-selection related contexts as well. Wrt. the range inference, these occurences are ignored.

It should be noted here, that explicit indices on the left hand side do not necessarily have to match the rank of the array they select from. For example, we have

```
{ [i] -> reshape( [2,2], [1,2,3,4])[[i]] }
    == reshape( [2,2], [1,2,3,4])              .
```

From the definition (6) we obtain that reshape([2,2], [1,2,3,4])[[i]] yields either [1,2] or [3,4] depending on i being 0 or 1, respectively. The set notation combines these subarrays in a way that ensures that non-scalar right hand side expressions per default constitute the inner axes of the result array. This can be changed by using .-symbols for indicating those axes that should constitute the result axis. Applying this to our last example, we obtain

```
{ [.,i] -> reshape( [2,2], [1,2,3,4])[[i]] }
    == reshape( [2,2], [1,3,2,4])              .
```

4.3   Axis Control

Although generalized selections and the set notation per se can be useful their real potential shows when they are used in combination. Together, they constitute means to control the axes a given operation is applied to.

The basic idea is to use generalized selections to extract the axes of interest, apply the desired operation to the extracted subarrays and then recombine the results to the overall array.

Fig. 4 shows how axis control can be used to sum up different hyperplanes of a rank 3 array. The first example shows how the **sum** operation is mapped on all vectors within the rightmost axis of the rank 3 array which results in a matrix

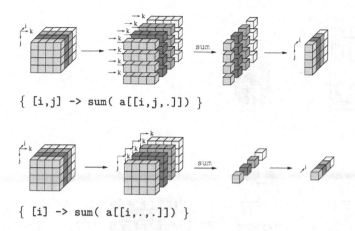

{ [i,j] -> sum(a[[i,j,.]]) }

{ [i] -> sum(a[[i,.,.]]) }

Fig. 4. Axis Control for summation of hyperplanes

of sums as indicated on the right hand side of the figure. The second example demonstrates how the summation can by applied to submatrices which results in a vector of sums.

Reduction operations, in general, are prone to axis control as they often need to be applied to one or several particular axes rather than an entire array. Other popular examples are the maximum (max) and minimum (min) operations which can now be used to compute local maxima or minima within selected hyperplanes.

Further demand for axis control arises in the context of array operations that are dedicated to one fixed axis (usually the outermost one) and that need to be applied to another one. An example for this situation is the concatenation operation (++). Fig. 5 shows how axis control can be used to drive the concatenation into non-leftmost axes. Essentially, the idea is to first split the matrices into vectors. Pairs of these vectors are then concatenated before the results of that operation are combined into the final result.

4.4   Examples

The array operations presented so far constitute a substantial subset of the functionality that is provided by array programming languages such as APL. When orchestrated properly, these suffice to express rather complex array operations very concisely. In the sequel, we present two examples that make use of this combined expressive power: matrix product and relaxation.

Matrix Product. The matrix product of two matrices A and B (denoted by $A\,B$) is defined as follows:

Provided A has as many columns as B has rows, the result of $A\,B$ has as many rows as A and as many columns as B. Each element $(A\,B)_{i,j}$ is defined as the scalar product of the i-th row of A and the j-th column of B, i.e., we have $(A\,B)_{i,j} = \sum_k A_{i,k} * B_{k,j}$.

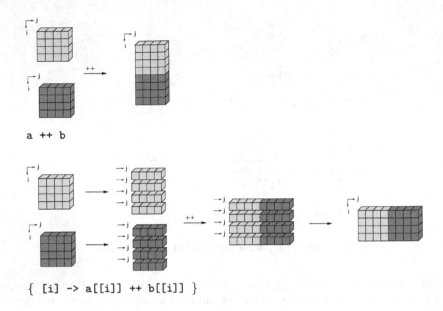

a ++ b

{ [i] -> a[[i]] ++ b[[i]] }

Fig. 5. Axis Control for concatenation on inner axes

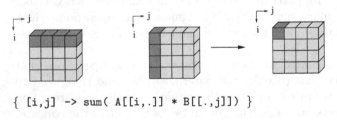

{ [i,j] -> sum(A[[i,.]] * B[[.,j]]) }

Fig. 6. Matrix product

Fig 6 shows how the matrix product can be defined in terms of axis control. The expression A[[i,.]] selects the i-th row of A, and B[[.,j]] refers to the j-th column of B. The index ranges for i and j are deduced from the accesses into A and B, respectively. A variable k as used in the mathematical specification is not required as we can make use of the array operations * and sum.

Relaxation. Numerical approximations to the solution of partial differential equations are often made by applying so-called **relaxation methods**. These require large arrays to be iteratively modified by so-called **stencil operations** until a certain convergence criterion is met. Fig. 7 illustrates such a stencil operation. A stencil operation re-computes all elements of an array by computing a weighted sum of all neighbor elements. The weights that are used solely depend on the positions relative to the element to be computed rather than the position in the result array. Therefore, we can conveniently specify these weights by a single matrix of weights as shown on the left side in the top of Fig. 7.

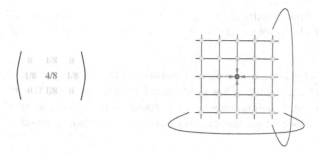

```
weights = [ [0d, 1d, 0d], [1d, 4d, 1d], [ 0d, 1d, 0d]] / 8d;
mat = ...
res = { [i,j] -> sum(
         { iv -> weights[iv] * rotate( iv-1, mat)}
                    [[...,i,j]] ) };
```

Fig. 7. A 5-point-stencil relaxation with cyclic boundaries

In this example, only 4 direct neighbor elements and the old value itself are taken into account for computing a new value. (Hence its name: **5-point-stencil operation**). As can be seen from the weights, a new value is computed from old ones by adding an eight-th each of the values of the upper, lower, left, and right neighbors to half of the old value.

As demonstrated on the right side in the top of Fig. 7 our example assumes so-called **cyclic boundary conditions**. This means that the missing neighbor elements at the boundaries of the matrix are taken from the opposite sides as indicated by the elliptic curves.

The code shown in the bottom of Fig. 7 shows the relevant part for computing a single relaxation step, i.e., the code for one re-computation of the entire array. At its core, all elements are re-computed by operations on the entire array rather than individual elements. This is achieved by applying `rotate` for each legal index position `iv` into the array of weights `weights`. Since the expression `{ iv -> weights[iv] * rotate( iv-1, mat)}` computes a 3 by 3 array of matrices (!) the reduction operation `sum` needs to be directed towards the leftmost two axes of that expression only. This is achieved through axis control using a selection index `[...,i,j]` within a set notation over i and j.

4.5 Exercises

Exercise 8. How can a selection of all elements of a rank 3 array `mat` be specified using generalized selections? Try to find all 9 possible solutions!

Exercise 9. Referring to Exercise 3, can generalized selections be used for selecting "over" empty axis? For example, can you specify a selection vector $< vec >$, so that `reshape([3,0,5], [])[< vec >]` == `reshape( [3,0], [])` holds?

Exercise 10. Which of the examples in Fig. 3 can be expressed in terms of the array operations defined in the previous sections?

Exercise 11. What results do you expect from the expressions in Fig. 3 if a or mat turn out to be empty matrices, e.g., the turn out to be identical to `reshape(` `[10,0]`, `[]`)?

Exercise 12. The `.`-symbol in the set notation allows us to direct a computation to any axes of the result. This is identical to first putting the result into the innermost axes and then transposing the result. Can you come up with a general scheme that translates set notations containing `.`-symbols into set notations that do without?

Exercise 13. The operation `take` is defined in a way that ensures inner axes to be taken completely in case the take vector does not provide enough entities for all axes. How can `take` be applied to an array so that the outermost axis remains untouched and the selections are applied to inner axes, starting at the second one? (You may assume, that the take vector has fewer elements than the array axes!) Can you specify a term that - according to a take vector of length 1 - takes from the innermost axis only?

Exercise 14. Can you merge two vectors of identical length element-wise? Extend your solution in a way that permits merging n-dimensional arrays on the leftmost axis.

Exercise 15. Another variant of relaxation problems requires the boundary elements to have a fixed value. Can you modify the above solution in a way that causes all boundary elements to be 0? [**Hint:** You may consider the boundary elements to actualy be located **outside** the matrix]

4.6   Further Reading

A more detailed definition of Axis Control Notation can be found in [GS03]. APL [Int84] does provide the notion of explicit array nesting as alternative means for controlling the function applications wrt. certain axes. The notion of nesting is introduced in [Ben91, Ben92]. Yet another alternative to the same effect is the rank operator as proposed in [Ber88, Hui95]. It is implemented as part of J [Ive91, Ive95].

5   SaC Basics

SaC (for Single Assignment C) is a functional language whose design targets array-intensive applications as they for example can be found in the areas of scientific applications or image processing.

5.1   Overall Design

The fundamental idea in the design of the language is to keep the language as close as possible to C but to nevertheless base the language on the principle

of context free substitutions. While the former may attract application programmers with an imperative background, the latter ensures the Church-Rosser
property which is crucial for extensive compile-time optimizations as well as
for non-sequential executions. Another key objective in the design of SAC is to
provide support for high-level array programming as introduced in the previous
sections.

Fig. 8 sketches the overall design of SAC. As can be seen in the middle of
the figure, a large part of standard C such as basic types and the fundamental
language constructs is adopted in SAC. Only a few language constructs of C
such as pointers and global variables need to be excluded in order to be able
to guarantee a side-effect-free setting. Instead, some new language constructs
are added pertaining to array programming. Besides a basic integration of n-
dimensional arrays as first-class citizens, the most important addition are the
so-called WITH-**loops**. They are versatile language constructs that allow all the
array operations as introduced in the previous sections to be defined within the
language itself.[1]

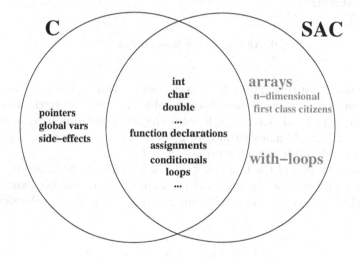

Fig. 8. The overall design of SAC

5.2   To Be and Not to Be Functional

The incorporation of most of the fundamental language constructs of C such as
loops, conditionals, and assignments into the functional setting of SAC allows
the programmer to stick to his preferred model of computation. To illustrate
this effect, let us consider the following function **foo**:

---

[1] In fact, all examples from the previous sections can be used in SAC without modification. They are implemented within the standard library of SAC.

```
int foo( int v, int w) {
    int r;

    r = v + w;
    r = r + 1;
    return(r);
}
```

It takes two arguments v and w, adds them up, and increments the result by one which yields the return value of foo.

An imperative interpretation of foo is shown in Fig. 9. In the imperative

```
int foo( int v, int w) {
    int r;

    r = v + w;
    r = r + 1;
    return(r);
}
```

v:	10	v:	10	v:	10
w:	10	w:	10	w:	10
r:		r:	20	r:	21

Fig. 9. An imperative look on foo

world, v, w, and r constitute names for box variables. During the execution of the body of foo, the content of these box variables is successively changed as indicated on the right hand side of Fig. 9 assuming an application to arguments 10 ans 10. After the final "modification" of r the last value it contains, i.e., 21, is returned as overall result of the function call of foo.

However, the definition of the function foo equally well can be interpreted as syntactic sugar for a let-based function definition as shown on the left-hand-side of Fig. 10. With this interpretation, v, w, and r become variables in a λ-calculus

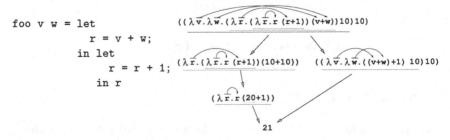

```
foo v w = let
            r = v + w;
          in let
            r = r + 1;
          in r
```

Fig. 10. A functional look on foo

sense. As we can see, the assignment to r has turned into two nested let-expression which effectively leads to two distinct variables r which are assigned to only once. A further transformation into an applied λ-calculus as shown on the right-hand-side of Fig. 10 identifies the potential for independent evaluations of subexpressions. The arrows on top of the λ-expressions indicate the static scoping of the individual variables. The lines under the expressions indicate the β-redices that are present. As indicated by the different reduction sequences the λ-calculus representation thus eases the identification of legal program transformations part of which may be performed at compile-time.

This duality in program interpretation is achieved by the choice of a subset of C which can easily be mapped into an applied λ-calculus whose semantics reflects that of the corresponding C program. A formal definition of the semantics of SAC is beyond the scope of this lecture. In the sequel, it suffices to expect all language constructs adopted from C to adhere to their operational behaviour in C.

5.3   The Type System of SAC

As mentioned in Section 5.1, the elementary types of C are available in SAC too. However, they constitute only a small subset of the types of SAC. For each elementary type in C there exists an entire hierarchy of array types in SAC. As an example, Fig 11 shows the hierarchy for integer arrays. It consists of three layers

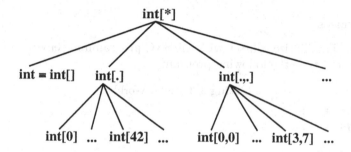

Fig. 11. A hierarchy of shapely types

of array types which differ wrt. the level of shape restrictions that is imposed on their constituents. On the top layer, we find int[*] which comprises all possible integer arrays. The second layer of types differentiates between arrays of different dimensionality. This layer comprises the standard type int which still denotes scalar integers only. All other types on this level are denoted by the elementary type followed by a vector of .-symbols. The number of .-symbols determines the rank of the arrays contained. On the bottom layer, the types are shape-specific. They are denoted by the elementary type followed by the shape. For example, int[3,2] denotes all integer matrices of shape [3,2].

Although a generic array programming style suggests a predominant use of the top layer types, the availability of the type hierarchy provides the programmer with additional expressiveness. Domain restrictions wrt. rank or shape of the arguments can be made explicit and support for function overloading eases rank/shape-specific implementations. Fig. 12 shows an example for such an overloading. Let us consider an implementation of a general solver for a set of linear

```
double[.] solve( double[.,.] A, double[.] b) {
  /* general solver */   ...
}

double[3] solve( double[3,3] A, double[3] b) {
  /* direct solver */   ...
}
```

Fig. 12. Overloading and function dispatch

equations `Ax = b` as indicated in the top of Fig. 12. For arrays of a certain shape it may be desirable to apply a different algorithm which has different runtime properties. The bottom of Fig. 12 shows how this functionality can be added in SAC by specifying a further instance of the function `solve` which is defined on a more restricted domain.

Besides the hierarchy of array types and function overloading it should be mentioned here that SACin contrast to C does not require the programmer to declare array types for variables. Type specifications are only mandatory for argument and return types of all function instances.

5.4   Exercises

Exercise 16. Familiarize yourself with the SAC programming environment. Start your editor and type the following program:

Listing 1.1. Hello World

```
use StdIO: all;
use Array: all;

int main()
{
  printf( "Hello World!\n");
  return(0);
}
```

As you can see, it has a strong resemblance to C. The major difference are the module use declarations at the beginning of the program. Their exact behaviour is beyond the scope of this lecture. For now, it suffices to keep in mind, that these two declarations for most experiments will do the job. Details on the module system as well as further introductory material can be found at <http://www.sac-home.org/>.

5.5   Further Reading

A more extended introduction into the language constructs of SAC can be found in [Sch03]. Formal definitions are contained in [Sch96]. More elaboration on the type system of SAC is provided in [Sch01] and details of the module system can be found in [HS04].

6   WITH-loops

Besides basic support for n-dimensional arrays as described in Section 2 all array operations in SAC are defined in terms of a language construct called WITH-loop. There are three variants of WITH-loops: the genarray-WITH-loop, the modarray-WITH-loop, and the fold-WITH-loop.

6.1   Genarray-WITH-loop

In essence, the genarray-WITH-loop can be considered an advanced version of the set notation as introduced in Section 4. Apart from the syntax, there are two major differences: the result shape is specified explicitly, and besides the expression that is associated with the index vector there is a second expression, called **default expression**, which does not depend on the index vector. Which of these expressions actually is used for a given index position depends on a so called **generator** which denotes a subset of the index range. For all indices within the generator range the associated expression is chosen, and for all others the default expression is taken.

Fig. 13 shows an example WITH-loop and the array it represents. A genarray-WITH-loop starts with the keyword **with** followed by the index variable (iv in the example) followed by two parts: the so-called **generator part** (here: second line) and the **operator part** (here: last line). The operator part contains the result shape (here: [4,5]) and the default expression *def.* The generator part consists of a range specification followed by the expression *e(iv)* that is associated to it. As shown in the lower part of Fig. 13, the result array has shape [4,5], all elements specified by the generator range i.e., those elements with indices between [1,1] and [2,3], are computed from the associated expression with the index variable iv being replaced with the respective index, and all remaining elements are identical to the default expression.

```
A = with (iv)
      ([1,1] <= iv < [3,4]) : e(iv);
    genarray( [4,5],  def );
```

$$A = \begin{pmatrix} def & def & def & def & def \\ def & e([1,1]) & e([1,2]) & e([1,3]) & def \\ def & e([2,1]) & e([2,2]) & e([2,3]) & def \\ def & def & def & def & def \end{pmatrix}$$

Fig. 13. A genarray-WITH-loop

Range specifications always take the form

$$lower\_bound \ rel\_op \ variable \ rel\_op \ upper\_bound$$

where *lower_bound* and *upper_bound* are expressions that evaluate to vectors of the same length and *rel_op* is one of < and <=. This deviation from C-style was made in order to stress the fact that more general range restrictions are not supported. Although more general predicates do not cause any conceptual problems, they can have a substantial effect on the level of code optimization that can be achieved. In order to prevent from "spurious" performance degradations due to unfavourable generator specifications we rule out more general predicates here.

The generator variable can be replaced by a vector of variables which implicitly fixes the result shape. For example, we have:

```
with([i])
    ( [0] <= [i] < [n]) : i;
genarray( [n], 0);
```

which computes an n-element vector containing the values 0 up to n-1, i.e.,

```
reshape( [n], [0, 1, 2, ...., n-1])
```

Similarily, we can compute a 10 by 10 element unit matrix by

```
with([i,j])
    ( [0,0] <= [i,j] <= [9,9]) : ( i==j ? 1 : 0);
genarray( [10,10], 0);
```

Note here that an expression of the form

(*predicate* ? *then_expr* : *else_expr*)

as in C denotes a conditional expression.

6.2   Modarray-WITH-loop

The difference between the modarray-WITH-loop and the genarray-WITH-loop lies in the way the result shape as well as the default expression are derived. Fig. 14 shows a prototypical example. As we can see, the only difference to a genarray-WITH-loop is the operator part. Rather than giving the result shape and the default expression explicitly, these are derived from an array *B*.

As a more concrete example, consider the following WITH-loop:

```
maxidx0 = shape( a)[[0]] - 1;
res = with([i])
        ( [0] <= [i] <= [maxidx0]): a[[maxidx0 - i]]
    modarray( a);
```

```
A = with (iv)
      ([1,1] <= iv < [3,4]) : e(iv)
      modarray( B );
```

$$A = \begin{pmatrix} B[[0,0]] & B[[0,1]] & B[[0,2]] & B[[0,3]] & B[[0,4]] \\ B[[1,0]] & e([1,1]) & e([1,2]) & e([1,3]) & B[[1,4]] \\ B[[2,0]] & e([2,1]) & e([2,2]) & e([2,3]) & B[[2,4]] \\ B[[3,0]] & B[[3,1]] & B[[3,2]] & B[[3,3]] & B[[3,4]] \end{pmatrix}$$

Fig. 14. A modarray-WITH-loop

It computes an array **res** whose shape is identical to that of **a**. The generator specifies that all subarrays of the result wrt. the leftmost axis are reversed. Asuming **a** to be a 2 by 3 matrix of the form:

$$\begin{pmatrix} 1 & 2 & 3 \\ 4 & 5 & 6 \end{pmatrix}$$

we obtain `maxidx0 == 1` and, thus, `[a[[1]], a[[0]]] == [ [4, 5, 6], [1, 2, 3]]` as a result.

6.3   Fold-WITH-loop

The fold-WITH-loop, again, is a variant in the operator part. As can be seen in Fig. 15, it denotes a binary folding operation $\oplus$ alongside with the neutral element *neutr* of that operation. The overall result of such a fold-WITH-loop stems from folding all the expressions associated with the generator. However, the order in which the folding eventually is done is intentionally left unspecified. To guarantee predictable results, the operation $\oplus$ needs to be associative and commutative.

With this construct, all reduction operations can be conveniently specified. For example, the **sum** operation as defined in Section 3 can be specified as

```
res = with(iv)
        ( 0*shape(a) <= iv < shape(a)): a[iv]
      fold( +, 0);
```

Assuming **a** to be of the form

$$\begin{pmatrix} 1 & 2 & 3 \\ 4 & 5 & 6 \end{pmatrix}$$

we obtain for the lower bound of the genrator `0*shape(a) == [0, 0]` and for the overall result:

```
A = with (iv)
      ([1,1] <= iv < [3,4]) : e(iv)
    fold( ⊕, neutr );
```

$$A = neutr \oplus e([1,1]) \oplus e([1,2]) \oplus e([1,3])$$
$$\oplus\ e([2,1]) \oplus e([2,2]) \oplus e([2,3])$$

(⊕ denotes associative, commutative binary function.)

Fig. 15. A fold-WITH-loop

```
0 + a[[0,0]] + a[[0,1]] + a[[0,2]] + a[[1,0]] + a[[1,1]] + a[[1,2]]
```
which reduces to 0 + 1 + 2 + 3 + 4 + 5 + 6 == 21.

6.4 Extensions

So far, the generator specification is rather limited. Only one dense range of indices can be specified. To provide more specificational flexibility, SAC provides a few optional extensions for the generator parts of WITH-loops.

Fig. 16 shows the first extension the so-called **step vectors**. They allow to specify grids of indices rather than dense index ranges. Each of the components of the step vector specified the stride wrt. one individual axis. As shown in the

```
A = with (iv)
      ([2,1] <= iv < [8,11] step [2,3]) : e(iv);
    genarray( [10,13],  def );
```

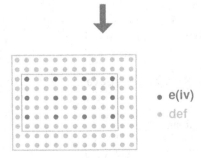

Fig. 16. Introducing step vectors

lower part of Fig. 16, in the example, this leads to a stride of **2** for the first axis and a stride **3** in the second.

These steps can be refined further by using so-called **width vectors**. Fig. 17 illustrates the use of width vectors. They allow the chosen grid elements not to

```
A = with (iv)
      ([2,1] <= iv < [8,11] ) step [3,4] width [2,3]) :  e(iv);
    genarray( [10,13],  def );
```

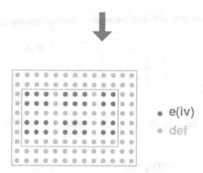

• e(iv)

• def

Fig. 17. Introducing width vectors

consist of one array element only but to consist of several adjacent elements. Again, the number of elements to be chosen can be specified on a per-axis basis.

Besides these potential extensions of individual generators, WITH-loops in SAC can contain more than just one generator part. In this case, the generators are subsequently executed in the order the are specified. Fig. 18 provides an example with two generators. The lower diagram shows how two separate generator ranges are computed according to the two (different) expressions *e1(iv)* and *e2(iv)*. All those elements not covered by any of the two generator ranges are copies of the default element.

6.5   Axis Control Revisited

As mentioned in Section 6.1, WITH-loops in SAC can be considered extended set notations. In fact, not only set notations but generalized selections as well can be defined in terms of WITH-loop.

For example, the generalized selection a[[.,1]] can be translated into

```
with( iv)
  ( 0 * shape( a)[[0]] <= iv < shape( a)[[0]])
  : a[ iv ++ [1]];
genarray( shape( a)[[0]], default);
```

which selects a vector of elements/subarrays of **a** as they are obtained when selecting with the second index being fixed to 1. The challenge of this WITH-loop is a correct specification of the default expression **default**. It needs to be

```
A = with (iv)
      ([1,1] <= iv < [6,4]) : e1(iv)
      ([3,4] <= iv < [8,9]) : e2(iv)
    genarray( [10,13],  def );
```

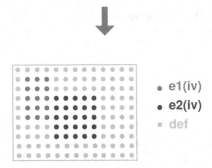

Fig. 18. A multi-generator WITH-loop

of the same shape as the subarrays of a are when selecting with two fixed indices.
This can be specified by yet another WITH-loop as

```
with( iv)
   ( 0 * drop( [2], shape( a)) <= iv < drop( [2], shape( a))
   : zero( a);
genarray( drop( [2], shape( a)), zero( a));
```

where `zero( a)` denotes the scalar 0.

Similarily, set notations can be translated into WITH-loops. Let us consider
the increment operation `{ [iv] -> a[iv] + 1 }` . The range inference yields
the shape of the result, which, in this example is identical to that of the array a:

```
with( iv)
   ( 0 * shape( a) <= iv < shape( a))
   : a[ iv ]
genarray( shape( a), default);
```

Again, the definition of the default expression, due to the lack of further information on the shape of a, requires another WITH-loop:

```
with( iv)
   ( 0 * drop( [dim(a)], shape( a)) <= iv
                        < drop( [dim(a)], shape( a))
   : zero( a);
genarray( drop( [dim(a)], shape( a)), zero( a));
```

6.6   Exercises

Exercise 17. Implement addition for arrays of arbitrary but identical shape as introduced in Section 3.2. Since this operation is already contained in the standard library you need to restrict the use of the modules from the standard library. You should import the scalar version of + by stating import ScalarArith:{+} and restrict the use of the library **Array** by excluding the array version for + contained in it. This can be achieved by a use statement of the form use Array:all except{+}. This will allow you to overload the scalar version of + by your own version of + for arrays.

Exercise 18. Implement a function **spread** that spreads an argument array a wrt. its first axis. It should insert elements / subarrays of value 0 between each two adjacent elements.

Modify your solution so that the "interim" values constitute the arithmetic mean of the formerly adjacent values.

Exercise 19. Extend your addition from Exercise 17 so that arrays of different shape but same dimensionality can be added. Find a consistent way in dealing with non-identical shapes!

Exercise 20. Extend the addition from Exercise 17 and Exercise 19 further so that mismatches in dimensionality can be handled as well. Do this by replicating the elements of the array that has fewer axes.

Exercise 21. Define an extended version of selection called over_sel. It should allow the selection vector to be an array of more than one axis. This index array should be considered an array of index vectors and the result should be an array of selected subarrays.

Examples:

$$
\text{over\_sel}\left(\begin{pmatrix} 1\ 0 \\ 1\ 1 \\ 1\ 1 \end{pmatrix}, \begin{pmatrix} 1\ 2\ 3 \\ 4\ 5\ 6 \end{pmatrix} \right) == \begin{pmatrix} 4 \\ 5 \\ 5 \end{pmatrix}
$$

$$
\text{over\_sel}\left(\begin{pmatrix} 1 \\ 1 \\ 0 \end{pmatrix}, \begin{pmatrix} 1\ 2\ 3 \\ 4\ 5\ 6 \end{pmatrix} \right) == \begin{pmatrix} 4\ 5\ 6 \\ 4\ 5\ 6 \\ 1\ 2\ 3 \end{pmatrix}
$$

6.7   Further Reading

Formal definitions of the WITH-loops as presented here can be found in [Gre01] and on the SaC home page <http::://www.sac-home.org/>. A formal translation scheme for generalized selections and the set notation is contained in [GS03].

7   Compilation Issues

The natural choice of a target language for the compilation of SaC is C. Compilation to C can be liberated from all hardware-specific low-level optimizations such as delay-slot utilization or register allocation, as this is taken care of by the C compiler for the target machine. Last not least, the strong syntactical similarity between the two languages allows the compilation efforts to be concentrated on adequate array representations and on optimizing the code for array operations. Other basic language constructs can be translated more or less one to one to their C counterparts.

The major phases of the actual SAC compiler are shown in Fig. 19. After scan-

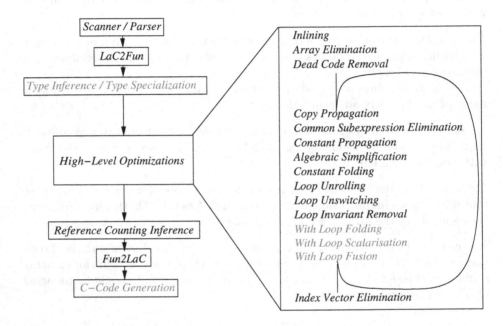

Fig. 19. Compiling SAC programs into C programs

ning and parsing the SAC-program to be compiled, its internal representation is simplified by a transformation called *LaC2Fun* which eliminates syntactical sugar such as loop constructs and (non-top-level) conditionals.

The next compilation phase implements a type inference algorithm based on the hierarchy of array types described in Section 5.3. To achieve utmost code optimizations, the actual implementation tries to specialize all array types to specific shapes. Starting from the designated main function, it traverses function bodies from outermost to innermost, propagating exact shapes as far as possible. In order to avoid non-termination, the number of potential function specializations is limited by a pre-specified number of instances. If this number is exceeded, the generic version is used instead.

The fourth compilation phase implements all the optimizations that can be done on the level of SAC itself. Of particular interest in this context are three SAC-specific optimizations which try to combine WITH-loops for avoiding the creation of arrays that hold intermediate results of the overall computation. These are

- WITH-LOOP-FOLDING eliminates intermediate arrays by folding consecutive WITH-loops into single ones. It constitutes the key optimization for achieving competitive runtimes.
- WITH-loop-fusion enables sharing of loop overhead between otherwise independent WITH-loops.
- WITH-loop-scalarization transform nested WITH-loops into non-nested ones which significantly improves the memory demands.

To improve the applicability of these optimizations, constants have to be propagated / inferred as far as possible, i.e., several standard optimizations have to be included in this compilation phase as well. It also turns out that on the SAC level these standard optimizations, due to the absence of side-effects, can be applied much more rigorously than in state-of-the-art C compilers. The standard optimizations implemented in the actual compiler include Function Inlining, Constant Folding, Constant Propagation, Dead Code Removal, etc. (cf. Fig. 19.).

Many of these optimizations interact with each other, e.g., constant folding may enable WITH-LOOP-FOLDING by inferring exact generator boundaries of WITH-loops which, in turn, may enable further constant folding within the body of the resulting WITH-loop. Therefore, the optimizations are applied in a cyclic fashion, as shown on the right hand side of Fig. 19. This cycle terminates if either there are no more code changes or if a pre-specified number of cycles has been performed.

The three final compilation phases transform the optimized SAC code step by step into a C program. The first phase, called *Reference Counting Inference*, adds for all non-scalar arr ays operations that handle the reference counters at runtime. The techniques used here are similar to those developed for SISAL.

The next phase, called *Fun2LaC*, is dual to *LaC2Fun*; it reverts tail-end recursive functions into loops and inlines functions that were created from non-top-level conditionals during *LaC2Fun*.

Finally, the SAC-specific language constructs are compiled into ANSI C code.

7.1 WITH-LOOP-FOLDING

Our first optimization technique, WITH-loop-folding, addresses the composition of WITH-loops that are used in a pipelined fashion. Consider, for example, a definition

    res = (a + b) + c;

where a, b, and c are all matrices of shape [10, 10]. Inlining the definition of + leads to two subsequent WITH-loops of the form

```
tmp = with(iv)
        ( [0,0] <= iv < [10,10]) : a[iv] + b[iv];
      genarray( [10,10], 0.0);
res = with(iv)
```

```
      ( [0,0] <= iv < [10,10]) : tmp[iv] + c[iv];
      genarray( [10,10], 0.0);
```

which can be combined into a single one

```
res = with(iv)
      ( [0,0] <= iv < [10,10]) : a[iv] + b[iv] + c[iv];
      genarray( [10,10], 0.0);          .
```

Technically spoken, WITH-loop-folding aims at identifying array references within the generator-associated expressions in WITH-loops. If the index expression is an affine function of the WITH-loop's index variable and if the referenced array is itself defined by another WITH-loop, the array reference is replaced by the corresponding element computation. Instead of storing an intermediate result in a temporary data structure and taking the data from there when needed, we forward-substitute the computation of the intermediate value to the place where it is actually needed.

The challenge of WITH-loop-folding lies in the identification of the correct expression which is to be forward-substituted. Usually, the referenced WITH-loop has multiple generators each being associated with a different expression. Hence, we must decide which of the index sets defined by the generators is actually referenced. To make this decision we must take into account the entire generator sequence of the referenced WITH-loop, the generator of the referencing WITH-loop that is associated with the expression which contains the array reference under consideration, and the affine function defining the index. The top of Fig. 20 shows an example for a more general situation. The generator ranges of both WITH-loops do not cover the entire array. Instead, they overlap without one being included within the other. As a consequence, the result of the folding step requires the computation of the intersection of the generators. In order to be able to do this in a uniform way, we first introduce further generators that make the default expressions explicit. The result of this extension is shown in the middle part of Fig. 20. In case of the first WITH-loop, we obtain 4 further generators with 0 being the associated expression. Similarily, the second WITH-loop has to be extended by 4 generators as well. However, since the second WITH-loop is a modarray-WITH-loop, the associated expression needs to be a selection into the array A. After this transformation, the generators within the WITH-loops constitute partitions of the result arrays. This facilitates the computation of generator intersections which then can be folded naively leading to the overall result shown in the bottom of Fig. 20.

7.2   WITH-**Loop-Fusion**

WITH-loop-fusion is similar to conventional loop fusion. It is characterized by two a more WITH-loops without data dependences that iterate over the same index space. Consider for example a function body where both, the maximum element as well as the minimum element of a given array A is needed. This can be specified as

```
A = with (iv)
      ([2,2] <= iv < [6,6]) : 2
    genarray( [10,12],  );
B = with (iv)
      ([4,4] <= iv < [9,9]) : A[iv] + 1
    modarray(  );
```

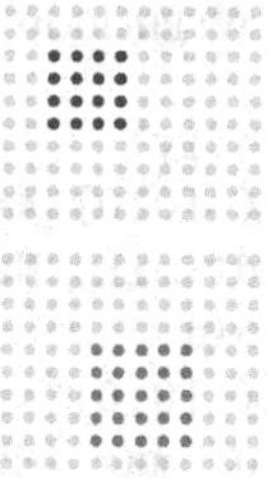

```
A = with (iv)
      ([0,0] <= iv < [ 2, 6]) : 0
      ([2,0] <= iv < [ 6, 2]) : 0
      ([2,2] <= iv < [ 6, 6]) : 2
      ([2,6] <= iv < [ 6,12]) : 0
      ([6,0] <= iv < [10,12]) : 0
    genarray( [10,12]);
B = with (iv)
      ([0,0] <= iv < [ 4,12]) : A[iv]
      ([4,0] <= iv < [ 9, 4]) : A[iv]
      ([4,4] <= iv < [ 9, 9]) : A[iv] + 1
      ([4,9] <= iv < [ 9,12]) : A[iv]
      ([9,0] <= iv < [10,12]) : A[iv]
    modarray(  );
```

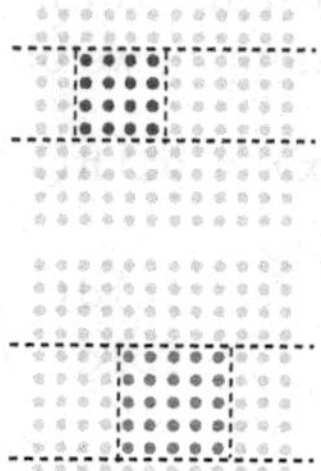

```
B = with (iv)
      ([0,0] <= iv < [ 2, 6]) : 0
      ([2,0] <= iv < [ 6, 2]) : 0

      ([2,2] <= iv < [ 4, 6]) : 2
      ([4,2] <= iv < [ 6, 4]) : 2
      ([4,4] <= iv < [ 6, 6]) : 2 + 1
      ([4,6] <= iv < [ 6, 9]) : 1
      ([6,4] <= iv < [ 9, 9]) : 1

      ([4,9] <= iv < [ 9,12]) : 0
      ([9,0] <= iv < [10,12]) : 0
    genarray( [10,12],  );
```

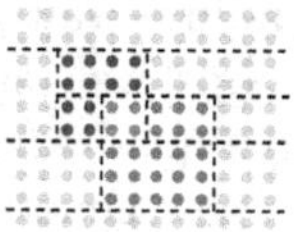

Fig. 20. WITH-loop-folding in the general case

```
minv = minval(A);
maxv = maxval(A);
```

Inlining the WITH-loop definitions for `minval` and `maxval` leads to

```
minv = with(iv)
          ( [0,0] <= iv < shape(A)): A[iv]
        fold( min, MaxInt());
maxv = with(iv)
          ( [0,0] <= iv < shape(A)): A[iv]
        fold( max, MinInt())
```

The idea of WITH-loop-fusion is to combine such WITH-loops into a more versatile internal representation named multi-operator WITH-loop. The major characteristic of multi-operator WITH-loops is their ability to define multiple array comprehensions and multiple reduction operations as well as mixtures thereof. For the example, we obtain:

```
minv, maxv = with(iv)
                ( [0,0] <= iv < shape(A)): A[iv], A[iv]
              fold( min, MaxInt())
              fold( max, MinInt())
```

As a consequence of the code transformation both values `minv` and `maxv` are computed in a single sweep. This allows us to share the overhead inflicted by the multi-dimensional loop nest. Furthermore, we change the order of array references at runtime. The intermediate code as shown above accesses large parts of array `A` in both WITH-loops. Assuming array sizes typical for numerical computing, elements of `A` are extremely likely not to reside in cache memory any more when they are needed for execution of the second WITH-loop. With the fused code both array references `A[iv]` occur in the same WITH-loop iteration and, hence, the second one always results in a cache hit.

Technically, WITH-loop-fusion requires systematically computing intersections of generators in a way similar to WITH-loop-folding. After identification of suitable WITH-loops, we compute the intersections of all pairs of generators. Whereas this leads to a quadratic increase in the number of generators for the worst case, many of the new generators turn out to be empty in practice.

7.3   WITH-Loop-Scalarization

So far, we have not paid any attention to the element types of the arrays involved. In SAC, complex numbers are not built-in, but they are defined as vectors of two elements of type double. As a consequence, an addition of two vectors of complex numbers such as

```
cv = [ Cplx(1.0,1.0), Cplx(-1.0,-1.0), Cplx(-1.0,0.0)];
res = cv + cv;
```

in fact is an addition of two matrices of doubles. However, since addition for complex arrays is defined in terms of a WITH-loop as is the scalar addition of complex numbers, after inlining we obtain

```
res = with(iv)
        ( [0] <= iv < [3]) :
        with(jv)
            ( [0] <= jv < [2]) :(cv[iv])[jv]+(cv[iv])[jv];
          genarray( [2], 0.0);
        genarray( [3], [ 0.0, 0.0]);
```

The idea of WITH-loop-scalarization is to get rid of these nestings of withloops and to transform them into WITH-loops that operate on scalar values. This is achieved by concatenating the bound and shape expressions of the WITH-loops involved and by adjusting the generator variables accordingly. For our example we obtain

```
res = with(iv)
        ( [0,0] <= iv < [3,2]) : cv[iv] + cv[iv]
      genarray( [3,2], [[ 0.0, 0.0], ...]);
```

When comparing this code against the non-scalarized version above we can observe several benefits. There are no more two-element vectors which results in less memory allocations and deallocations at runtime. Furthermore, the individual values are directly written into the result arrays without any copying from temporary vectors.

7.4   Further Reading

Material on the basic compilation scheme can be found in [Sch96, Sch03]. Cache related aspects of the compilation of WITH-loops are covered in [GKS00]. Elaboration on how to make use of various levels of shape information for generating efficient code is provided in [Kre03]. Issues around the heap management as well as compilation into concurrently executable code are presented in [Gre01]. Formal descriptions of the individual optimizations can be found in [Sch98, GST04, Sch03]. Several further papers on performance comparisons can be found on the SAC home page <http://www.sac-home.org/>.

Besides the SAC-specific publications, there is a large body of literature on optimizing array computations in general. Good starting points are books such as [ZC91, Wol95, AK01]. In the context of functional languages, papers on optimizations towards high-performance array computations can also be found in the context of the programming language SISAL [Feo91, Can92, Can93, Can89]. Optimizations for n-dimensional array operations similar to WITH-loop-fusion in SAC can be found in the context of ZPL [Lin96, LLS98].

WITH-loop-folding and WITH-loop-fusion are based on principles that can be found in optimization techniques for algebraic data types as well. The corresponding optimization techniques are referred to as fusion and as tupling, respectively. Papers such as [Chi93, Chi94, Chi95, Gil96, HI97, NP98, Chi99, vAvGS03] contain work on these optimizations.

References

[AK01]   R. Allen and K. Kennedy. *Optimizing Compilers for Modern Architectures*. Morgan Kaufmann Publishers, 2001. ISBN 1-55860-286-0.

[Ass87] I.P Sharp & Associates. *SHARP APL Release 19.0 Guide for APL Programmers*. I.P Sharp & Associates, Ltd., 1987.

[Ben91] J.P. Benkard. Extending Structure, Type, and Expression in APL-2. In *Proceedings of the International Conference on Array Processing Languages (APL'91), Palo Alto, California, USA*, volume 21 of *APL Quote Quad*, pages 20–29. ACM Press, 1991.

[Ben92] J.P. Benkard. Nested Arrays and Operators — Some Issues in Depth. In *Proceedings of the International Conference on Array Processing Languages (APL'92), St.Petersburg, Russia*, APL Quote Quad, pages 7–21. ACM Press, 1992.

[Ber88] R. Bernecky. An Introduction to Function Rank. In *Proceedings of the International Conference on Array Processing Languages (APL'88), Sydney, Australia*, volume 18 of *APL Quote Quad*, pages 39–43. ACM Press, 1988.

[Bro85] J. Brown. Inside the APL2 Workspace. *SIGAPL Quote Quad*, 15:277–282, 1985.

[Bur96] C. Burke. *J and APL*. Iverson Software Inc., Toronto, Canada, 1996.

[Can89] D.C. Cann. Compilation Techniques for High Performance Applicative Computation. Technical Report CS-89-108, Lawrence Livermore National Laboratory, LLNL, Livermore California, 1989.

[Can92] D.C. Cann. Retire Fortran? A Debate Rekindled. *Communications of the ACM*, 35(8):81–89, 1992.

[Can93] D.C. Cann. *The Optimizing SISAL Compiler: Version 12.0*. Lawrence Livermore National Laboratory, LLNL, Livermore California, 1993. Part of the SISAL distribution.

[Chi93] W.N. Chin. Towards an Automated Tupling Strategy. In *Proceedings of the ACM SIGPLAN Symposium on Partial Evaluation and Semantic-Based Program Manipulation (PEPM'97), Copenhagen, Denmark*, pages 119–132. ACM Press, 1993.

[Chi94] W.-N. Chin. Safe Fusion of Functional Expressions II: Further Improvements. *Journal of Functional Programming*, 4(4):515–550, 1994.

[Chi95] W.N. Chin. Fusion and Tupling Transformations: Synergies and Conflicts. In *Proceedings of the Fuji International Workshop on Functional and Logic Programming, Susono, Japan*, pages 106–125. World Scientific Publishing, 1995.

[Chi99] O. Chitil. Type Inference Builds a Short Cut to Deforestation. In *Proceedings of the 1999 ACM SIGPLAN International Conference on Functional Programming (ICFP '99)*, pages 249–160. ACM Press, 1999. ACM Sigplan Notices, 34(9).

[CK01]   M.M.T. Chakravarty and G. Keller. Functional Array Fusion. In X. Leroy, editor, *Proceedings of ICFP'01*. ACM-Press, 2001.

[CK03]   Manuel M.T. Chakravarty and Gabriele Keller. An Approach to Fast Arrays in Haskell. In Johan Jeuring and Simon Peyton Jones, editors, *Summer School and Workshop on Advanced Functional Programming, Oxford, England, UK, 2002*, volume 2638 of *Lecture Notes in Computer Science*, pages 27–58. Springer-Verlag, Berlin, Germany, 2003.

[Feo91]   J.T. Feo. *Arrays in Sisal*, chapter 5, pages 93–106. Arrays, Functional Languages, and Parallel Systems. Kluwer Academic Publishers, 1991.

[Gil96]   A. Gill. *Cheap Deforestation for Non-strict Functional Languages*. PhD thesis, Glasgow University, 1996.

[GKS00]   C. Grelck, D. Kreye, and S.-B. Scholz. On Code Generation for Multi-Generator WITH-Loops in SAC. In P. Koopman and C. Clack, editors, *Proc. of the 11th International Workshop on Implementation of Functional Languages (IFL'99), Lochem, The Netherlands, Selected Papers*, volume 1868 of *LNCS*, pages 77–95. Springer, 2000.

[Gre01]   C. Grelck. *Implicit Shared Memory Multiprocessor Support for the Functional Programming Language SAC - Single Assignment C*. PhD thesis, Institut für Informatik und Praktische Mathematik, Universität Kiel, 2001.

[GS00]   C. Grelck and S.B. Scholz. HPF vs. SAC – A Case Study. In A. Bode, T. Ludwig, and R. Wismüller, editors, *Euro-Par 2000 Parallel Processing*, volume 1900 of *LNCS*, pages 620–624. Springer, 2000.

[GS03]   C. Grelck and S.B. Scholz. Axis Control in SaC. In T. Arts and R. Peña, editors, *Proceedings of the 14th International Workshop on Implementation of Functional Languages (IFL'02), Madrid, Spain, Selected Papers*, volume 2670 of *LNCS*, pages 182–198. Springer-Verlag, Berlin, Germany, 2003.

[GST04]   C. Grelck, S.-B. Scholz, and K. Trojahner. WITH-Loop Scalarization – Merging Nested Array Operations. In G. Michaelson and P. Trinder, editors, *Proc. of the 15th International Workshop on Implementation of Functional Languages (IFL'03), Edinburgh, UK, Selected Papers*, volume 3145 of *LNCS*, pages 118–134. Springer, 2004.

[HI97]   Z. Hu and H. Iwasaki. Tupling Calculation Eliminates Multiple Data Traversals. In *Proceedings of the 2nd ICFP*. ACM-Press, 1997.

[HS04]   S. Herhut and S.-B. Scholz. Towards Fully Controlled Overloading Across Module Boundaries. In c. Grelck and F. Huch, editors, *Proceedings of the 16th International Workshop on the Implementation and Application of Functional Languages (IFL'04), Lübeck, Germany*, pages 395–408. University of Kiel, 2004.

[Hui95]   R. Hui. Rank and Uniformity. *APL Quote Quad*, 25(4):83–90, 1995.

[Int84]   International Standards Organization. International Standard for Programming Language APL. Iso n8485, ISO, 1984.

[Ive62]   K.E. Iverson. *A Programming Language*. Wiley, New York, 1962.

[Ive91]   K.E. Iverson. *Programming in J*. Iverson Software Inc., Toronto, Canada, 1991.

[Ive95]   K.E. Iverson. *J Introduction and Dictionary*. Iverson Software Inc., Toronto, Canada, 1995.

[JF99]   M.A. Jenkins and P. Falster. Array Theory and NIAL. Technical Report 157, Technical University of Denmark, ELTEK, Lyngby, Denmark, 1999.

[JG89]   M.A. Jenkins and J.I. Glasgow. A Logical Basis for Nested Array Data Structures. *Computer Languages Journal*, 14(1):35–51, 1989.

[JJ93]   M.A. Jenkins and W.H. Jenkins. *The Q'Nial Language and Reference Manuals*. Nial Systems Ltd., Ottawa, Canada, 1993.

[Kre03]   D.J. Kreye. *A Compiler Backend for Generic Programming with Arrays*. PhD thesis, Institut für Informatik und Praktische Mathematik, Universität Kiel, 2003.

[Lin96]   C. Lin. ZPL Language Reference Manual. UW-CSE-TR 94-10-06, University of Washington, 1996.

[LLS98]   E.C. Lewis, C. Lin, and L. Snyder. The Implementation and Evaluation of Fusion and Contraction in Array Languages. In *Proceedings of the ACM SIGPLAN '98 Conference on Programming Language Design and Implementation*. ACM, 1998.

[MJ91]   L.M. Restifo Mullin and M. Jenkins. A Comparison of Array Theory and a Mathematics of Arrays. In *Arrays, Functional Languages and Parallel Systems*, pages 237–269. Kluwer Academic Publishers, 1991.

[Mul88]   L.M. Restifo Mullin. *A Mathematics of Arrays*. PhD thesis, Syracuse University, 1988.

[NP98]   L. Nemeth and S. Peyton Jones. A Design for Warm Fusion. In C. Clack, T. Davie, and K. Hammond, editors, *Proceedings of the 10th International Workshop on Implementation of Functional Languages*, pages 381–393. University College, London, 1998.

[PW93]   S.L. Peyton Jones and P. Wadler. Imperative functional programming. In *POPL '93, New Orleans*. ACM Press, 1993.

[Sch96]   S.-B. Scholz. *Single Assignment C – Entwurf und Implementierung einer funktionalen C-Variante mit spezieller Unterstützung shape-invarianter Array-Operationen*. PhD thesis, Institut für Informatik und Praktische Mathematik, Universität Kiel, 1996.

[Sch98]   S.-B. Scholz. With-loop-folding in SAC–Condensing Consecutive Array Operations. In C. Clack, K.Hammond, and T. Davie, editors, *Implementation of Functional Languages, 9th International Workshop, IFL'97, St. Andrews, Scotland, UK, September 1997, Selected Papers*, volume 1467 of *LNCS*, pages 72–92. Springer, 1998.

[Sch01]   S.-B. Scholz. A Type System for Inferring Array Shapes . In T. Arts and M. Mohnen, editors, *Proceedings of the 13th International Workshop on Implementation of Functional Languages (IFL'01), Stockholm, Sweden*, pages 65–82. Ericsson Computer Science Laboratory, 2001.

[Sch03]   Sven-Bodo Scholz. Single Assignment C — efficient support for high-level array operations in a functional setting. *Journal of Functional Programming*, 13(6):1005–1059, 2003.

[SSH+06]   A. Shafarenko, S.-B. Scholz, S. Herhut, C. Grelck, and K. Trojahner. Implementing a numerical solution for the KPI equation using Single Assignment C: lessons and experience. In A. Butterfield, editor, *Implementation and Application of Functional Languages, 17th INternational Workshop, IFL'05*, volume ??? of *LNCS*. Springer, 2006. to appear.

[vAvGS03]   D. van Arkel, J. van Groningen, and S. Smetsers. Fusion in Practice. In R. Peña and T. Arts, editors, *Proceedings of the 14th International Workshop on Implementation of Functional Languages (IFL'02), Madrid, Spain, Selected Papers*, volume 2670 of *Lecture Notes in Computer Science*, pages 51–67. Springer-Verlag, Berlin, Germany, 2003.

[vG97]   J. van Groningen. The Implementation and Efficiency of Arrays in Clean
          1.1. In Werner Kluge, editor, *Implementation of Functional Languages,
          8th International Workshop, Bad Godesberg, Germany, September 1996,
          Selected Papers*, volume 1268 of *LNCS*, pages 105–124. Springer, 1997.
[Wol95]   M.J. Wolfe.   *High-Performance Compilers for Parallel Computing*.
          Addison-Wesley, 1995. ISBN 0-8053-2730-4.
[ZC91]   H. Zima and B. Chapman. *Supercompilers for Parallel and Vector Com-
          puters*. Addison-Wesley, 1991.

Exploiting Purely Functional Programming to Obtain Bounded Resource Behaviour: The Hume Approach

Kevin Hammond

School of Computer Science,
University of St Andrews, St Andrews, Scotland
Tel.:+44-1334-463241; Fax:+44-1334-463278
kh@dcs.st-and.ac.uk

Abstract. This chapter describes Hume: a functionally-based language for programming with bounded resource usage, including time and space properties. The purpose of the Hume language design is to explore the expressibility/costability spectrum in resource-constrained systems, such as real-time embedded or control systems. It is unusual in being based on a combination of λ-calculus and finite state machine notions, rather than the more usual propositional logic, or flat finite-state-machine models. The use of a strict, purely functional programming notation allows the construction of a strong cost model for expressions, which can then be embedded into a simple cost model for processes.

In this chapter, we introduce Hume, describe the Hume Abstract Machine implementation, and show how a high-level cost model can be constructed that relates costs from the abstract machine to Hume source programs. We illustrate our approach with an example adapted from the literature: a simple vending machine controller.

1 Introduction

Hume is a functionally-based research language aimed at applications requiring bounded time and space behaviour, such as real-time embedded systems. Historically, the majority of embedded systems were implemented using low-level notations, often machine code. This was dictated by, firstly, the need to interface to devices at a very low level of abstraction; and, secondly, the need to minimise overall system costs by producing code that was highly efficient in both time and space usage. Since embedded applications were historically both small and simple, they could be (relatively) easily re-implemented if a change to a new architecture proved necessary. Encouraged by major improvements in the price/performance ratio of low- and mid-range devices, the demand for ever more complex applications, such as those found in mobile telephony, has, however, mandated a move to higher level languages such as C++, Ada or even perhaps Java. In this way, some precise low-level control has been sacrificed in favour of advantages of portability, speed of coding and code reuse. This trend is projected to continue with the introduction of Systems-on-a-(Programmable)-Chip. The

Z. Horváth (Ed.): CEFP 2005, LNCS 4164, pp. 100–134, 2006.

challenge that must be met in designing future languages for embedded systems work is to preserve the essential properties of costability and low-level interfacing whilst providing as high-level a programming environment as possible.

Hume has three main research objectives: firstly, to explore the tension between expressibility and costability in order to determine how much abstraction can be included in a language design without losing strong formal properties of cost; secondly, to act as a "virtual laboratory" to allow the construction of new, advanced cost models and analyses in a relatively constrained setting; and thirdly to explore whether functional programming languages can plausibly be used to program real-time embedded systems.

1.1 Properties of a Real-Time Language

We can identify a number of essential or desirable properties for a language that is aimed at real-time embedded systems [18, 30].

- *determinacy* – the language should allow the construction of determinate systems, by which we mean that under identical environmental constraints, all executions of the system should be *observationally equivalent*;
- *bounded time/space* – the language must allow the construction of systems whose resource costs are statically bounded – so ensuring that *hard real-time* and *real-space* constraints can be met;
- *asynchronicity* – the language must allow the construction of systems that are capable of responding to inputs as they are received without imposing total ordering on environmental or internal interactions;
- *concurrency* – the language must allow the construction of systems as communicating units of independent computation;
- *correctness* – the language must allow a high degree of confidence that constructed systems meet their formal requirements [1].

Since functional languages have strong properties of determinacy and correctness, they are potentially good fits to the real-time systems domain provided it is possible to incorporate the remaining properties of concurrency, asynchronicity (where this is required), and above all boundedness. We will now explore this fit in the context of existing functional language designs.

1.2 Functional Languages and Real-Time Systems

Real-time systems can be categorised as being either *hard real-time* or *soft real-time*. Soft real-time has been described as a situation where "nothing really serious happens if a time constraint is not met" [4]. Conversely, hard real-time is characterised by situations of systems failure, mission loss, and even personal injury or death. Since issues of cost and performance conflict with the high-level expressibility that is the general goal of most functional language designs, the majority of functional languages that have even considered real-time issues to date have focused on soft real-time rather than hard real-time. In soft real-time

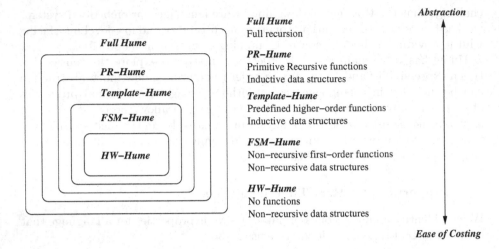

Fig. 1. Expressibility versus Costability in the Hume Design

systems, time boundedness is, of course, non-critical; however, space boundedness may still be essential if memory overflows etc. are to be avoided.

The most widely used soft real-time functional language is the impure, strict
language Erlang [5]. Erlang has been used by Ericsson to construct a number of
successful telecommunications and related applications [3], including the Ericsson AXD301 ATM switch [8] and the soft real-time distributed database management system, Mnesia [50]. In Erlang, concurrent processes are constructed using
explicit spawn operations, with communication occurring through explicit send
and receive operations to nominated processes. While Erlang therefore supports
asynchronicity, there is thus no strong notion of process network.

Another functional language targetting soft real-time systems is the exper-
imental Embedded Gofer language [49]. Embedded Gofer is a strongly-typed
purely functional programming language based on the standard non-strict functional language Haskell. Embedded Gofer has a two-level structure, where concurrent asynchronously communicating processes are defined using a monadic
notation. These processes are then defined in terms of purely functional computations. As part of the monadic process level, Embedded Gofer includes explicit
register access, process creation and communication primitives. This gives a direct, but relatively low-level approach to programming soft real-time systems,
similar to that adopted by existing imperative languages, but with type guarantees providing separation between the two programming levels. Since Embedded
Gofer has a non-strict evaluation model, however, it is not possible to provide
strong behavioural guarantees on either time or space behaviour, as we require
for bounded resource programming.

A similar approach to Embedded Gofer has also been taken by Fijma and
Udink, who introduced special language constructs in a purely functional

program ::=	$decl_1$; ... ; $decl_n$	$n \geq 1$
decl ::=	*boxdecl* | *vardecl* | *fundecl* | *datadecl* | *wiredecl*	
boxdecl ::=	**box** *boxid* *ins* *outs* **fair/unfair** *matches*	
ins/outs ::=	($wireid_1$,... , $wireid_n$)	$n \geq 0$
matches ::=	$match_1$; ... ; $match_n$	$n \geq 1$
match ::=	pat_1 ... pat_n $\rightarrow$ *exp*	$n \geq 1$
pat ::=	*int* | *float* | *char* | *bool* | *string* | varid | _ | *	
	| conid $varid_1$ ... $varid_n$	$n \geq 0$
	| (pat_1 , ... , pat_n)	$n \geq 2$
	| ⟨⟨ pat_1 , ... , pat_n ⟩⟩	$n \geq 0$
exp ::=	*int* | *float* | *char* | *bool* | *string* | varid | *	
	| funid exp_1 ... exp_n	$n \geq 1$
	| varid exp_1 ... exp_n	$n \geq 1$
	| primid exp_1 ... exp_n	$0 < n \leq 3$
	| conid exp_1 ... exp_n	$n \geq 0$
	| (exp_1 , ... , exp_n)	$n \geq 2$
	| ⟨⟨ exp_1 , ... , exp_n ⟩⟩	$n \geq 0$
	| **if** exp_1 **then** exp_2 **else** exp_3	
	| **case** *exp* **of** *matches*	
	| *exp* **within** *constraint*	
	| *exp* **as** τ	
	| *exp* :: τ	
	| **let** $vardecl_1$; ... ; $vardecl_n$ **in** *exp*	$n \geq 1$
constraint ::=	timeconst | spaceconst	
vardecl ::=	varid = *exp*	
fundecl ::=	funid *matches*	
datadecl ::=	**data** typeid $tvarid_1$ ... $tvarid_n$ = *constrs*	$n \geq 0$
constrs ::=	$constr_1$ | ... | $constr_n$	$n \geq 1$
constr ::=	conid τ_1 ... τ_n	$n \geq 0$
τ ::=	typeid τ_1 ... τ_n | tvarid | τ_1 $\rightarrow$ τ_2	$n \geq 0$
wiredecl ::=	**wire** $port_1$ **to** $port_2$	
port ::=	boxid . wireid | deviceid	

Fig. 2. Hume Abstract Syntax (Main Constructs)

language to control a robot arm [16]; and the Timber language also uses *monadic* constructs for specifying strong real-time properties [33].

Finally, a number of functional languages have been designed for programming reactive systems, without considering real-time properties. Such languages will typically incorporate concurrent process creation, inter-process communication and synchronisation constructs. Examples include Concurrent Clean [32], Concurrent ML [42], Concurrent Haskell [40] and Eden [11]. One recent example is Frob (Functional Robotics) [37], which provides monadic support for timed events, tasks and behaviours, and which has been used successfully on the Yale robotics course. Frob is primarily intended to explore issues of high-level expressibility, rather than control systems, real-time systems or bounded space.

1.3   The Hume Design Philosophy

Like many of the reactive functional languages described above, and also like Embedded Gofer, Hume takes a two-level approach to language design, where a purely functional expression layer is embedded within a process layer that describes communicating processes. Where Embedded Gofer uses monads to encapsulate processes, Eden uses a process construct within a functional expression, and Concurrent ML uses side-effecting process creation and communication constructs, Hume makes the separation more explicit by introducing a syntactically distinct process notation, and uses implicit communication.

Costability is, of course, key to the Hume design. Rather than attempting to apply cost modelling and correctness proving technology to an existing language framework either directly or by altering the language to a greater or lesser extent as with e.g. RTSj [9], our approach is to design Hume in such a way that we are *certain* that formal cost models and the associated correctness proofs can be constructed for all Hume language constructs. In order to provide structure to these notions of cost, we envisage a series of overlapping language subsets as shown in Figure 1, where each superset adds expressibility to the expression layer, but either loses some aspect of decidability over our formal properties or increases the difficulty of providing formal correctness/cost models. By choosing an appropriate language level, the programmer can obtain the required balance between expressibility and costability.

2   Boxes and Coordination

In order to support concurrency, Hume requires both computation and coordination constructs. The fundamental unit of computation in Hume is the *box*, which defines a finite mapping from inputs to outputs in a functional manner. Boxes are *wired* into (static) networks of concurrent processes using wiring directives. Each box introduces one process. This section introduces such notions informally.

Figure 2 shows the abstract syntax of Hume. We have chosen to use a rule-based approach to our language design, with a fairly conventional purely-functional expression notation embedded in an asynchronous process model. This simplifies both correctness proofs and the construction of cost models at the expression level. There are four unconventional expression forms: $\langle\langle \ \ldots \ \rangle\rangle$ is a vector pattern or expression; *exp* **within** *constraint* expresses a checkable constraint on time- or space-usage; *exp* **as** τ indicates a dynamic coercion to the specified type τ; and * is used to define asynchronous programs, as described in Section 2.3.

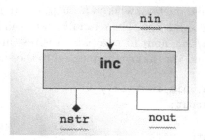

Fig. 3. System diagram for a simple incrementing box

Boxes are abstractions of processes that correspond to (usually finite) state machines. A single Hume box comprises a set of pattern-directed rules, rewriting a set of inputs to a set of outputs, plus appropriate exception handlers and type information. The left-hand-side (pattern part) of each rule defines the situations in which that rule may be active. The right-hand-side of each rule is an expression specifying the results of the box when the rule is activated and matches the corresponding pattern. A box becomes active when any of its rules may match the inputs that have been provided. For example, we can define a box `inc` that simultaneously increments its input `nin` and outputs it as a fixed-width string as follows. Figure 3 shows a system diagram of this box.

```
box inc
in   (nin :: int 32)
out (nout ::int 32, nstr::string 11)
match
 n -> (n+1, n as string 10 ++ "\n");
```

We first specify the types of the inputs (the singleton `nin`, an integer) and outputs (the pair `nout`, an integer, and `nstr`, a string) to the box. We then specify the single pattern-matching rule that takes a single integer value n and produces two outputs: the incremented value of n; and the original input value converted to a fixed-width string using the **as** construct. The Hume design requires the use of explicit type-coercion in order to make clear that time and space costs may be incurred at this point in the program.

2.1   Wiring

Boxes are connected using wiring declarations to form a static process network, with each wire mapping a specific box output to a specific input. Each box output must be connected to precisely one input, and each input must have precisely one output connected to it. In addition to the usual wires connecting boxes, inputs/outputs may be wired from/to external devices, such as I/O streams or ports attached to hardware devices. It is also possible to specify the initial value that appears on a wire. This is typically used to seed computations, such as wires carrying explicit state parameters, where an output wire from a box is wired to an input wire from the same box. For example, we could wire the `inc` box as follows, where `inc.nin`/`inc.nout` form a pair of wires carrying an explicit state that is initialised to 0, and `inc.nstr` is connected to the standard output stream.

```
wire inc.nout to inc.nin initially 0;
wire inc.nstr to output;

stream output to "std_out";
```

2.2   Coordination

Having considered how a static process network can be constructed from a set of boxes, we now turn our attention to how boxes are executed and scheduled. The basic box execution cycle in Hume is:

1. check input availability for all box inputs and latch the input values;
2. match box inputs against the box rules in turn;
3. consume all box inputs;
4. bind variables to input values and evaluate the RHS of the selected rule;
5. write box outputs to the corresponding wires.

A key issue is the management of input and output values on wires. As we have seen, in the Hume model, there is a one-to-one correspondance between input- and output-wires. Each of these wires is *single-buffered*. Since we require data types to convey bounded size information , this ensures that communication buffers are also of bounded size. It also avoids the synchronisation problems that can occur if no buffering is used. In particular, a box may write an output to one of its own inputs, so creating an explicit representation of state, as shown in the `inc` example above.

Values for all available inputs are latched atomically, but are not removed from the wire buffer (*consumed*) until a rule is matched. Consuming an input removes the lock on the wire buffer, resetting the availability for that input. Outputs are written atomically: if any output cannot be written to its buffer because a previous value has not yet been consumed, the box blocks. This reduces concurrency by preventing boxes from proceeding if their inputs could be made available but the producer is blocked on some other output, so potentially introducing deadlock/livelock in some situtations. However, it also improves strong notions of *causality* [43]: if a value has appeared as input on a wire the box that produced that input has certainly generated all of its outputs.

Once a box execution cycle has completed and all outputs have been written to the corresponding wire buffers, the box becomes available for execution in the next scheduling cycle as described in Section 2.4. This improves concurrency, by avoiding unnecessary synchronisation. Note that individual Hume boxes will never terminate. Program termination occurs when no box is runnable and no external input can become available in future. This reflects the requirements of the embedded systems domain that we are targetting: programs should not normally terminate, but should be available to react to any external inputs that may become available at any point during their execution.

2.3 Asynchronous Coordination Constructs

So far, we have described an essentially synchronous coordination model. However, many real-time applications benefit from asynchronicity in its various forms. One of the interesting features of Hume is that it goes beyond the usual synchronous programming models such as Lustre [13], Signal [17] or Esterel [10], whilst maintaining the strong cost properties that are required for embedded systems programming. The two primary coordination constructs that are used to introduce asynchronous coordination are to *ignore* certain inputs/outputs and to introduce *fair matching*. In order to deal with these asynchronous constructs, it is necessary to alter the basic box execution cycle as follows (changes are italicised):

1. check input availability *against possible matches* and latch *available* input values;
2. match *available* inputs against box rules in turn;
3. consume *those inputs that have been matched and which are not ignored in the selected rule*;
4. bind variables to input values and evaluate the RHS of the selected rule;
5. write *non-ignored* outputs to the corresponding wires;
6. *reorder match rules according to the fairness criteria.*

Note that: i) inputs are now consumed after rules have been selected rather than before; ii) only some inputs/outputs may be involved in a given box cycle, rather than all inputs/outputs being required; and iii) rules may be reordered if the box is engaged in fair matching. This new model in which inputs can be ignored in certain patterns or in certain output positions can be considered to be similar to *non-strictness* at the box level.

We use the accepted notion of *fairness* whereby each rule will be used equally often given a stream of inputs that match all rules [2]. *Channel fairness* [2] is not enforced, however: it is entirely possible, for example, for a programmer to write a sequence of rules that will treat the input from different sources unfairly. It is the programmer's responsibility to ensure that channel fairness is maintained, if required.

For example, a fair merge operation, which selects values alternately from its two inputs, can be defined as:

```
box merge
in ( xs  :: int 32, ys :: int 32)
out ( xys :: int 32)
fair
  (x, *) -> x
| (*, y) -> y
;
```

The *-pattern indicates that the corresponding input position should be ignored, that is the *-pattern matches *any* input, without consuming it. Note the difference between *-patterns and wildcard/variable patterns: in the latter cases, successful matching will mean that the corresponding input value (and all of that value) is removed from the input buffer. * can be used as an expression. In this case no output is produced on the corresponding wire, and consequently the box cannot be blocked on that output.

Fair merging is an example of an operation that cannot be expressed easily in a single-layer purely functional notation, since it is non-deterministic at the box level. There have been several attempts in the literature to resolve this problem, including *hiatons* [48] (empty values similar in effect to our * notation, but which incur cost even if no value is present on an input), computations over *sets* of values [23], the introduction of *non-deterministic monads* [28], and the use of explicit concurrency in the Eden language [11]. We argue that the two-layer approach used in Hume offers a simple and clean solution to this problem, by properly encapsulating the notion of a process as a separate construct not embedded into the single functional layer. In this way, all underlying properties of the functional language are preserved without the need for complex analyses to determine whether a computation might be non-deterministic, as is required with Eden [35].

Note that despite this local idea of non-determinacy in Hume (which is an essential part of the specification of this problem), *the system as a whole* is still deterministic. Since we use a least-recently used notion of fairness on rules, systems may be replayed from any known intermediate state, yielding identical results to those originally obtained.

2.4 Thread Scheduling

The prototype Hume Abstract Machine implementation maintains a vector of threads (*thread*), one per box, each with its own *thread state record*, containing state information and links to input/output wires. Each wire comprises a pair of a value (*value*) and a validity flag (*available*). used to ensure correct locking between input and output threads. The flag is atomically set to *true* when an output is written to the wire, and is reset to *false* when an input is consumed.

Threads are scheduled under the control of a built-in scheduler, which currently implements round-robin scheduling. A thread is deemed to be *runnable* if all the required inputs are available for any of its rules to be executed (Figure 4). A compiler-specified matrix is used to determine whether an input is needed: for some thread t, $thread[t].required[r, i]$ is true if input i is required to run rule r of that thread. Since wires are single-buffered, a thread will consequently block when writing to a wire which contains an output that has not yet been consumed. In order to ensure a consistent semantics, a single check is performed on all output wires immediately before any output is written. No output will be written until all the input on all output wires has been consumed. The check ignores * output positions.

```
for i = 1 to nThreads do
  runnable := false;
  for j = 1 to thread[i].nRules do
    if ¬ runnable then
      runnable := true;
      for k = 1 to thread[i].nIns do
        runnable &= thread[i].required[j, k] ⇒ thread[i].ins[k].available
      endfor
    endif
  endfor
  if runnable then schedule (thread[i]) endif
endfor
```

Fig. 4. Hume Abstract Machine Thread Scheduling Algorithm

2.5   Hume Example: A Vending Machine

We will now illustrate Hume with a simple, but more realistic, example from the reactive systems literature, suggested to us at CEFP 2005 by Pieter Koopman: the control logic for a simple vending machine. A system diagram is shown in Figure 5. We will show Hume code only for the most important part of the system: the *control* box. This box responds to inputs from the keypad box and the cash holder box representing presses of a button (for tea, coffee, or a refund) or coins (nickels/dimes) being loaded into the cash box. In a real system, these boxes would probably be implemented as hardware components. If a drinks button (tea/coffee) is pressed, then the controller determines whether a sufficient value of coins has been deposited for the requested drink using the do_dispense function. If so, the vending unit is instructed to produce the requested drink. Otherwise, the button press is ignored. If the cancel button is pressed, or the control unit does not respond within 30s of a button being pressed, then the cash box is instructed to refund the value of the input coins to the consumer.

First we define some basic types representing the value of coins held in the machine (**Cash**), the different types of coins (**Coins**), the drinks that can be dispensed (**Drinks**) and the buttons that can be pressed (**Buttons**). We also define the maximum value of coins that can be input by a single consumer (**MAX_VALUE**).

```
type Cash = int 8;

data Coins = Nickel | Dime;
data Drinks = Coffee | Tea;
data Buttons = BCoffee | BTea | BCancel;

constant MAX_VALUE = 100;
```

Now we can define the control box itself. This box uses *asychronous* constructs to react to each of the two input possibilities: either an inserted coin or a button-press. As with the inc box, state is maintained explicity through a feedback wire: the value' output will be wired directly to the value input. For simplicity, the

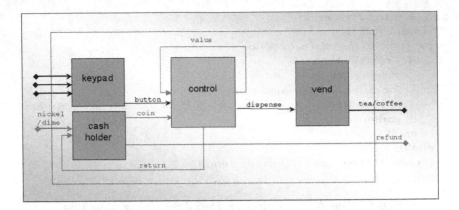

Fig. 5. Hume example: vending machine box diagram

box uses unfair matching, which will prioritise coin inputs over simultaneous button presses. If the cancel button (BCancel) is pressed, no drink will be dispensed (shown by *), but the internal cash value will be reset to zero and the cash holder instructed to refund the current value of coins held (value) through the return wire. A timeout has the same effect as explicitly pressing the cancel button.

```
-- vending machine control box

box control
in  ( coin :: Coins, button :: Buttons, value :: Cash )
out ( dispense :: Drinks, value' :: Cash, return :: Cash )
match
    ( Nickel, *,        v )  ->  add_value v 5
  | ( Dime,   *,        v )  ->  add_value v 10
  | ( *,      BCoffee, v )  ->  do_dispense Coffee 10 v
  | ( *,      BTea,    v )  ->  do_dispense Tea 5 v
  | ( *,      BCancel, v )  ->  ( *, 0, v )
handle
  TimeOut ( *, *, v) -> ( *, 0, v );
```

The control box logic makes use of two auxiliary functions: do_dispense calculates whether sufficient coins have been deposited and instructs the vend box accordingly; and add_value increments the value held in the cash box by the value of the deposited coin. Note the use of * as a return value in the function definition: this is permitted only in positions which correspond to top-level outputs. Note also that the box corresponds to the FSM-Hume level of Section 1.3: it uses first-order non-recursive functions as part of its definition.

```
do_dispense drink cost v =
  if v >= cost then ( drink, v-cost, * )
            else ( *,     v,      * );
```

```
add_value v coin =
   let v' = v + coin in
   if v' > MAX_VALUE then ( *, v,   coin )
                     else ( *, v', *    );
```

Finally, we wire the control box to the other boxes shown in the system diagram. Note that the button wire is instructed to carry a 30s timeout, and the value/value' pair are wired together with an initial value of 0. This ensures that the system is properly initialised and can proceed when started.

```
wire cashbox.coin_in        to control.coin;
wire keypad.button_pressed  to control.button timeout 30s;
wire control.value'         to control.value initially 0;
wire control.dispense       to vend.dispense;
wire control.return         to cashbox.refund;
```

3   Hume Abstract Machine Design

We will now show how Hume programs may be compiled into an abstract machine representation which will allow concrete time and space cost information to be extracted. The goal of the prototype Hume Abstract Machine (pHAM) design is to provide a credible basis for research into bounded time and space computation, allowing formal cost models to be verified against a realistic implementation. An important part of this work is to provide a formal and precise translation scheme as given in Section 4. We have therefore defined the pHAM at a level which is similar to, but slightly more abstract than, the JVM [29], giving a formalised description of the abstract machine in terms of a simple abstract register language which can be easily mapped to machine code. Absolute space- and time-performance (while an important long-term objective for Hume) is thus less important in this initial design than predictability, simplicity and ease of implementation.

3.1   Outline Design

The prototype Hume Abstract Machine is loosely based on the design of the classical G-Machine [6] or SECD-Machine [27]. with extensions to manage concurrency and asynchronicity. Each Hume box is implemented as a thread with its own dynamic stack (S) and heap (H) and associated stack and heap pointers (sp and hp). These and the other items that form part of the individual *thread state record* are shown in Figure 6. Each function and box has an associated *ruleset* (Figure 7). The ruleset is used for two purposes: it gives the address of the next rule to try if matching fails; and it is used to reorder rules if fair matching is specified. The box ruleset is specified as the *base* field of the thread state record. Function rulesets are set as part of a function call.

   The motivation for a separate stack for each thread is to maintain independence between thread states. Similarly, separate heaps allow a simple, real-time

name	interpretation
S	stack
H	heap
sp	stack pointer
hp	heap pointer
fp	frame pointer
mp	match pointer
inp	input pointer
rs	current ruleset
$base$	base ruleset

name	interpretation
pc	program counter
pcr	restart program counter
$blocked$	box blocked
$blockedon$	output on which blocked
$EXNPC$	exception program counter
ins	input buffers
$outs$	output buffers
$nIns$	number of inputs
$nOuts$	number of outputs
$timeout$	current timeout value
$thandler$	pc for timeout handler

Fig. 6. Thread-specific registers, constants and memory areas – the *thread state record*

name	interpretation
$rules$	array of rule entry points
$nRules$	number of rules
rp	current rule pointer

Fig. 7. Ruleset-specific registers and constants

model of garbage collection where the *entire heap* for a box becomes garbage each time a thread completes, and all heaps can therefore be allocated from the same common dynamic memory area. The sizes of all stack and heap spaces are fixed at compile-time using the static analysis described in Section 5, and in principle, small pointer ranges (e.g. 8 bits) can be used in either case. The main disadvantage of our present design is that we cannot use physically- or virtually-shared heap to communicate arguments and results between threads. Rather, such values are copied between heaps at the beginning and end of thread execution as explicit values within wire buffers. In effect, we have a simple copying garbage collector for which liveness can be trivially determined.

There is an analogy with the *working copies* of global variables that may be obtained by implementations of the JVM [29]. However, variable accesses in the JVM may occur at any point during thread execution, not only at the beginning/end as in the pHAM. Moreover, unlike the pHAM, which is stateless, the JVM maintains a virtually shared heap containing *master copies* of each variable. Our design is thus closer to that of Eden [11]: a reactive functional language based on Haskell.

The pHAM design uses a pure stack calling convention. Function arguments are followed by a three-item subframe containing the return address, a pointer to the previous ruleset, and the previous frame pointer. In the rules that follow, the size of this subframe is given by the constant S_{frame}. The local frame pointer fp points immediately after this subframe, to the address of the first local variable.

For consistency, the same layout is used at the outer thread level. In this case, the box inputs are stored in the argument position, and the return address item is redundant. All values on the stack other than the saved return address, ruleset and frame pointer are local heap pointers (i.e. they are *boxed* [38]). Moreover, in the current design there is no separate *basic value stack* to handle scalar values as in some versions of the G-Machine [38], STG-Machine [39] etc. nor are scalars and heap objects mixed on the stack as in the JVM [29].

MkBool b	$H[hp] := \textbf{Bool } b; S[sp] := hp; {+}{+}sp; hp := hp + \mathcal{H}_{bool}; {+}{+}pc$
MkChar c	$H[hp] := \textbf{Char } c; S[sp] := hp; {+}{+}sp; hp := hp + \mathcal{H}_{char}; {+}{+}pc$
MkInt32 i	$H[hp] := \textbf{Int32 } i; S[sp] := hp; {+}{+}sp; hp := hp + \mathcal{H}_{int32}; {+}{+}pc$
MkFloat32 f	$H[hp] := \textbf{Float32 } f; S[sp] := hp; {+}{+}sp;$
	$hp := hp + \mathcal{H}_{float32}; {+}{+}pc$
MkString s	$H[hp] := \textbf{String } s; S[sp] := hp; {+}{+}sp; hp := hp + ssize(s); {+}{+}pc$
...	
MkNone	$H[hp] := \textbf{None}; S[sp] := hp; {+}{+}sp; hp := hp + \mathcal{H}_{none}; {+}{+}pc$
MkCon c n	$H[hp] := \textbf{Con } c\ n\ (S[sp-1])\ ...\ (S[sp-n-1]); sp := sp - n;$
	$S[sp-1] := hp; hp := hp + \mathcal{H}_{con} + n; {+}{+}pc$
MkTuple n	$H[hp] := \textbf{Tuple } n\ (S[sp-1])\ ...\ (S[sp-n-1]); sp := sp - n;$
	$S[sp-1] := hp; hp := hp + \mathcal{H}_{tuple} + n; {+}{+}pc$
MkVector n	$H[hp] := \textbf{Vector } n\ (S[sp-1])\ ...\ (S[sp-n-1]); sp := sp - n;$
	$S[sp-1] := hp; hp := hp + \mathcal{H}_{vector} + n; {+}{+}pc$
MkFun f m n	$H[hp] := \textbf{Fun } f\ m\ n\ (S[sp-1])\ ...\ (S[sp-n-1]); sp := sp - n;$
	$S[sp-1] := hp; hp := hp + \mathcal{H}_{fun} + n; {+}{+}pc$
Push n	$sp := sp + n; {+}{+}pc$
Pop n	$sp := sp - n; {+}{+}pc$
Slide n	$S[sp-n-1] := S[sp-1]; sp := sp - n; {+}{+}pc$
SlideVar n	$S[sp-n-1] := S[sp-1]; sp := sp - n; {+}{+}pc$
Copy n	$S[sp] := S[sp-n-1]; {+}{+}sp; {+}{+}pc$
CopyArg n	$S[sp] := S[fp - S_{frame} - n - 1]; {+}{+}sp; {+}{+}pc$
CreateFrame n	$S[sp] := fp; fp := sp + 1; sp := sp + n + 1; {+}{+}pc$
PushVar n	$S[sp] := S[fp + n]; {+}{+}sp; {+}{+}pc$
MakeVar n	$S[fp + n] := S[sp-1]; {-}{-}sp; {+}{+}pc$

Fig. 8. Hume Abstract Machine Instructions (Heap and Stack Manipulation)

3.2   The Hume Abstract Machine Instructions

The abstract machine instructions implement the abstract machine design described above. An operational description of these instructions is given in Figures 8–13. We use a number of auxiliary definitions: *copy* creates a copy of a wire value in the appropriate heap/wire; *getchar* reads a character from the specified stream; *putvalue* writes a representation of its value argument to the specified stream; and *reschedule* terminates the current box execution, passing control to the abstract machine scheduler. $\mathcal{H}_{con}$, $\mathcal{H}_{int32}$ etc. are constants defining the sizes of heap objects. A number of pseudo-instructions: **Box**, **Stream**, **Wire**, **Label**, **Function**, **Rule** and **Require** are also used to provide information about program structure that is exploited by the abstract machine implementation (Figure 11).

Heap Object Creation and Stack Manipulation (Figure 8). Tagged objects are created in the heap, and pointers to the new object stored on the top of the stack. For scalar values (booleans, characters, integers, floats and strings – **MkInt32** etc.), the actual value is taken directly from the instruction stream. For strings, this value is a pointer into a global shared string table). The instruction **MkNone** creates a special value **None**, which is tested in the **CheckOutputs/Write** instructions. Finally, **MkCon** builds user-defined data structures of a given size, **MkTuple** builds tuples and **MkVector** builds vectors.

The abstract machine uses a number of simple and conventional stack manipulation operations: **Push** and **Pop** manipulate the stack pointer directly; and

Goto l	$pc := l$
If l	**if** $S[sp - 1] = true$ **then** $pc := l$ **else** $++pc$ **endif**; $--sp$
Call f	$S[sp] := pc + 1; S[sp + 1] := rs; ++sp;$ $rs := f.ruleset; rs.rp := 0; pc := rs.rules[0]$
Return l	$rs := S[fp - 2]; pc := S[fp - 3]; sp' := fp - S_{frame};$ $fp := S[fp - 1]; S[sp'] := S[sp - 1]; sp := sp' + 1$
CallPrim1 p	$S[sp] := p\ (S[sp]); ++pc$
CallPrim2 p	$S[sp - 1] := p\ (S[sp])\ (S[sp - 1]); --sp; ++pc$
CallPrim3 p	$S[sp - 1] := p\ (S[sp])\ (S[sp - 1])\ (S[sp - 2]); sp := sp - 2; ++pc$

CallVar $v\ x$	**let** $H[v]$ be **Fun** $f\ m\ n\ a_1 \ldots a_m$ **in**
	if $m + x \geq n$ **then**
	  for $i = 1$ **to** m **do**
	    $S[sp + i - 1] := a_i;$
	  $sp := sp + m;$
	  Call f;
	else
	  $H[hp] := $ **Fun** $f\ (m + x)\ n\ a_1\ \ldots\ a_m\ S[sp - 1]\ \ldots\ S[sp - x - 1];$
	  $sp := sp - x; S[sp - 1] := hp; hp := hp + \mathcal{H}_{fun} + m + x; ++pc$

AP n	$--sp;$ CallVar$(S[sp])n;$

Fig. 9. Hume Abstract Machine Instructions (Control)

MatchRule	$mp := fp - S_{frame} + 1; inp := 0; pc := rs.rules[rp]; {+}{+}rp$
MatchNone	$--mp; {+}{+}inp; {+}{+}pc$
MatchAvailable	**if** $\neg\ ins[inp].available$ **then** $pc := rules[rp]$ **endif**; $inp := inp + 1$
MatchBool b	$--mp;$ **if** $H[S[mp]] \neq$ **Bool** b **then** $pc := rules[rp]$ **endif**
MatchChar c	$--mp;$ **if** $H[S[mp]] \neq$ **Char** c **then** $pc := rules[rp]$ **endif**
MatchString s	$--mp;$ **if** $H[S[mp]] \neq$ **String** s **then** $pc := rules[rp]$ **endif**
MatchInt32 i	$--mp;$ **if** $H[S[mp]] \neq$ **Int32** i **then** $pc := rules[rp]$ **endif**
MatchFloat32 f	$--mp;$ **if** $H[S[mp]] \neq$ **Float32** f **then** $pc := rules[rp]$ **endif**
...	
MatchCon $c\ n$	$--mp;$ **if** $H[S[mp]] \neq$ **Con** $c\ n$ **then** $pc := rules[rp]$ **endif**
MatchTuple n	$--mp;$ **if** $H[S[mp]] \neq$ **Tuple** n **then** $pc := rules[rp]$ **endif**
MatchVector s	$--mp;$ **if** $H[S[mp]] \neq$ **Vector** s **then** $pc := rules[rp]$ **endif**
Unpack	**let** offset $=$ **if** $H[S[--sp]] =$ **Tuple** n **then** 2 **else if** $H[S[sp]] =$ **Con** $c\ n$ **then** 3 **in** **else if** $H[S[sp]] =$ **Vector** n **then** 2 **in** **for** $i = 0$ **to** $n - 1$ **do** $S[sp{+}{+}] := H[hp + \text{offset} + i];$ **endfor**; ${+}{+}pc$
StartMatches	$pc := base.rules[0]$

Reorder	**let** $n = rs.nRules - 1; r = rs.rules[rp]$ **in**
	 for $i = rp$ **to** n **do**
	 $rs.rules[i] := rs.rules[i + 1]$
	 endfor;
	 $rs.rules[n] := r; {+}{+}pc$

Fig. 10. Hume Abstract Machine Instructions (Pattern Matching)

Copy and **CopyArg** copy stack locations or function arguments to the top of the stack. Two operations are used to restore stack frames following a call: **Slide** pops the stack frame, removing the function arguments after a call, but leaving the result on the top of the stack; **SlideVar** has a similar purpose, but is used where the call has been made indirectly through a closure. Three operations manipulate variables: **PushVar** copies a local variable to the stack; **PushVarF** (not shown) does the same for non-local variables; and **MakeVar** sets the value of a local variable.

Control Operations (Figure 9). The Hume abstract machine control instructions are shown in Figure 9. **Goto** sets the pc to the appropriate instruction. **If** does the same conditionally on the value on the top of the stack. **Call** calls the specified function, saves the current ruleset on the stack, and updates the ruleset. **CallPrim1/2/3** call primitive (built-in) functions with the corresponding numbers of arguments.

Label l	l labels the next instruction
Function f l_1 ... l_n	Function f has rules at labels l_1 ... l_n
Box b h s i o r	Box b has heap h, stack s, i inputs, o outputs and r rules
Rule b l_1 ... l_n	Box b has rules at labels l_1 ... l_n
Require b x_1 ... x_n	Box b requires inputs x_1 ... x_n
Stream s In/Out h s	Stream h has heap h and stack s
Wire wi i wo o h	Wire connects input $wi.i$ to output $wo.o$ with heap h

Fig. 11. Hume Abstract Machine Pseudo-Instructions

Raise x	$H[hp] := \mathbf{Exn}\ x\ (S[sp-1]);\ S[sp-1] := hp;$
	$hp := hp + \mathcal{H}_{exn};\ pc := EXNPC$
Within l t	$S[sp] := timeout;\ S[sp+1] := thandler;\ sp := sp+2;$
	$timeout := t;\ thandler := l;$
RaiseWithin x	$timeout := NEVER;\ {+}{+}pc;$
DoneWithin	$thandler := S[--sp];\ timeout := S[--sp];$

Fig. 12. Hume Abstract Machine Instructions (Exceptions)

Pattern Matching (Figure 10). We use a set of high level pattern matching instructions rather than compiling into a series of case matches as with e.g. the STG-Machine [39]. Thread matching is initiated by the **StartMatches** instruction, which sets the program counter to the first rule in the base ruleset. Identical matching operations are used both for box inputs and for function arguments. The operations are divided into three sets: the **MatchRule** operation which initialises the matching for a rule; the **MatchAvailable** and **MatchNone** operations which check box input availability (**MatchNone** for *-patterns); and the value matching operations such as **MatchInt32** or **MatchCon**, which use the current match pointer, mp. Nested matching is achieved by unpacking the arguments onto the stack using **Unpack**. Finally rules may be reordered if fair matching is required using **Reorder**.

Exceptions (Figure 12). Exceptions are raised by the **Raise** instruction, which constructs the relevant exception value and then transfer control to the box's exception handler (EXNPC). **within**-expressions are managed by three instructions, which manipulate $timeout$ and $thandler$: provided the new timeout t is earlier than the current timeout, $timeout$, the **Within** instruction will stack the previous timeout value, together with the timeout handler, $thandler$. If a timeout occurs, then control will be transferred to the timeout handler, whose first action will be to use a **RaiseWithin** instruction to disable the timeout, by setting the timeout so that it will never occur. Finally, if the expression doesn't trigger a timeout, then **DoneWithin** will restore the previous $timeout$

CopyInput n	$S[sp] := copy\ (ins[n].value); {+}{+}sp; {+}{+}pc$
Consume n	$ins[n].available := false; {+}{+}pc$
CheckOutputs	**for** $i = 0$ **to** $nOuts$ **do**
	$\qquad$ **if** $H[S[sp-i-1]] \neq$ **None and** $outs[i].available$ **then**
	$\qquad\qquad blocked := true; blockedon := i; pcr := pc; reschedule;$
	$\qquad$ **endif;**
	endfor; ${+}{+}pc$
Write n	**if** $H[S[{-}{-}sp]] \neq$ **None then**
	$\qquad outs[n].value := copy(H[S[sp]]); outs[n].available := true;$
	endif; ${+}{+}pc$
Input s	**let** $c = getchar\ s$ **in**
	$\qquad H[hp] := $ Char $c; S[sp] := hp; {+}{+}sp;$
	$\qquad hp := hp := hp + \mathcal{H}_{char}; {+}{+}pc$
Output s	$putvalue(s, S[sp-1]); {-}{-}sp; {+}{+}pc$
Schedule	$reschedule$

Fig. 13. Hume Abstract Machine Instructions (Threads)

and *thandler* values from the stack. Similar instructions (not shown here) are used to handle space restrictions.

Thread Input/Output and Rescheduling Operations (Figure 13). Thread input and output on wires is handled by two sets of operations. The **CopyInput** instruction copies the specified input from the input wire into the heap and places it on the top of the stack prior to matching. If matching is successful, input is *consumed* using the **Consume** operation, which resets the availability flag for the appropriate input wire, thereby permitting subsequent **Write** instructions to succeed for that wire.

Thread output is handled by two analagous operations. The **Write** operation writes the value on the top of the stack to the specified output wire. Before this can be done, the **CheckOutputs** operation is used to ensure that all required **Write** instructions will succeed. This is achieved by checking that all output wire buffers are empty, as indicated by the wire's *available* flag. If not, then the thread blocks until the value on the wire has been consumed, and the *available* flag has been cleared. If the heap value is **None** (corresponding to * on the output), then the **Write** will not actually write anything to the output wire, and the *available* flag is therefore ignored by **CheckOutputs**.

Control is returned to the scheduler either when a thread blocks, either as a consequence of being unable to write some output during the **CheckOutputs** operation, or explicitly when a thread terminates as a consequence of executing the **Schedule** operation. In either case, the scheduler will select a new runnable thread to execute. If there is no runnable thread, then in the current implementation the system will terminate. In a distributed system, it would be necessary to check for global termination, including outstanding communications that could awaken some thread.

Finally, two operations are provided to manage stream and device input/output. A special I/O thread is attached to each stream/device by the **Stream** pseudo-instruction (Figure 11). Executing the **Input** operation blocks this thread if no input is available, but otherwise reads input into the thread's heap. The **Output** operation simply writes the top stack value to the appropriate device. Normal wire operations are used to interface other threads to these special I/O threads. For simplicity, we only show character-level I/O, but more complex I/O can also be managed in a similar way.

4   Compilation Scheme

This section outlines a formal compilation scheme for translating Hume programs into pHAM instructions. Our intention is to demonstrate that a formal (and ultimately provable) model of compilation can be constructed for Hume. By constructing a formal translation to real machine code from pHAM code, it is then possible to verify both correctness of the compiler output and time/space cost models.

Figures 14–18 outline rules for compiling Hume abstract syntax forms into the abstract machine instructions described in Section 3, as a formal compilation scheme similar to that for the G-machine [6]. These rules have been used to construct a compiler from Hume source code to the pHAM, whose main component is a 500-line Haskell module translating abstract syntax to pHAM instructions.

The compilation scheme makes extensive use of a simple sequence notation: $\langle i_1, \ldots, i_n \rangle$ denotes a sequence of n items. The $+\!\!+$ operation concatenates two such sequences. Many rules also use an environment ρ which maps identifiers to $\langle depth, offset \rangle$ pairs.

Four auxiliary functions are used, but not defined here: $maxVars$ calculates the maximum number of variables in a list of patterns; $bindDefs$ augments the environment with bindings for the variable definitions taken from a declaration sequence – the $depth$ of these new bindings is 0, whilst the depth of existing variable bindings in the environment is incremented by 1; $bindVars$ does the same for a sequence of patterns; and $labels$ generates new labels for a set of function/box rules. Note that where labels lt, ln, lx etc. are used, these are assumed to be unique in the obvious way: there is at most one **Label** pseudo-instruction for each label in the translated program. Labels for boxes and function blocks are derived in a standard way from the (unique) name of the box or function. Finally, priming (e.g. ρ') has no semantic significance as in mathematics: it is used here for naming purposes only.

The rules are structured by abstract syntax class. The rules for translating expressions ($\mathcal{C}_E$ etc. – Figures 14–15) are generally straightforward, but note

$$\mathcal{C}_E\ \rho\ (c\ e_1\ \ldots\ e_n) \quad = \quad \mathcal{C}_E\ \rho\ e_n\ \mathbin{+\!\!+}\ \ldots\ \mathbin{+\!\!+}\ \mathcal{C}_E\ \rho\ e_1\ \mathbin{+\!\!+}\ \langle\ \mathbf{MkCon}\ c\ n\ \rangle$$
$$\mathcal{C}_E\ \rho\ (p\ e_1\ \ldots\ e_n) \quad = \quad \mathcal{C}_E\ \rho\ e_n\ \mathbin{+\!\!+}\ \ldots\ \mathbin{+\!\!+}\ \mathcal{C}_E\ \rho\ e_1\ \mathbin{+\!\!+}\ \langle\ \mathbf{CallPrim}n\ p\ \rangle$$

$$\mathcal{C}_E\ \rho\ (f\ e_1\ \ldots\ e_n) \quad = \quad \mathbf{let}\ a\ =\ arity\ f\ \mathbf{in}$$
$$\mathcal{C}_E\ \rho\ e_n\ \mathbin{+\!\!+}\ \ldots\ \mathbin{+\!\!+}\ \mathcal{C}_E\ \rho\ e_1\ \mathbin{+\!\!+}$$
$$\mathbf{if}\ n = a\ \mathbf{then}\ \ \langle\ \mathbf{Call}\ f, \mathbf{Slide}\ n\ \rangle$$
$$\mathbf{else\ if}\ n < a\ \mathbf{then}\ \ \langle\ \mathbf{MkFun}\ \rangle$$
$$\mathbf{else}\ \ \langle\ \mathbf{Call}\ f,\ \mathbf{Slide}\ n,\ \mathbf{AP}\ (n - a)\ \rangle$$

$$\mathcal{C}_E\ \rho\ (v\ e_1\ \ldots\ e_n) \quad = \quad \mathcal{C}_E\ \rho\ e_n\ \mathbin{+\!\!+}\ \ldots\ \mathbin{+\!\!+}\ \mathcal{C}_E\ \rho\ e_1\ \mathbin{+\!\!+}$$
$$\langle\ \mathbf{CallVar}\ v\ n, \mathbf{SlideVar}\ v\ \rangle$$

$$\mathcal{C}_E\ \rho\ (i) \quad = \quad \langle\ \mathbf{MkInt32}\ i\ \rangle$$
$$\ldots$$
$$\mathcal{C}_E\ \rho\ (*) \quad = \quad \langle\ \mathbf{MkNone}\ \rangle$$

$$\mathcal{C}_E\ \rho\ (\ e_1\ ,\ \ldots\ ,\ e_n\ ) \quad = \quad \mathcal{C}_E\ \rho\ e_n\ \mathbin{+\!\!+}\ \ldots\ \mathbin{+\!\!+}\ \mathcal{C}_E\ \rho\ e_1\ \mathbin{+\!\!+}\ \langle\ \mathbf{MkTuple}\ n\ \rangle$$
$$\mathcal{C}_E\ \rho\ \langle\ \langle\ e_1\ ,\ \ldots\ ,\ e_n\ \rangle\ \rangle \quad = \quad \mathcal{C}_E\ \rho\ e_n\ \mathbin{+\!\!+}\ \ldots\ \mathbin{+\!\!+}\ \mathcal{C}_E\ \rho\ e_1\ \mathbin{+\!\!+}\ \langle\ \mathbf{MkVector}\ n\ \rangle$$

$$\mathcal{C}_E\ \rho\ (var) \quad = \quad \langle\ \mathbf{PushVar}\ n\ \rangle$$

Fig. 14. Compilation Rules for Expressions (1)

that function frames are created to deal with *let*-expressions and other similar structures, which then exploit the function calling mechanism. This allows the creation of local stack frames. It would obviously be possible to eliminate the function call for *let*-expressions provided the stack frame was properly set up in order to allow access to non-local definitions. Note also the three cases for function application: respectively corresponding to the usual first-order case, to under-application of a function (where a closure will be created using **MkFun**), and to over-application of a function (where the closure will be applied to the additional arguments using **Ap**).

In order to avoid the increase in closure sizes that would result from lambda-lifting [22], we instead use a *static link pointer* approach, where each new stack frame is linked at runtime to the frame corresponding to the function that statically encloses the current function body. This gives a space and time cost model that can be more easily related to the source, since we will not transform value definitions into functions as a result of lifting free variables. It also reduces the number and size of functional closures that must be created. However, it does increase the (fixed) size for each stack frame, since a static link pointer to the enclosing scope must be stored in each frame. In order to exploit this approach, we introduce variants of the **PushVar**, **SlidaVar**, **CallVar** instructions that use the static link pointer to locate the variable definition from the correct statically linked frame. For simplicity, we have omitted these instructions here.

The rules for translating box and function declarations are shown in Figure 16. These rules create new stack frames for the evaluation of the box or function,

$$\mathcal{C}_E \ \rho \ (\textbf{if } c \textbf{ then } t \textbf{ else } f) \ = \ \mathcal{C}_E \ \rho \ c \ +\!\!+ \ \langle \textit{ If lt } \rangle \ +\!\!+ \ \mathcal{C}_E \ \rho \ f \ +\!\!+$$
$$\langle \textit{ Goto ln}, \textit{ Label lt } \rangle \ +\!\!+ \ \mathcal{C}_E \ \rho \ t \ +\!\!+$$
$$\langle \textit{ Label ln } \rangle$$

$$\mathcal{C}_E \ \rho \ (\textbf{case } e \textbf{ of } ms) \ = \ \mathcal{C}_E \ \rho \ e \ +\!\!+ \ \langle \textit{ Call lc}, \textit{ Slide } 1, \textit{ Goto ln}, \textit{ Label lc } \rangle \ +\!\!+$$
$$\mathcal{C}_{Case} \ \rho \ ms \ +\!\!+$$
$$\langle \textit{ Label ln}, \textit{ Function lc (labels lc) } \rangle$$

$$\mathcal{C}_E \ \rho \ (\textbf{let } d_1 \ \dots \ d_n \textbf{ in } e) \ = \ \textbf{let } \rho' \ = \ \textit{bindDefs } \langle \ d_1 \ ; \ \dots \ ; \ d_n \ \rangle \ \rho \textbf{ in}$$
$$\langle \textit{ Call ll}, \textit{ Goto ln}, \textit{ Label ll}, \textit{ CreateFrame } n \ \rangle \ +\!\!+$$
$$\mathcal{C}_{Let} \ \rho \ 0 \ d_1 \ +\!\!+ \ \dots \ +\!\!+ \ \mathcal{C}_{Let} \ \rho \ (n-1) \ d_n \ +\!\!+$$
$$\mathcal{C}_E \ \rho' \ e \ +\!\!+ \ \langle \textit{ Return}, \textit{ Label ln } \rangle \ +\!\!+$$
$$\langle \textit{ Function ll } \langle\rangle \ \rangle$$

$$\mathcal{C}_E \ \rho \ (\ e \textbf{ as } \tau) \ = \ \mathcal{C}_E \ \rho \ e \ +\!\!+ \ \langle \textit{ CallPrim1 Coerce} - \tau \ \rangle$$

$$\mathcal{C}_E \ \rho \ (\ e \textbf{ within } c) \ = \ \langle \textit{ Within lw c } \rangle \ +\!\!+ \ \langle \ \mathcal{C}_E \ \rho \ e \ +\!\!+ \ \langle \textit{ Goto ln } \rangle \ +\!\!+$$
$$\langle \textit{ Label lw}, \textit{ RaiseWithin } \rangle \ +\!\!+$$
$$\langle \textit{ MkTuple } 0, \textit{ Raise Timeout/HeapOverflow } \rangle \ +\!\!+$$
$$\langle \textit{ Label ln}, \textit{ DoneWithin } \rangle$$

$$\mathcal{C}_E \ \rho \ (\textbf{raise } exnid \ e) \ = \ \mathcal{C}_E \ \rho \ e \ +\!\!+ \ \langle \textit{ Raise exnid } \rangle$$

$$\mathcal{C}_E \ \rho \ (e :: \tau) \ = \ \mathcal{C}_E \ \rho \ e$$

$$\mathcal{C}_{Case} \ \rho \ \langle \ r_1, \dots, r_m \ \rangle \ = \ \textbf{let } n \ = \ \textit{maxVars } \langle \ r_1, \ \dots, \ r_m \ \rangle \textbf{ in}$$
$$\langle \textit{ CreateFrame } n \ \rangle \ +\!\!+$$
$$\mathcal{C}_F \ \rho \ \langle \ r_1, \dots, r_m \ \rangle$$

$$\mathcal{C}_{Let} \ \rho \ n \ (v = e) \ = \ \mathcal{C}_E \ \rho \ e \ +\!\!+ \ \langle \textit{ MakeVar } n \ \rangle$$

Fig. 15. Compilation Rules for Expressions (2)

label the entry points and introduce appropriate pseudo-instructions. In the case of box declarations, it is also necessary to copy inputs to the stack using **CopyInput** instructions and to deal with fair matching.

Box bodies are compiled using $\mathcal{C}_R/\mathcal{C}_{R'}$ (Figure 17). These rules compile matches for the outer level patterns using $\mathcal{C}_P$, then compile inner pattern matches using $\mathcal{C}_A$, before introducing **Consume** instructions for non-* input positions. The RHS can now be compiled. If more than one result is to be produced, the tuple of outputs is unpacked onto the stack. A **CheckOutputs** is inserted to verify that the outputs can be written using appropriate **Write** instructions. Finally, a **Reorder** is inserted if needed to deal with fair matching, and a **Schedule** returns control to the scheduler. The compilation of function/handler bodies using $\mathcal{C}_F/\mathcal{C}_{F'}$ is similar, except that $\mathcal{C}_{P'}$ is used rather than $\mathcal{C}_P$, there is no need to deal with box inputs/outputs or fair matching, and a **Return** rather than **Schedule** is inserted at the end of each compiled rule.

$$\mathcal{C}_D \; \rho \; (\mathbf{box} \; b \; ins \; outs \; \mathbf{fair} \; rs \; \mathbf{handle} \; xs) \;\; = \;\; \mathcal{C}_B \; \rho \; true \; b \; ins \; outs \; rs$$
$$\mathcal{C}_D \; \rho \; (\mathbf{box} \; b \; ins \; outs \; \mathbf{unfair} \; rs \; \mathbf{handle} \; xs) \;\; = \;\; \mathcal{C}_B \; \rho \; false \; b \; ins \; outs \; rs$$

$$\mathcal{C}_D \; \rho \; (v \; = \; e) \;\; = \;\; \langle \; \text{Label} \; v, \; \text{CreateFrame} \; 0 \; \rangle \; +\!\!+ \; \mathcal{C}_E \; \rho \; e \; +\!\!+ \; \langle \; \text{Return} \; \rangle$$

$$\mathcal{C}_D \; \rho \; (f \; = \; p_1 \; \rightarrow \; e_1 \; ; \; \ldots \; p_n \; ; \; \rightarrow \; e_n) =$$
$$\quad \mathbf{let} \; n \; = \; maxVars \; \langle \; p_1, \; \ldots, \; p_n \; \rangle \; \mathbf{in}$$
$$\quad \langle \; \text{Label} \; f, \; \text{CreateFrame} \; n \; \rangle \; +\!\!+$$
$$\quad \mathcal{C}_F \; \rho \; \langle \; p_1 \; \rightarrow \; e_1 \; \ldots \; p_n \; \rightarrow \; e_n \; \rangle \; +\!\!+$$
$$\quad \langle \; \text{Function} \; f \; (labels \; f) \; \rangle$$

$$\mathcal{C}_D \; \rho \; (\mathbf{wire} \; p_1 \; \mathbf{to} \; p_2) = \;\; \langle \; \text{Wire} \; \ldots \; \rangle$$

$$\mathcal{C}_D \; \rho \; (\mathbf{data} \; t \; v_1 \; \ldots \; v_n \;) = \;\; \langle \; \rangle$$

$$\mathcal{C}_B \; \rho \; f \; b \; (in_1, \ldots, in_i) \; (out_1, \ldots, out_m) \; rs \;\; =$$
$$\quad \mathbf{let} \; n \; = \; maxVars \; rs \; \mathbf{in}$$
$$\quad \langle \; \text{Label} \; b \; \rangle \; +\!\!+$$
$$\quad \langle \; \text{CopyInput} \; (i-1), \; \ldots, \; \text{CopyInput} \; 0 \; \rangle \; +\!\!+$$
$$\quad \langle \; \text{Push} \; 2, \; \text{CreateFrame} \; n \; \rangle \; +\!\!+$$
$$\quad (\mathbf{if} \; f \; \mathbf{then} \; \langle \; \text{StartMatches} \; \rangle \; \mathbf{else} \; \langle \; \rangle) \; +\!\!+ \; \mathcal{C}_R \; \rho \; f \; m \; rs \; +\!\!+$$
$$\quad \langle \; \text{Box} \; b \; \ldots \; \rangle$$

Fig. 16. Compilation Rules for Declarations and Box Bodies

Finally patterns are compiled using $\mathcal{C}_P/\mathcal{C}_{P'}$ (Figure 18), where $\mathcal{C}_P$ inserts the **MatchNone/ MatchAvailable** instructions that are needed at the box level, and $\mathcal{C}_{P'}$ compiles simple patterns. Constructed values are matched in two stages: firstly the constructor is matched, and then if the match is successful, the matched object is deconstructed on the stack to allow its inner components to be matched against the inner patterns. These nested patterns are compiled using $\mathcal{C}_A$ and $\mathcal{C}_{A'}$. $\mathcal{C}_{A'}$ inserts either **CopyArg** and **Unpack** instructions to decompose function/box arguments, or **Copy** and **Unpack** instructions to deal with nested pattern matches, where it is only necessary to replicate arguments that are already in the local stack frame.

4.1 Compilation Example: The Vending Machine

Figure 19 shows the pHAM instructions for the vending machine example of Section 2.5. First, in the preamble to the box, the inputs are copied into the local heap using `CopyInput` instructions and a dummy stack frame is constructed to hold values of the matched variables. Each rule is then compiled separately. For illustration, we show instructions corresponding to the first and third rules only. The LHS of each rule is bracketed in a pair of `MatchRule..MatchedRule` instructions, where individual `MatchX` instructions perform the matching of inputs against patterns. `MatchAvailable` is used to ensure that the input is available

$$\mathcal{C}_R\ \rho\ f\ m\ \langle\ r_1\ ;\ \ldots\ ;\ r_n\ \rangle \quad = \quad \mathcal{C}_{R'}\ \rho\ f\ m\ r_1\ +\!\!+\ \ldots\ +\!\!+\ \mathcal{C}_{R'}\ \rho\ f\ m\ r_n$$

$$\mathcal{C}_{R'}\ \rho\ f\ m\ (p_1\ \ldots\ p_n\ \rightarrow\ e) \quad = \quad \langle\ \text{Label}\ lr,\ \text{MatchRule}\ \rangle\ +\!\!+$$
$$\mathcal{C}_P\ p_1\ +\!\!+\ \ldots\ +\!\!+\ \mathcal{C}_P\ p_n\ +\!\!+$$
$$\mathcal{C}_A\ p_1\ +\!\!+\ \ldots\ +\!\!+\ \mathcal{C}_A\ p_n\ +\!\!+$$
$$\mathcal{C}_C\ 0\ p_1\ +\!\!+\ \ldots\ +\!\!+\ \mathcal{C}_C\ (n-1)\ p_n\ +\!\!+$$
$$\mathcal{C}_E\ \rho\ e\ +\!\!+$$
$$(\textbf{if}\ m\ >\ 1\ \textbf{then}\ \langle\ \text{Unpack}\ \rangle\ \textbf{else}\ \langle\ \rangle)\ +\!\!+$$
$$\langle\ \text{CheckOutputs}\ \rangle\ +\!\!+$$
$$\langle\ \text{Write}\ (n-1),\ \ldots,\ \text{Write}\ 0\ \rangle\ +\!\!+$$
$$(\textbf{if}\ f\ \textbf{then}\ \langle\ \text{Reorder}\ \rangle\ \textbf{else}\ \langle\ \rangle)\ +\!\!+$$
$$\langle\ \text{Schedule}\ \rangle$$

$$\mathcal{C}_C\ n\ (\textbf{*}) \quad = \quad \langle\ \rangle$$
$$\mathcal{C}_C\ n\ (p) \quad = \quad \langle\ \text{Consume}\ n\ \rangle$$

$$\mathcal{C}_F\ \rho\ (r_1\ ;\ \ldots\ ;\ r_n) \quad = \quad \mathcal{C}_{F'}\ \rho\ r_1\ +\!\!+\ \ldots\ +\!\!+\ \mathcal{C}_{F'}\ \rho\ r_n$$
$$\mathcal{C}_{F'}\ \rho\ (p_1\ \ldots\ p_n\ \rightarrow\ e) \quad = \quad \textbf{let}\ \rho'\ =\ bindVars\ \langle\ p_1\ ,\ \ldots,\ p_n\ \rangle\rho\ \textbf{in}$$
$$\langle\ \text{Label}\ lf,\ \text{MatchRule}\ \rangle\ +\!\!+$$
$$\mathcal{C}_{P'}\ p_1\ +\!\!+\ \ldots\ +\!\!+\ \mathcal{C}_{P'}\ p_n\ +\!\!+$$
$$\mathcal{C}_A\ p_1\ +\!\!+\ \ldots\ +\!\!+\ \mathcal{C}_A\ p_n\ +\!\!+$$
$$\mathcal{C}_E\ \rho'\ e\ +\!\!+$$
$$\langle\ \text{Return}\ \rangle$$

Fig. 17. Compilation Rules for Rule Matches and Functions

$$\mathcal{C}_P\ (\textbf{*}) \quad = \quad \langle\ \text{MatchNone}\ \rangle$$
$$\mathcal{C}_P\ (p) \quad = \quad \langle\ \text{MatchAvailable}\ \rangle\ +\!\!+\ \mathcal{C}_{P'}\ p$$

$$\mathcal{C}_{P'}\ (i) \quad = \quad \langle\ \text{MatchInt32}\ i\ \rangle$$
$$\ldots$$
$$\mathcal{C}_{P'}\ (c\ p_1\ \ldots\ p_n) \quad = \quad \langle\ \text{MatchCon}\ c\ n\ \rangle$$
$$\mathcal{C}_{P'}\ (\ p_1\ \ldots\ p_n\ ) \quad = \quad \langle\ \text{MatchTuple}\ n\ \rangle$$
$$\mathcal{C}_{P'}\ \langle\!\langle\ p_1\ \ldots\ p_n\ \rangle\!\rangle \quad = \quad \langle\ \text{MatchVector}\ n\ \rangle$$
$$\mathcal{C}_{P'}\ (var) \quad = \quad \langle\ \text{MatchVar}\ var\ \rangle$$
$$\mathcal{C}_{P'}\ \_ \quad = \quad \langle\ \text{MatchAny}\ \rangle$$

$$\mathcal{C}_A\ (c\ p_1\ \ldots\ p_n) \quad = \quad \mathcal{C}_{A'}\ \text{CopyArg}\ \langle\ p_1,\ldots,\ p_n\ \rangle$$
$$\mathcal{C}_A\ (\ p_1,\ \ldots,\ p_n\ ) \quad = \quad \mathcal{C}_{A'}\ \text{CopyArg}\ \langle\ p_1,\ldots,\ p_n\ \rangle$$
$$\mathcal{C}_A\ (x\ p) \quad = \quad \mathcal{C}_{A'}\ \text{CopyArg}\ \langle\ p\ \rangle$$
$$\mathcal{C}_A\ p \quad = \quad \langle\ \rangle$$

$$\mathcal{C}_{A'}\ i\ \langle\ p_1,\ldots,\ p_n\ \rangle \quad = \quad \langle\ i,\text{Unpack}\ \rangle\ +\!\!+$$
$$\mathcal{C}_{A'}\ \text{Copy}\ p_1\ +\!\!+\ \ldots\ +\!\!+\ \mathcal{C}_{A'}\ \text{Copy}\ p_n\ +\!\!+$$
$$\mathcal{C}_{P'}\ p_1\ +\!\!+\ \ldots\ +\!\!+\ \mathcal{C}_{P'}\ p_n$$

Fig. 18. Compilation Rules for Patterns

before matching a concrete value or variable; MatchNone corresponds to a *-pattern, and is used to indicate that the particular input need not be matched. Any match failure transfers control to label corresponding to the next rule. Finally, the inputs that have been matched are consumed.

The expression corresponding to RHS of the rule is compiled in a fairly conventional manner with arguments pushed on the stack before each function call, and the stack cleaned up using a Slide)instruction and the result unpacked from a tuple onto the stack using an Unpack instruction.

Finally, it is necessary to check that the thread does not need to block (this is done using CheckOutputs); if not, then each of the results is written to the correct wire using a Write instruction, and finally control is returned to the scheduler using a Schedule instruction.

5   Modelling Space Costs

A major goal of our research is to provide good cost models for Hume programs. We have already defined a simple space cost model for FSM-Hume that predicts upper bound stack and heap space limits for the pHAM [19]. We will reprise and extend this model here to illustrate how Hume aids the construction of cost models for resource-bounded programming.

The stack and heap requirements for the boxes and wires represent the only dynamically variable memory requirements for the pHAM implementation: all other memory costs can be fixed at compile-time based on the number of wires, boxes, functions and the sizes of static strings. In the absence of recursion, we can provide precise static memory bounds on rule evaluation. Predicting the stack and heap requirements for an FSM-Hume program thus provides complete static information about system memory requirements.

5.1   Memory Costs in the pHAM

Figure 20 defines values in the pHAM for all the constants $\mathcal{H}_{int32}$ etc. used above. In the prototype implementation, all heap cells are *boxed* [39] with tags distinguishing different kinds of objects. Furthermore, tuple structures require *size* fields, and data constructors also require a *constructor tag* field. All data objects in a structure are referenced by pointer. For simplicity each field is constrained to occupy one word of memory. Clearly, it would be easy to considerably reduce heap usage using a more compact representation such as that used by the state-of-the-art STG-Machine [39]. For now, we are, however, primarily concerned with bounding and predicting memory usage. Small changes to data representations can be easily incorporated into both models and implementations at a future date without affecting the fundamental results described here, except by reducing absolute costs of both model and implementation.

We can now define concrete costs for each of the first-order pHAM instructions from Section 3 as shown in Figure 21. This effectively gives a small-step operational semantics for cost based on the translation of FSM-Hume source programs to pHAM instructions that was defined earlier.

```
Label "control"
CopyInput 2    # latch inputs
CopyInput 1
CopyInput 0
Push 3         # new frame
CreateFrame 1  # one matched var.
```

```
Label "control_0"                        Label "control_2"
MatchRule         # LHS of rule 1        MatchRule        # LHS of rule 3
MatchAvailable # coin = Nickel?          MatchNone        # match *
MatchCon "Nickel" 0                      MatchAvailable # button = Coffee?
MatchNone         # match *              MatchCon "BCoffee" 0
MatchAvailable # match v                 MatchAvailable # match v
MatchVar 0                               MatchVar 0
Consume 0         # consume coin         Consume 1        # consume button
Consume 2         # consume value        Consume 2        # consume value
MatchedRule       # end of LHS           MatchedRule      # end of LHS

# add_value v 5                          # do_dispense Coffee 10 v
MkInt 5           # push 5               PushVar 0        # push v
PushVar 0         # push v               MkInt 10         # push 10
Call "f_add_value"                       MkCon "Coffee" 0 # push Coffee
Slide 2           # pop 2 args.          Call "f_do_dispense"
Unpack            # unpack result        Slide 3          # pop 3 args.
                                         Unpack           # unpack result

CheckOutputs      # OK to write?         CheckOutputs     # OK to write?
Write 0           # write dispense       Write 0          # write dispense
Write 1           # write value'         Write 1          # write value'
Write 2           # write return         Write 2          # write return
Schedule          # end of rule 1        Schedule         # end of rule 3 ...
```

```
...

...
```

```
Wire "control" 0 "cashbox" 0 3 0 NullT
Wire "control" 1 "keypad" 1 3 0 NullT
Wire "control" 2 "control" 1 2 0 NullT
Wire "vend" 0 "control" 0 3 0 NullT
Wire "cashbox" 1 "control" 2 2 0 NullT
```

Fig. 19. pHAM instructions for the Vending Machine Example

5.2 Space Cost Rules

Figures 22–23 give stack- and heap-space cost rules for a representative subset of FSM-Hume expressions, based on an operational interpretation of the Hume abstract machine implementation. Heap and stack costs are each integer values of type Cost, labelled h and s, respectively. Each rule produces a pair of such values

constant	value (words)
$\mathcal{H}_{con}$	3
$\mathcal{H}_{tuple}$	2
$\mathcal{H}_{bool}$	2
$\mathcal{H}_{char}$	2
$\mathcal{H}_{int32}$	2

constant	value (words)
$\mathcal{H}_{float32}$	2
$\mathcal{H}_{none}$	1
$\mathcal{H}_{exn}$	1
$\mathcal{H}_{fun}$	4
...	...
$\mathcal{S}_{frame}$	4

Fig. 20. Sizes from the prototype Hume Abstract Machine

Instruction	stack	heap
MkBool b	1	2
MkInt32 n	1	2
MkFloat32 f	1	2
MkNone	1	1
MkCon c n	1	$n+3$
MkTuple n	1	$n+2$
MkVector n	1	$n+2$
MkFun f m n	1	$m+4$
Push n	n	0
Pop n	$-n$	0
Slide n	$-n$	0
Copy n	1	0
CopyArg n	1	0
CreateFrame n	$n+3$	0
PushVar n	1	0
MakeVar n	0	0

Instruction	stack	heap
MatchRule	0	0
MatchAvailable	0	0
MatchNone	0	0
MatchBool	0	0
MatchInt32	0	0
MatchFloat32	0	0
MatchCon	0	0
MatchTuple	0	0
MatchVector	0	0
Unpack n-tuple	n	0
Unpack n-vector	n	0
Unpack $constr(c,n)$	n	0
StartMatches	0	0
Reorder	0	0
CopyInput n τ	0	$sizeof(\tau)$
Consume	0	0
CheckOutputs	0	0
Write	0	0
Input	1	2
Output	-1	0
Schedule	0	0

Fig. 21. Memory Costs for each pHAM instruction (first-order constructs)

representing an independent upper bound on the stack and heap usage. The result is produced in the context of an environment, E, that maps function names to the space (heap and stack) requirements associated with executing the body of the function. This environment is derived from the top-level program declarations plus standard prelude definitions. Rules for building the environment are omitted here, except for local declarations, but can be trivially constructed.

The heap cost of a standard integer is given by $\mathcal{H}_{int32}$ (rule 1), with other scalar values costed similarly. The cost of a function application is the cost of evaluating the body of the function plus the cost of each argument (rule 2). Each evaluated argument is pushed on the stack before the function is applied, and this must be taken into account when calculating the maximum stack usage. The cost

$$\boxed{\text{E} \overset{\text{space}}{\vdash} exp \Rightarrow \text{Cost}, \text{Cost}}$$

(1) $$\frac{}{\text{E} \overset{\text{space}}{\vdash} n \Rightarrow \mathcal{H}_{int32}, 1}$$

...

(2) $$\frac{\text{E}\,(varid) = \langle h, s \rangle \qquad \forall i.\ 1 \leq i \leq n,\ \text{E} \overset{\text{space}}{\vdash} exp_i \Rightarrow h_i, s_i}{\text{E} \overset{\text{space}}{\vdash} funid\ exp_1\ \ldots\ exp_n \Rightarrow \sum_{i=1}^{n} h_i + h,\ \max_{i=1}^{n}\ (s_i + (i-1)) + s}$$

(3) $$\frac{\forall i.\ 1 \leq i \leq n,\ \text{E} \overset{\text{space}}{\vdash} exp_i \Rightarrow h_i, s_i}{\text{E} \overset{\text{space}}{\vdash} conid\ exp_1\ \ldots\ exp_n \Rightarrow \sum_{i=1}^{n} h_i + n + \mathcal{H}_{con},\ \max_{i=1}^{n}\ (s_i + (i-1))}$$

(4) $$\frac{\forall i.\ 1 \leq i \leq n,\ \text{E} \overset{\text{space}}{\vdash} exp_i \Rightarrow h_i, s_i}{\text{E} \overset{\text{space}}{\vdash} (\ exp_1,\ \ldots,\ exp_n\ ) \Rightarrow \sum_{i=1}^{n} h_i + n + \mathcal{H}_{tuple},\ \max_{i=1}^{n}\ (s_i + (i-1))}$$

(5) $$\frac{\forall i.\ 1 \leq i \leq n,\ \text{E} \overset{\text{space}}{\vdash} exp_i \Rightarrow h_i, s_i}{\text{E} \overset{\text{space}}{\vdash} \langle\langle\ exp_1,\ \ldots,\ exp_n\ \rangle\rangle \Rightarrow \sum_{i=1}^{n} h_i + n + \mathcal{H}_{vector},\ \max_{i=1}^{n}\ (s_i + (i-1))}$$

Fig. 22. Space cost axioms for expressions (1)

of building a new data constructor value such as a user-defined constructed type (rule 3) is similar to a function application, except that pointers to the arguments must be stored in the newly created closure (one word per argument), and fixed costs $\mathcal{H}_{con}$ are added to represent the costs of tag and size fields. Tuples and vectors are costed analogously to constructors (rules 4 and 5).

The heap usage of a conditional (rule 6) is the heap required by the condition part plus the maximum heap used by either branch. The maximum stack requirement is simply the maximum required by the condition and either branch. Case expressions (omitted) are costed analogously. The cost of a let-expression (rule 7) is the space required to evaluate the value definitions (including the stack required to store the result of each new value definition) plus the cost of the enclosed expression. The local declarations are used to derive a quadruple comprising total heap usage, maximum stack required to evaluate any value definition, a count of the value definitions in the declaration sequence (used to calculate the size of the stack frame for the local declaratons), and an envi-

$$(6) \quad \frac{E \overset{space}{\vdash} exp_1 \Rightarrow h_1, s_1 \qquad E \overset{space}{\vdash} exp_2 \Rightarrow h_2, s_2 \qquad E \overset{space}{\vdash} exp_3 \Rightarrow h_3, s_3}{E \overset{space}{\vdash} \text{if } exp_1 \text{ then } exp_2 \text{ else } exp_3 \Rightarrow h_1 + max(h_2, h_3), max(s_1, s_2, s_3)}$$

$$(7) \quad \frac{E \overset{decl}{\vdash} decls \Rightarrow h_d, s_d, s'_d, E' \qquad E' \overset{space}{\vdash} exp \Rightarrow h_e, s_e}{E \overset{space}{\vdash} \text{let decls in } exp \Rightarrow h_d + h_e, max(s_d, s'_d + s_e)}$$

$$(8) \quad \frac{E \overset{space}{\vdash} exp \Rightarrow h_e, s_e \qquad E \models matches \Rightarrow h_m, s_m}{E \overset{space}{\vdash} \text{case } exp \text{ of } matches \Rightarrow h_e + h_m, max(s_e, s_m)}$$

$$(9) \quad \frac{E \overset{space}{\vdash} exp \Rightarrow h_e, s_e}{E \overset{space}{\vdash} exp \text{ within } h, s \Rightarrow min(h_e, h), min(s_e, s)}$$

$$(10) \quad \frac{E \overset{space}{\vdash} exp \Rightarrow h_e, s_e \qquad coerce \ \tau \ = \ (h_c, s_c)}{E \overset{space}{\vdash} exp \text{ as } \tau \Rightarrow h_e + h_c, max(s_e, s_c)}$$

$$(11) \quad \frac{E \overset{space}{\vdash} exp \Rightarrow h_e, s_e}{E \overset{space}{\vdash} exp :: \tau \Rightarrow h_e, s_e)}$$

Fig. 23. Space cost axioms for expressions (2)

ronment mapping function names to heap and stack usage. The body of the
let-expression is costed in the context of this extended environment. The cost
of a case=expression (rule 8) is derived from the maximum heap used by any
RHS or the matched expression e, and the greatest stack used by any individual
match or the matched expression e. Note that in calculating the stack usage, it
is necessary to account both for the stack frame which is needed to record the
local variable definitions in each match, and for any structured values which are
unpacked onto the stack during matching.

Finally, the rule for within-expressions (rule 9) restricts the costs to the smaller
of the space that is estimated to be used by the sub-expression or the specified restriction; as-expressions must account for any space used by the coercion
(rule 10); but type restrictions have no cost component (rule 11).

5.3   Costing Example: The Vending Machine

We illustrate the cost analysis by showing how stack and heap limits can be derived structurally for the do_dispense function taken from the vending machine
example.

```
do_dispense drink cost v =
   if v >= cost then ( drink, v-cost, * )
              else ( *,      v,       * );
```

```
Label "f_do_dispense"
CreateFrame 3    # 3 local vars.

Label "f_do_dispense_0"          Label "t"
MatchRule                        MkNone         # *
MatchVar 0     # bind drink      PushVar 1      # cost
MatchVar 1     # bind cost       PushVar 2      # v
MatchVar 2     # bind v          CallPrim "-"   # v-cost
MatchedRule                      PushVar 0      # drink
                                 MkTuple 3      # make result
                                 Return
PushVar 1      # cost
PushVar 2      # v
CallPrim ">="  # v >= cost?
If "t"         # branch if so

MkNone         # *
PushVar 2      # v
MkNone         # *
MkTuple 3      # (*,v,*)
Return


Function "f_do_dispense" "f_do_dispense_0"
```

Fig. 24. pHAM instructions for the do_dispense function

Figure 24 shows the pHAM bytecode for this function, which follows the translation of Section 4. The costs for each expression are shown below, where $e : s/h$ is the relative change in stack (s) and heap (h) incurred by evaluating expression e:

$$\frac{v : 1/0 \quad cost : 1/0}{v \geq cost : 2/2} \qquad \frac{\dfrac{v : 1/0 \quad cost : 1/0}{v - cost : 2/2} \quad * : 1/1 \quad drink : 1/0}{(drink, v - cost, *) : 3/8} \qquad (*, v, *) : 3/7$$

$$if\ v \geq cost\ then\ (drink, v - cost, *)\ else\ (*, v, *) : max(3,3)/2 + max(7,8)$$

```
$ phamc coffee.hume
Prototype Hume Abstract Machine Compiler 0.8t
importing coffee.hume
Function costs:

do_dispense: stack = 16; heap = 10
add_value: stack = 23; heap = 13
...


Box costs:
Box control: stack = 31, heap = 23
...
```

Results from a sample execution of the program on a 1.67GHz PowerPC G4 (Apple Macintosh Powerbook) show that stack and heap costs are consistent with the limits given by the analysis: 26 words of stack used versus a limit of 31 word; and 20 words of heap versus a limit of 23 words. The differences are due to the need to reserve heap memory for all wires in calculating an upper bound limit for heap usage, even though, in the actual execution path, only one of coin or button is active at any time; and to the existence of program paths that require additional stack, but which are not explored in the test examples.

The control box takes a maximum of 630μs to execute, with maximum response time on any of the control wires being 0.186ms. These figures are consistent with genuine real-time requirements.

```
Box Statistics:

control: CALLS = 14, MAXTIME = 0.00063s, MAXHP = 20, MAXSP = 26
...

Wire Statistics:

control.0: MAX DELAY = 0.045ms, MAXHP = 3
control.1: MAX DELAY = 0.082ms, MAXHP = 3
control.2: MAX DELAY = 0.186ms, MAXHP = 2

Memory usage for boxes:

control: Heap 20(23) Stack 26(31) -- wires Heap 8(8) Stack 0(0)
...

Total heap usage: 72 (87 est)
Total stack usage: 49 (57 est)
```

6   Other Related Work

As discussed in Section 1.2, because of the difficulty of constructing strong bounded cost models, functional languages have not historically been applied to hard real-time systems. Hume is therefore highly novel in its approach. There has, however, been much recent theoretical interest both in the problems associated with costing functional languages [41,25,12,46,36] and in bounding space/ time usage [24,45,21], including work on automatically generating heap bounded functional programs [44].

Synchronous dataflow languages such as Lustre [13] or Signal [17] have been widely used for programming hard real-time systems. Like Hume, such designs tend to separate computation from communication. Compared with Hume, however, such notations tend to lack expressibility. For example, they will usually provide only first order functions and flat data structures, compared with the higher-order functions and recursive data structures that Hume supports. They also generally eschew constructs such as exception handling, and are also, of course, restricted to synchronous communication rather than the asynchronous approach described here. The advantage of these notations lies in providing a powerful and simple model of time costs, by eliminating the timing complexities associated with asynchronicity. One interesting new design that attempts to marry the advantages of synchronous and asynchronous languages is Lucid Synchrone [15]. This language combines both synchronous and asynchronous communication within a single language framework.

Cost issues are relevant not only for programming real-time systems, but also for producing hardware designs, or even hardware/software co-designs. There have been several functionally-based notations for hardware design [20,14,26,34, 31], similar in scope to the HW-Hume level described here, but usually including hardware-specific issues such as on-chip circuit layout.

Finally, there has, of course, been much work on applying conventional language technology to the problems of hard real-time, bounded space programming. Amongst recent language designs, two extreme approaches are SPARK Ada [7] and the real-time specification for Java (RTSJ) [9]. SPARK Ada aims to ensure strong formal properties by eliminating difficult-to-model behaviours from the general-purpose language Ada. However, this excludes highly desirable features such as concurrency and asynchronous communication.

A contrasting approach is taken by RTSj, which provides specialised runtime and library support for real-time systems work, including manually controlled region-based dynamic memory allocation, but which makes no absolute performance guarantees. One major limitation of the approach is that standard Java libraries cannot normally be used, since the usual object allocation and garbage collection mechanisms are not supported. Thus, SPARK Ada provides a minimal, highly controlled environment for real-time programming emphasising *correctness by construction* [1], whilst Real-Time Java provides a much more expressible, but less controlled environment, without formal guarantees. Our objective with the Hume design is to maintain strong formal correctness whilst also providing high levels of expressibility that match the demands of real-time systems programming.

7   Expressibility Versus Costability

In Section 5 we have shown that formal space cost models can be easily constructed for FSM-Hume. Although we have not yet proven the formal correctness of these models, we have verified the accuracy of these cost models against the pHAM implementation and shown that such models have practical application in the pHAM compiler. Moreover the pHAM implementation technology is competitive in both time and space usage with similar technologies proposed for embedded Java applications, for example. We anticipate that it should be possible to construct equally usable time-cost models using a similar approach, but that these must be tailored to specific processor architectures in order to obtain usable real-time guarantees.

We have obtained accurate cost models by sacrificing expressibility: FSM-Hume is devoid of recursive or higher-order functions and possesses only non-recursive data structure such as tuples. Features such as asynchronous concurrency and box iteration do compensate to some extent and will allow the construction of moderately complex programs. Our more theoretical work [41] suggests that we should be able to incorporate higher-order functions into FSM-Hume (to form Template-Hume) while still being able to construct good quality cost models. We have also constructed prototype cost models that include automatic cost analysis of primitive recursive function definitions, and have obtained results that are equivalent to hand analysis for some simple recursive functions [47]. Our hope is that this work will allow us to construct PR-Hume, incorporating primitive recursive functions and a range of recursive data structures such as lists. Such a result would show that it is possible to combine both a very high level of expressibility and accurate cost models.

8   Conclusions and Further Work

This paper has introduced Hume, a concurrent functionally-based language aimed at resource-limited systems such as real-time embedded systems. Hume is novel in being built on a combination of finite-state-machine and λ-calculus concepts. It is also novel in aiming to provide a high level of programming abstraction whilst maintaining good formal properties, including bounded time and space behaviour and provably correct rule-based translation. We achieve this by synthesising recent advances in theoretical computer science into a coherent pragmatic framework. In this paper, we have formally described the Hume abstract machine implementation, shown how this is related to Hume source programs through a formal set of translation rules, and finally shown how a source-level cost model can consequently be constructed for Hume. We believe that this work helps to open up the in-principle use of functional programming techniques in resource-constrained situations.

While we have not yet optimised our implementations, Hume has been designed to allow good compiler optimisations to be exploited – time performance *without* optimisation is roughly 10 times that for Sun's embedded KVM Java Virtual Machine or about 50% of that of optimised C++, and dynamic space usage is both guaranteed to be bounded and a fraction of that required by either Java or C++. For example, we have constructed a complete implementation for a Renesas M32C bare development board using less than 16KB RAM, including all runtime, operating system, user code and library support.

A number of important limitations remain to be addressed:

1. space and time cost models must be defined for additional Hume levels and language features, including higher-order functions (Template-Hume) and (primitive) recursion (PR-Hume);
2. these cost models must be used to construct high-quality static analyses;
3. we must incorporate interrupt handling and some other low-level features into our design and implementation;

4. more sophisticated scheduling algorithms could improve performance, however, these must be balanced with the need to maintain correctness; and finally
5. no attempt is made to avoid deadlock situations: a suitable model checker must be desgned and implemented.

Acknowledgements

This work has been generously supported by EU Framework VI grant IST-2004-510255 (EmBounded) and by EPSRC Grant EPC/0001346.

References

1. P. Amey. Correctness by Construction: Better can also be Cheaper. *CrossTalk: the Journal of Defense Software Engineering*, pages 24–28, March 2002.
2. K.R. Apt and E.-R. Olderog. *Verification of Sequential and Concurrent Programs.* Springer Verlag, 1997. 2nd Edition.
3. J. Armstrong. Erlang — a Survey of the Language and its Industrial Applications. In *Proc. INAP'96 — The 9th Exhibitions and Symposium on Industrial Applications of Prolog*, pages 16–18, Hino, Tokyo, Japan, 1996.
4. J. Armstrong. The Development of Erlang. In *Proc. 1997 ACM Intl. Conf. on Functl. Prog. (ICFP '97)*, pages 196–203, Amsterdam, The Netherlands, 1997.
5. J. Armstrong, S.R. Virding, and M.C. Williams. *Concurrent Programming in Erlang.* Prentice-Hall, 1993.
6. L. Augustsson. *Compiling Lazy Functional Languages, Part II.* PhD thesis, Dept. of Computer Science, Chalmers University of Technology, Göteborg, Sweden, 1987.
7. J.G.P. Barnes. *High Integrity Ada: the Spark Approach.* Addison-Wesley, 1997.
8. S. Blau and J. Rooth. AXD-301: a New Generation ATM Switching System. *Ericsson Review*, 1, 1998.
9. G. Bollela and et al. *The Real-Time Specification for Java.* Addison-Wesley, 2000.
10. F. Boussinot and R. de Simone. The Esterel Language. *Proceedings of the IEEE*, 79(9):1293–1304, September 1991.
11. S. Breitinger, R. Loogen, Y. Ortega-Mallén, and R. Pe na. The Eden Coordination Model for Distributed Memory Systems. In *Proc. High-Level Parallel Programming Models and Supportive Environments (HIPS '97), Springer-Verlag LNCS 1123.* Springer-Verlag, 1997.
12. R. Burstall. Inductively Defined Functions in Functional Programming Languages. Technical Report ECS-LFCS-87-25, Dept. of Comp. Sci., Univ. of Edinburgh, 1987.
13. P. Caspi, D. Pilaud, N. Halbwachs, and J. Place. Lustre: a Declarative Language for Programming Synchronous Systems. In *Proc. POPL '87 – 1987 Symposium on Principles of Programming Languages, München, Germany*, pages 178–88, January 1987.
14. K. Claessen and M. Sheeran. A Tutorial on Lava: a Hardware Description and Verification System, unpublished report, chalmers university of technology, sweden. August 2000.
15. J.-L. Colaço, B. Pagano, and M. Pouzet. A Conservative Extension of Synchronous Data-flow with State Machines. In *Proc. ACM International Conference on Embedded Software (EMSOFT'05)*, Jersey City, New Jersey, USA, September 2005.

16. D.H. Fijma and R.T. Udink. A Case Study in Functional Real-Time Programming. Technical report, Dept. of Computer Science, Univ. of Twente, The Netherlands, 1991. Memoranda Informatica 91-62.

17. T. Gautier, P. Le Guernic, and L. Besnard. Signal: A declarative language for synchronous programming of real-time systems. In G. Kahn, editor, *Proc. Intl. Conf. on Functional Programming Languages and Computer Architecture (FPCA '87), Springer-Verlag LNCS 274*, pages 257–277, 1987.

18. K. Hammond and G.J. Michaelson. Hume: a Domain-Specific Language for Real-Time Embedded Systems. In *Proc. 2003 Conf. on Generative Programming and Component Engineering (GPCE '03), Springer-Verlag LNCS 2830*, pages 37–56, 2003.

19. K. Hammond and G.J. Michaelson. Predictable Space Behaviour in FSM-Hume. In *Proc. Implementation of Functional Langs.(IFL '02), Madrid, Spain*, number 2670 in Lecture Notes in Computer Science. Springer-Verlag, 2003.

20. J. Hawkins and A.E. Abdallah. Behavioural Synthesis of a Parallel Hardware JPEG Decoder from a Functional Specification. In *Proc. EuroPar 2002, Paderborn, Germany*, pages 615–619. Springer-Verlag LNCS 2400, August 2002.

21. M. Hofmann and S. Jost. Static Prediction of Heap Space Usage for First-Order Functional Programs. In *POPL'03 — Symposium on Principles of Programming Languages*, pages 185–197, New Orleans, LA, USA, January 2003. ACM Press.

22. R.J.M. Hughes. The Design and Implementation of Programming Languages, DPhil Thesis, Programming Research Group, Oxford. July 1983.

23. R.J.M. Hughes and J.T. O'Donnell. Expressing and reasoning about non-deterministic functional programs. In *Proceedings of the 1989 Glasgow Workshop on Functional Programming*, pages 308–328, London, UK, 1990. Springer-Verlag.

24. R.J.M. Hughes and L. Pareto. Recursion and Dynamic Data Structures in Bounded Space: towards Embedded ML Programming. In *ICFP'99 — International Conference on Functional Programming*, pages 70–81, Paris, France, September 1999. ACM Press.

25. R.J.M. Hughes, L. Pareto, and A. Sabry. Proving the Correctness of Reactive Systems Using Sized Types. In *POPL'96 — Symposium on Principles of Programming Languages*, pages 410–423, St. Petersburg Beach, Florida, January 1996. ACM.

26. J. Launchbury J. Matthews and B. Cook. Microprocessor Specification in Hawk. In *Proc. International Conference on Computer Languages*, pages 90–101, 1998.

27. P. Landin. The Mechanical Evaluation of Expressions. *The Computer Journal*, 6(4):308–320, Jan 1964.

28. S. Liang, P. Hudak, and M.P. Jones. Monad transformers and modular interpreters. In ACM, editor, *Proc. POPL '95 — 1995 Symposium on Principles of Programming Languages: San Francisco, California*, pages 333–343, New York, NY, USA, 1995. ACM Press.

29. T. Lindholm and F. Yellin. *The Java Virtual Machine Specification, Second Edition*. Addison-Wesley, April 1999.

30. J. McDermid. *Engineering Safety-Critical Systems*, pages 217–245. Cambridge University Press, 1996.

31. A. Mycroft and R. Sharp. Hardware/software co-design using functional languages. In *Proc. Tools and Algorithms for Construction and Analysis of Systems (TACAS '01)*, pages 236–251, 2001.

32. E.G.J.M.H. Nöcker, J.E.W. Smetsers, M.C.J.D. van Eekelen, and M.J. Plasmeijer. Concurrent Clean. In *Proc. Parallel Architectures and Languages Europe (PARLE '91)*, pages 202–219. Springer-Verlag LNCS 505, 1991.

33. J. Nordlander, M. Carlsson, and M. Jones.   Programming with Time-Constrained Reactions (unpublished report). http://www.cse.ogi.edu/pacsoft/projects/Timber/publications.htm. 2006.
34. J.T. O'Donnell. The Hydra Hardware Description Language. In *Domain-Specific Program Generation*. Spinger-Verlag LNCS 3016, 2004.
35. R. Peña and C. Segura. A polynomial cost non-determinism analysis. In *Proc. IFL'01 – 13th International Workshop on Implementation of Functional Languages, Spinger-Verlag LNCS 2312*, pages 121–137, 2002.
36. R. Peña and C. Segura. A First-Order Functl. Lang. for Reasoning about Heap Consumption. In *Draft Proc. International Workshop on Implementation and Application of Functional Languages (IFL '04)*, 2004.
37. J. Peterson, P. Hudak, and C. Elliot. Lambda in Motion: Controlling Robots with Haskell. In *Proc. ACM Conference on Practical Applications of Declarative Languages (PADL '99)*, September 1999.
38. S. L. Peyton Jones and D. Lester. *Implementing Functional Languages: a Tutorial*. Prentice-Hall, 1992.
39. S.L. Peyton Jones. Implementing Lazy Functional Languages on Stock Hardware:the Spineless Tagless G-Machine. *Journal of Functional Programming*, 2(2):127–202, 1992.
40. S.L. Peyton Jones, A.D. Gordon, and S.O. Finne. Concurrent Haskell. In *Proc. POPL'96 — ACM Symp. on Principles of Programming Languages*, pages 295–308, January 1996.
41. A.J. Rebón Portillo, K. Hammond, H.-W. Loidl, and P. Vasconcelos. A Sized Time System for a Parallel Functional Language (Revised). In *Proc. Implementation of Functional Langs.(IFL '02), Madrid, Spain*, pages 1–16. Springer-Verlag LNCS 2670, 2003.
42. J.H. Reppy. CML: a Higher-Order Concurrent Language. In *Proc. 1991 ACM Conf. on Prog. Lang. Design and Impl. (PLDI '91)*, pages 293–305, June 1991.
43. R. Schwarz. Causality in distributed systems. In *Proc. EW 5: 5th ACM SIGOPS European workshop*, pages 1–5, New York, NY, USA, 1992. ACM Press.
44. W. Taha, S. Ellner, and H. Xi. Generating Heap-Bounded Programs in a Functional Setting. In *Proc. ACM International Conference on Embedded Software (EMSOFT '03)*, pages 340–355, 2003.
45. M. Tofte and J.-P. Talpin. Region-Based Memory Management. *Information and Computation*, 132(2):109–176, 1 February 1997.
46. D.A. Turner. Elementary Strong Functional Programming. In *Proc. 1995 Symp. on Functl. Prog. Langs. in Education — FPLE '95*, LNCS. Springer-Verlag, December 1995.
47. P.B. Vasconcelos. *Cost Inference and Analysis for Recursive Functional Programs*. PhD thesis, University of St Andrews, 2006. in preparation.
48. W.W. Wadge and E.A. Ashcroft. *LUCID, the dataflow programming language*. Academic Press, 1985.
49. M. Wallace and C. Runciman. Extending a Functional Programming System for Embedded Applications. *Software: Practice & Experience*, 25(1), January 1995.
50. C. Wikström and H. Nilsson. Mnesia — an Industrial Database with Transactions, Distribution and a Logical Query Language. In *Proc. 1996 International Symposium on Cooperative Database Systems for Advanced Applications*, 1996.

The Essence of Dataflow Programming

Tarmo Uustalu[1] and Varmo Vene[2]

[1] Inst. of Cybernetics at Tallinn Univ. of Technology,
Akadeemia tee 21, EE-12618 Tallinn, Estonia
tarmo@cs.ioc.ee
[2] Dept. of Computer Science, Univ. of Tartu,
J. Liivi 2, EE-50409 Tartu, Estonia
varmo@cs.ut.ee

Abstract. We propose a novel, comonadic approach to dataflow (stream-based) computation. This is based on the observation that both general and causal stream functions can be characterized as coKleisli arrows of comonads and on the intuition that comonads in general must be a good means to structure context-dependent computation. In particular, we develop a generic comonadic interpreter of languages for context-dependent computation and instantiate it for stream-based computation. We also discuss distributive laws of a comonad over a monad as a means to structure combinations of effectful and context-dependent computation. We apply the latter to analyse clocked dataflow (partial stream based) computation.

1 Introduction

Shall we be pure or impure? Today we shall be very pure. It must always be possible to contain impurities (i.e., non-functionalities), in a pure (i.e., functional) way.

The program

```
fact x  = if x <= 1 then 1 else fact (x - 1) * x
```

for factorial encodes a *pure function*.

The programs

```
factM x = (if x == 5 then raise else
             if x <= 1 then 1 else factM (x - 1) * x)
          'handle' (if x == 7 then 5040 else raise)
```

and

```
factL x = if x <= 1 then 1 else factL (x - 1) * (1 'choice' x)
```

represent "lossy" versions of the factorial function. The first yields an error on 5 and 6 whereas the second can fail to do some of the multiplications required for the normal factorial. These *impure* "functions" can be made sense of in the paradigms of *error raising/handling* and *non-deterministic* computations. Ever

Z. Horváth (Ed.): CEFP 2005, LNCS 4164, pp. 135–167, 2006.

since the work by Moggi and Wadler [26,40,41], we know how to reduce impure computations with errors and non-determinism to purely functional computations in a structured fashion using the maybe and list *monads*. We also know how to explain other types of *effect*, such as *continuations*, *state*, even *input/output*, using monads!

But what is more unnatural or hard about the following program?

```
pos  = 0 fby (pos + 1)
fact = 1 fby (fact * (pos + 1))
```

This represents a *dataflow* computation which produces two discrete-time signals or streams: the enumeration of the naturals and the graph of the factorial function. The syntax is essentially that of Lucid [2], which is an old *intensional* language, or Lustre [17] or Lucid Synchrone [11,31], the newer *French synchronous dataflow* languages. fby reads 'followed by' and means initialized unit delay of a discrete-time signal (cons of a stream).

Could it be that monads are capable of structuring notions of dataflow computation as well? No, there are simple reasons why this must be impossible. (We will discuss these.) As a substitute for monads, Hughes has therefore proposed a laxer framework that he has termed *arrow types* [19] (and Power et al. [32] proposed the same under the name of *Freyd categories*). But this is—we assert—overkill, at least as long as we are interested in dataflow computation. It turns out that something simpler and more standard, namely *comonads*, the dual of monads, does just as well. In fact, comonads are even better, as there is more structure to comonads than to arrow types. Arrow types are too general.

The message of this paper is just this last point: While notions of dataflow computation cannot be structured with monads, they can be structured perfectly with comonads. And more generally, comonads have received too little attention in programming language semantics compared to monads. Just as monads are good for speaking and reasoning about notions of functions that produce effects, comonads can handle context-dependent functions and are hence highly relevant. This has been suggested earlier, e.g., by Brookes and Geva [8] and Kieburtz [23], but never caught on because of a lack of compelling examples. But now dataflow computation provides clear examples and it hints at a direction in which there are more.

The paper contributes a novel approach to dataflow computation based on comonads. We show that general and causal stream functions, the basic entities in intensional resp. synchronous dataflow computation, are elegantly described in terms of comonads. Imitating monadic interpretation, we develop a generic comonadic interpreter. By instantiation, we obtain interpreters of a Lucid-like intensional language and a Lucid Synchrone-like synchronous dataflow language. Remarkably, we get elegant higher-order language designs with almost no effort whereas the traditional dataflow languages are first-order and the question of the meaningfulness or right meaning of higher-order dataflow has been seen as controversial. We also show that clocked dataflow (i.e., partial-stream based computation) can be handled by distributive laws of the comonads for stream functions over the maybe monad.

The organization of the paper is as follows. In Section 2, we give a short introduction to dataflow programming. In Section 3, we give a brief review of the Moggi-Wadler monad-based approach to programming with effect-producing functions in a pure language and to the semantics of corresponding impure languages. In particular, we recall monadic interpretation. In Section 4, we show that certain paradigms of computation, notably stream functions, do not fit into this framework, and introduce the substitute idea of arrow types/Freyd categories. In Section 5, we introduce comonads and argue that they structure computation with context-dependent functions. We show that both general and causal stream functions are smoothly described by comonads and develop a comonadic interpreter capable of handling dataflow languages. In Section 6, we show how effects and context-dependence can be combined in the presence of a distributive law of the comonad over the monad, show how this applies to partial-stream functions and present a distributivity-based interpreter which copes with clocked dataflow languages. Section 7 is a summary of related work, while Section 8 lists our conclusions.

We assume that the reader is familiar with the basics of functional programming (in particular, Haskell programming) and denotational semantics and also knows about the Lambek-Lawvere correspondence between typed lambda calculi and cartesian closed categories (the types-as-objects, terms-as-morphisms correspondence). The paper contains a brief introduction to dataflow programming, but acquaintance with languages such as Lucid and Lustre or Lucid Synchrone will be of additional help. Concepts such as monads, comonads etc. are defined in the paper.

The paper is related to our earlier paper [37], which discussed comonad-based dataflow programming, but did not treat comonad-based processing of dataflow languages. A short version of the present paper (without introductions to dataflow languages, monads, monadic interpretation and arrows) appeared as [38].

2   Dataflow Programming

We begin with an informal quick introduction to dataflow programming as supported by languages of the Lucid family [2] and the Lustre and Lucid Synchrone languages [11,31]. We demonstrate a neutral syntax which we will use throughout the paper.

Dataflow programming is about programming with streams, thought about as signals in discrete time. The style of programming is functional, but any expression denotes a stream (a signal), or more exactly, the element of a stream at an understood position (the value of a signal the time instant understood as the present). Since the position is not mentioned, the stream is defined uniformly across all of its positions. Compare this to physics, where many quantities vary in time, but the time argument is always kept implicit and there is never any explicit dependency on its value.

All standard operations on basic types are understood pointwise (so in particular constants become constant streams). The if-construct is also understood pointwise.

x	x_0	x_1	x_2	x_3	x_4	x_5	$\cdots$
y	y_0	y_1	y_2	y_3	y_4	y_5	$\cdots$
x + y	$x_0 + y_0$	$x_1 + y_1$	$x_2 + y_2$	$x_3 + y_3$	$x_4 + y_4$	$x_5 + y_5$	$\cdots$
z	t	f	t	t	f	t	$\cdots$
if z then x else y	x_0	y_1	x_2	x_3	y_4	x_5	$\cdots$

If we had product types, the projections and the pairing construct would also be pointwise. With function spaces, it is not obvious what the design should be and we will not discuss any options at this stage. As a matter of fact, most dataflow languages are first-order: expressions with variables are of course allowed, but there are no first-class functions.

With the pointwise machinery, the current value of an expression is always determined by the current values of its variables. This is not really interesting. We should at least allow dependencies on the past values of the variables. This is offered by a construct known as fby (pronounced "followed by"). The expression e0 fby e1 takes the initial value of e0 at the beginning of the history, and at every other instant of time it takes the value that e1 had at the immediately preceding instant. In other words, the signal e0 fby e1 is the unit delay of the signal e1, initialized with the initial value of e0.

x	x_0	x_1	x_2	x_3	x_4	x_5	$\cdots$
y	y_0	y_1	y_2	y_3	y_4	y_5	$\cdots$
x fby y	x_0	y_0	y_1	y_2	y_3	y_4	$\cdots$

With the fby operator, one can write many useful recursive definitions where the recursive calls are guarded by fby and there is no real circularity. Below are some classic examples of such feedback through a delay.

```
pos    = 0 fby pos + 1
sum x  = x + (0 fby sum x)
diff x = x - (0 fby x)
ini x  = x fby ini x
fact   = 1 fby (fact * (pos + 1))
fibo   = 0 fby (fibo + (1 fby fibo))
```

The value of pos is 0 at the beginning of the history and at every other instant it is the immediately preceding value incremented by one, i.e., pos generates the enumeration of all natural numbers. The function sum finds the accumulated sum of all values of the input up to the current instant. The function diff finds the difference between the current value and the immediately preceding value of the input. The function ini generates the constant sequence of the initial value of the input. Finally, fact and fibo generate the graphs of the factorial and Fibonacci functions respectively. Their behaviour is illustrated below.

pos	0	1	2	3	4	5	6	...
sum pos	0	1	3	6	10	15	21	...
diff pos	0	1	1	1	1	1	1	...
ini pos	0	0	0	0	0	0	0	...
fact	1	1	2	6	24	120	720	...
fibo	0	1	1	2	3	5	8	...

An expression written with pointwise constructs and fby is always causal in the sense that its present value can only depend on the past and present values of its variables. In languages à la Lucid, one can also write more general expressions with physically unrealistic dependencies on future values of the variables. This is supported by a construct called **next**. The value of next e at the current instant is the value of e at the immediately following instant, so the signal next e is the unit anticipation of the signal e.

x	x_0	x_1	x_2	x_3	x_4	x_5	...
next x	x_1	x_2	x_3	x_4	x_5	x_6	...

Combining next with recursion, it is possible to define functions whose present output value can depend on the value of the input in unboundedly distant future. For instance, the sieve of Eratosthenes can be defined as follows.

```
x wvr y = if ini y then x fby (next x wvr next y)
                   else (next x wvr next y)

sieve x = x fby sieve (x wvr x mod (ini x) /= 0)
eratosthenes = sieve (pos + 2)
```

The filtering function **wvr** (pronounced "whenever") returns the substream of the first input stream consisting of its elements from the positions where the second input stream is true-valued. (This is all well as long as there always is a future position where the second input stream has the value true, but poses a problem, if from some point on it is constantly false.) The function **sieve** outputs the initial element of the input stream and then recursively calls itself on the substream of the input stream that only contains the elements not divisible by the initial element.

x	x_0	x_1	x_2	x_3	x_4	x_5	...
y	t	f	t	t	f	t	...
x wvr y	x_0	x_2	x_3	x_5	...		
pos + 2	2	3	4	5	6	7	...
eratosthenes	2	3	5	7	11	13	...

Because anticipation is physically unimplementable and the use of it may result in unbounded lookaheads, most dataflow languages do not support it. Instead, some of them provide means to define partial streams, i.e., streams where some elements can be undefined (denoted below by −). The idea is that different signals may be on different clocks. Viewed as signals on the fastest (base) clock, they are not defined at every instant. They are only defined at those instants of the base clock that are also instants of their own clocks.

One possibility to specify partial streams is to introduce new constructs `nosig` and `merge` (also known as "default"). The constant `nosig` denotes a constantly undefined stream. The operator `merge` combines two partial streams into a partial stream that is defined at the positions where at least one of two given partial streams is defined (where both are defined, there the first one takes precedence).

nosig	–	–	–	–	–	–	...
x	x_0	–	–	x_3	–	–	...
y	–	–	y_2	y_3	–	y_5	...
merge x y	x_0	–	y_2	x_3	–	y_5	...

With the feature of partiality, it is possible to define the sieve of Eratosthenes without anticipation.

```
sieve x = if (tt fby ff) then x
          else sieve (if (x mod ini x /= 0) then x else nosig)
eratosthenes = sieve (pos + 2)
```

The initial element of the result of `sieve` is the initial element of the input stream whereas all other elements are given by a recursive call on the modified version of the input stream where all positions containing elements divisible by the initial element have been dropped.

pos + 2	2	3	4	5	6	7	8	9	10	11	...
eratosthenes	2	3	–	5	–	7	–	–	–	11	...

3   Monads and Monadic Interpreters

3.1   Monads and Effect-Producing Functions

Now we proceed to monads and monadic interpreters. We begin with a brief recapitulation of the monad-based approach to representing effectful functions [26,40,41,6].

A *monad* (in extension form) on a category C is given by a mapping $T : |C| \to |C|$ together with a $|C|$-indexed family η of maps $\eta_A : A \to TA$ of C (*unit*), and an operation $-^\star$ taking every map $k : A \to TB$ in C to a map $k^\star : TA \to TB$ of C (*extension operation*) such that

1. for any $f : A \to TB$, $k^\star \circ \eta_A = k$,
2. $\eta_A{}^\star = \mathrm{id}_{TA}$,
3. for any $k : A \to TB$, $\ell : B \to TC$, $(\ell^\star \circ k)^\star = \ell^\star \circ k^\star$.

Monads are a construction with many remarkable properties, but the central one for programming and semantics is that any monad $(T, \eta, -^\star)$ defines a category C_T where $|C_T| = |C|$ and $C_T(A, B) = C(A, TB)$, $(\mathrm{id}_T)_A = \eta_A$, $\ell \circ_T k = \ell^\star \circ k$ (*Kleisli category*) and an identity on objects functor $J : C \to C_T$ where $Jf = \eta_B \circ f$ for $f : A \to B$.

In the monadic approach to effectful functions, the underlying object mapping T of a monad is seen as an abstraction of the kind of effect considered and assigns to any type A a corresponding type TA of "computations of values" or "values with an effect". An effectful function from A to B is identified with a map $A \to B$ in the Kleisli category, i.e., a map $A \to TB$ in the base category. The unit of the monad makes it possible to view any pure function as an effectful one while the extension operation provides composition of effect-producing functions. Of course monads capture the structure that is common to all notions of effectful function. Operations specific to a particular type of effect are not part of the corresponding monad structure.

There are many standard examples of monads in semantics. Here is a brief list of examples. In each case, the object mapping T is a monad.

- $TA = A$, the identity monad,
- $TA = \mathsf{Maybe}\, A = A + 1$, error (undefinedness), $TA = A + E$, exceptions,
- $TA = \mathsf{List}\, A = \mu X.1 + A \times X$, non-determinism,
- $TA = E \Rightarrow A$, readable environment,
- $TA = S \Rightarrow A \times S$, state,
- $TA = (A \Rightarrow R) \Rightarrow R$, continuations,
- $TA = \mu X.A + (U \Rightarrow X)$, interactive input,
- $TA = \mu X.A + V \times X \cong A \times \mathsf{List}V$, interactive output,
- $TA = \mu X.A + FX$, the free monad over F,
- $TA = \nu X.A + FX$, the free completely iterative monad over F [1].

(By μ and ν we denote the least and greatest fixpoints of functors.)

In Haskell, monads are implemented as a type constructor class with two member functions (in the Prelude):

```
class Monad t where
  return :: a -> t a
  (>>=)  :: t a -> (a -> t b) -> t b

mmap :: Monad t => (a -> b) -> t a -> t b
mmap f c = c >>= (return . f)
```

return is the Haskell name for the unit and $(\gg\!=)$ (pronounced 'bind') is the extension operation of the monad. Haskell also supports a special syntax for defining Kleisli arrows, but in this paper we will avoid it.

In Haskell, every monad is strong in the sense that carries an additional operation, known as strength, with additional coherence properties. This happens because the extension operations of Haskell monads are necessarily internal.

```
mstrength :: Monad t => t a -> b -> t (a, b)
mstrength c b = c >>= \ a -> return (a, b)
```

The identity monad is Haskell-implemented as follows.

```
newtype Id a = Id a

instance Monad Id where
  return a  = Id a
  Id a >>= k = k a
```

The definitions of the maybe and list monads are the following.

```
data Maybe a = Just a | Nothing

instance Monad Maybe where
  return a        = Just a
  Just a  >>= k = k a
  Nothing >>= k = Nothing

data [a] = [] | a : [a]

instance Monad [] where
  return a        = [a]
  []       >>= k = []
  (a : as) >>= k = k a ++ (as >>= k)
```

The exponent and state monads are defined in the following fashion.

```
newtype Exp e a = Exp (e -> a)

instance Monad (Exp e) where
  return a       = Exp  (\ _ -> a)
  Exp  f >>= k = Exp  (\ e -> case k (f e) of
                                  Exp f' -> f' e)

newtype State s a = State (s -> (a, s))

instance Monad (State s) where
  return a       = State (\ s -> (a, s))
  State f >>= k = State (\ s -> case f s of
                                  (a, s') -> case k a of
                                      State f' -> f' s')
```

In the case of these monads, the operations specific to the type of effect they characterize are raising and handling an error, nullary and binary nondeterministic choice, consulting and local modification of the environment, consulting and updating the state.

```
raise :: Maybe a
raise = Nothing

handle :: Maybe a -> Maybe a -> Maybe a
Just a  'handle' _ = Just a
Nothing 'handle' c = c

deadlock :: [a]
deadlock = []

choice :: [a] -> [a] -> [a]
choice as0 as1 = as0 ++ as1
```

```
askE :: Exp e e
askE = Exp id

localE :: (e -> e) -> Exp e a -> Exp e b
localE g (Exp f) = Exp (f . g)

get :: State s s
get = State (\ s -> (s, s))

put :: s -> State s ()
put s = State (\ _ -> ((), s))
```

3.2   Monadic Semantics

Monads are a perfect tool for formulating denotational semantics of languages for programming effectful functions. If this is done in a functional (meta-)language, one obtains a reference interpreter for free. Let us recall how this project was carried out by Moggi and Wadler. Of course we choose Haskell as our metalanguage.

We proceed from a simple strongly typed purely functional (object) language with two base types, integers and booleans, which we want to be able to extend with various types of effects. As particular examples of types of effects, we will consider errors and non-determinism.

The first thing to do is to define the syntax of the object language. Since Haskell gives us no support for extensible variants, it is simplest for us to include the constructs for the two example effects from the beginning. For errors, these are error raising and handling. For non-determinism, we consider nullary and binary branching.

```
type Var = String

data Tm = V Var | L Var Tm | Tm :@ Tm
        | N Integer | Tm :+ Tm | ...
        | Tm :== Tm | ... | TT | FF | Not Tm | ... | If Tm Tm Tm
        -- specific for Maybe
        | Error | Tm 'Handle' Tm
        -- specific for []
        | Deadlock | Tm 'Choice' Tm
```

In the definition above, the constructors V, L, (:@) correspond to variables, lambda-abstraction and application. The other names should be self-explanatory.

Next we have to define the semantic domains. Since Haskell is not dependently typed, we have to be a bit coarse here, collecting the semantic values of all object language types (for one particular type of effect) into a single type. But in reality, the semantic values of the different object language types are integers, booleans and functions, respectively, with no confusion. Importantly, a function takes a value to a value with an effect (where the effect can only be trivial in the pure case). An environment is a list of variable-value pairs, where the first occurrence of a variable in a pair in the list determines its value.

```
data Val t = I Integer | B Bool | F (Val t -> t (Val t))

type Env t = [(Var, Val t)]
```

We will manipulate environment-like entities via the following three functions. (The safe lookup, that maybe returns a value, will be unnecessary, since we can type-check an object-language term before evaluating it. If this succeeds, we can be sure we will only be looking up variables in environments where they really occur.)

```
empty :: [(a, b)]
empty = []

update :: a -> b -> [(a, b)] -> [(a, b)]
update a b abs = (a, b) : abs

unsafeLookup :: Eq a => a -> [(a, b)] -> b
unsafeLookup a0 ((a,b):abs) = if a0 == a then b else unsafeLookup a0 abs
```

The syntax and the semantic domains of the possible object languages described, we can proceed to evaluation.

The pure core of an object language is interpreted uniformly in the type of effect that this language supports. Only the unit and bind operations of the corresponding monad have to be known to describe the meanings of the core constructs.

```
class Monad t => MonadEv t where
  ev :: Tm -> Env t -> t (Val t)

evClosed :: MonadEv t => Tm -> t (Val t)
evClosed e = ev e empty

_ev :: MonadEv t => Tm -> Env t -> t (Val t)
_ev (V x)        env = return (unsafeLookup x env)
_ev (L x e)      env = return (F (\ a -> ev e (update x a env)))
_ev (e :@ e')    env = ev e  env >>= \ (F k)  ->
                           ev e' env >>= \ a       ->
                           k a
_ev (N n)        env = return (I n)
_ev (e0 :+ e1)   env = ev e0 env >>= \ (I n0) ->
                           ev e1 env >>= \ (I n1) ->
                           return (I (n0 + n1))
...
_ev TT           env = return (B True )
_ev FF           env = return (B False)
_ev (Not e)      env = ev e  env >>= \ (B b)  ->
                           return (B (not b))
...
_ev (If e e0 e1) env = ev e  env >>= \ (B b)  ->
                       if b then ev e0 env else ev e1 env
```

To interpret the "native" constructs in each of the extensions, we have to use the "native" operations of the corresponding monad.

```
instance MonadEv Id where
  ev e env = _ev e env

instance MonadEv Maybe where
  ev Raise             env = raise
  ev (e0 'Handle' e1) env = ev e0 env 'handle' ev e1 env
  ev e                 env = _ev e env

instance MonadEv [] where
  ev Deadlock          env = deadlock
  ev (e0 'Choice' e1) env = ev e0 env 'choice' ev e1 env
  ev e                 env = _ev e env
```

We have achieved nearly perfect reference interpreters for the three languages. But there is one thing we have forgotten. To accomplish anything really interesting with integers, we need some form of recursion, say, the luxury of general recursion. So we would actually like to extend the definition of the syntax by the clause

```
data Tm = ... | Rec Tm
```

It would first look natural to extend the definition of the semantic intepretation by the clause

```
_ev (Rec e) env = ev  e        env >>= \ (F k) ->
                  _ev (Rec e) env >>= \ a      ->
                  k a
```

But unfortunately, this interprets Rec too eagerly, so no recursion will ever stop. For every recursive call in a recursion, the interpreter would want to know if it returns, even if the result is not needed at all.

So we have a problem. The solution is to use the MonadFix class (from Control.Monad.Fix), an invention of Erkök and Launchbury [16], which specifically supports the monadic form of general recursion [1]:

```
class Monad t => MonadFix t where
  mfix :: (a -> t a) -> t a

  -- the ideal uniform mfix which doesn't work
  -- mfix k = mfix k >>= k
```

The identity, maybe and list monads are instances (in an ad hoc way).

---

[1] Notice that 'Fix' in 'MonadFix' refers as much to fixing an unpleasant issue as it refers to a fixpoint combinator.

```
fix :: (a -> a) -> a
fix f = f (fix f)

instance MonadFix Id where
  mfix k = fix (k . unId)
          where unId (Id a) = a

instance MonadFix Maybe where
  mfix k = fix (k . unJust)
          where unJust (Just a) = a

instance MonadFix [] where
  mfix k = case fix (k . head) of
             []       -> []
             (a : _) -> a : mfix (tail . k)
```

Now, after subclassing MonadEv from MonadFix instead of Monad

```
class MonadFix t => MonadEv t where ...
```

we can define the meaning of Rec by the clause

```
_ev (Rec e) env = ev e  env >>= \ (F k) ->
                  mfix k
```

After this dirty fix (where however all dirt is contained) everything is clean and working. We can interpret our pure core language and the two extensions. The examples from the Introduction are handled by the interpreter exactly as expected. We can define:

```
fact = Rec (L "fact" (L "x" (
                 If (V "x" :<= N 1)
                    (N 1)
                    ((V "fact" :@ (V "x" :- N 1)) :* V "x"))))

factM = Rec (L "fact" (L "x" (
                (If (V "x" :== N 5)
                    Raise
                    (If (V "x" :<= N 1)
                        (N 1)
                        ((V "fact" :@ (V "x" :- N 1)) :* V "x")))
                 'Handle'
                (If (V "x" :== N 7)
                    (N 5040)
                    Raise))))

factL = Rec (L "fact" (L "x" (
                If (V "x" :<= N 1)
                   (N 1)
                   ((V "fact" :@ (V "x" :- N 1)) :*
                                           (N 1 'Choice' V "x")))))
```

Testing these, we get exactly the results we would expect.

```
> evClosed (fact   :@ N 6) :: Id (Val Id)
Id 720
> evClosed (factM :@ N 4) :: Maybe (Val Maybe)
Just 24
> evClosed (factM :@ N 6) :: Maybe (Val Maybe)
Nothing
> evClosed (factM :@ N 8) :: Maybe (Val Maybe)
Just 40320
> evClosed (factL :@ N 5) :: [Val []]
[1,5,4,20,3,15,12,60,2,10,8,40,6,30,24,120]
```

4   Arrows

Despite their generality, monads do not cater for every possible notion of impure function. In particular, monads do not cater for stream functions, which are the central concept in dataflow programming.

In functional programming, Hughes [19] has been promoting what he has called arrow types to overcome this deficiency. In semantics, the same concept was invented for the same reason by Power and Robinson [32] under the name of a Freyd category.

Informally, a Freyd category is a symmetric premonoidal category together and an inclusion from a base category. A symmetric premonoidal category is the same as a symmetric monoidal category except that the tensor need not be bifunctorial, only functorial in each of its two arguments separately.

The exact definition is a bit more complicated: A *binoidal* category is a category $\mathcal{K}$ binary operation $\otimes$ on objects of $\mathcal{K}$ that is functorial in each of its two arguments. A map $f : A \rightarrow B$ of such a category is called *central* if the two composites $A \otimes C \rightarrow B \otimes D$ agree for every map $g : C \rightarrow D$ and so do the two composites $C \otimes A \rightarrow D \otimes B$. A natural transformation is called central if its components are central. A *symmetric premonoidal category* is a binoidal category $(\mathcal{K}, \otimes)$ together with an object I and central natural transformations ρ, α, σ with components $A \rightarrow A \otimes I$, $(A \otimes B) \otimes C \rightarrow A \otimes (B \otimes C)$, $A \otimes B \rightarrow B \otimes A$, subject to a number of coherence conditions. A *Freyd category* over a Cartesian category $\mathcal{C}$ is a symmetric premonoidal category $\mathcal{K}$ together with an identity on objects functor $J : \mathcal{C} \rightarrow \mathcal{K}$ that preserves the symmetric premonoidal structure of $\mathcal{C}$ on the nose and also preserves centrality.

The pragmatics for impure computation is to have an inclusion from the base category of pure functions to a richer category of which is the home for impure functions (arrows), so that some aspects of the Cartesian structure of the base category are preserved. Importantly the Cartesian product $\times$ of $\mathcal{C}$ is bifunctorial, so $(B \times g) \circ (f \times C) = (f \times D) \circ (A \times g) : A \times C \rightarrow B \times D$ for any $f : A \rightarrow B$ and $g : C \rightarrow D$, but for the corresponding tensor operation $\oplus$ of $\mathcal{K}$ this is only mandatory if either f or g is pure (the idea being that different sequencings of impure functions must be able to give different results).

The basic example of a Freyd category is the Kleisli category of a strong monad. Another standard one is that of stateful functions. For a base category $\mathcal{C}$, the maps of the Freyd category are the maps $A \times S \to B \times S$ of $\mathcal{C}$ where S is some fixed object of $\mathcal{C}$. This is not very exciting, since if $\mathcal{C}$ also has exponents, the maps $A \times S \to B \times S$ are in a natural bijection with the maps $A \to S \Rightarrow B \times S$, which means that the Freyd category is essentially the same as the Kleisli category of the state monad. But probably the best known and most useful example is that of stream functions. In this case the maps $A \to B$ of the Freyd category are the maps $\mathsf{Str}A \to \mathsf{Str}B$ of $\mathcal{C}$ of $\mathcal{C}$ where $\mathsf{Str}A = \nu X.A \times X$ is the type of streams over the type A. Notice that differently from stateful functions from A to B, stream functions from A to B just cannot be viewed as Kleisli arrows.

In Haskell, arrow type constructors are implemented by the following type constructor class (appearing in Control.Arrow).

```
class Arrow r where
  pure :: (a -> b) -> r a b
  (>>>) :: r a b -> r b c -> r a c
  first :: r a b -> r (a, c) (b, c)


returnA :: Arrow r => r a a
returnA = pure id

second :: Arrow r => r c d -> r (a, c) (a, d)
second f = pure swap >>> first f >>> pure swap
```

pure says that every function is an arrow (so in particular identity arrows arise from identity functions). (>>>) provides composition of arrows and first provides functoriality in the first argument of the tensor of the arrow category.

In Haskell, Kleisli arrows of monads are shown to be an instance of arrows as follows (recall that all Haskell monads are strong).

```
newtype Kleisli t a b = Kleisli (a -> t b)

instance Monad t => Arrow (Kleisli t) where
  pure f = Kleisli (return . f)
  Kleisli k >>> Kleisli l = Kleisli ((>>= l) . k)
  first (Kleisli k) = Kleisli (\ (a, c) -> mstrength (k a) c)
```

Stateful functions are a particularly simple instance.

```
newtype StateA s a b = StateA ((a, s) -> (b, s))

instance Arrow (State A s) where
  pure f = StateA (\ (a, s) -> (f a, s))
  StateA f >>> StateA g = StateA (g . f)
  first (StateA f) = StateA (\ ((a, c), s) -> case f (a, s) of
                                        (b, s') -> ((b, c), s'))
```

Stream functions are declared to be arrows in the following fashion, relying on streams being mappable and zippable. (For reasons of readability that will become apparent in the next section, we introduce our own list and stream types with our own names for their nil and cons constructors. Also, although Haskell does not distinguish between inductive and coinductive types because of its algebraically compact semantics, we want to make the distinction, as our work also applies to other, finer semantic models.)

```
data Stream a = a :< Stream a                    -- coinductive


mapS :: (a -> b) -> Stream a -> Stream b
mapS f (a :< as) = f a :< mapS f as


zipS :: Stream a -> Stream b -> Stream (a, b)
zipS (a :< as) (b :< bs) = (a, b) :< zipS as bs


unzipS :: Stream (a, b) -> (Stream a, Stream b)
unzipS abs = (mapS fst abs, mapS snd abs)


newtype SF a b = SF (Stream a -> Stream b)

instance Arrow SF where
  pure f = SF (mapS f)
  SF k >>> SF l = SF (l . k)
  first (SF k) = SF (uncurry zipS . (\ (as, ds) -> (k as, ds)) . unzipS)
```

Similarly to monads, every useful arrow type constructor has some operation specific to it. The main such operation for stream functions are the initialized unit delay operation 'followed by' of intensional and synchronous dataflow languages and the unit anticipation operation 'next' that only exists in intensional languages. These are really the cons and tail operations of streams.

```
fbySF :: a -> SF a a
fbySF a0 = SF (\ as -> a0 :< as)


nextSF :: SF a a
nextSF = SF (\ (a :< as) -> as)
```

5   Comonads

5.1   Comonads and Context-Dependent Functions

While Freyd categories or arrow types are certainly general and cover significantly more notions of impure functions than monads, some non-monadic impurities should be explainable in more basic terms, namely via comonads, which are the dual of monads. This has been suggested [8,23,25], but there have been few useful examples. One of the goals of this paper is to show that general and causal stream functions are excellent new such examples.

A *comonad* on a category $\mathcal{C}$ is given by a mapping $D : |\mathcal{C}| \to |\mathcal{C}|$ together with a $|\mathcal{C}|$-indexed family ε of maps $\varepsilon_A : DA \to A$ (*counit*), and an operation $-^\dagger$ taking every map $k : DA \to B$ in $\mathcal{C}$ to a map $k^\dagger : DA \to DB$ (*coextension operation*) such that

1. for any $k : DA \to B$, $\varepsilon_B \circ k^\dagger = k$,
2. $\varepsilon_A{}^\dagger = \mathrm{id}_{DA}$,
3. for any $k : DA \to B$, $\ell : DB \to C$, $(\ell \circ k^\dagger)^\dagger = \ell^\dagger \circ k^\dagger$.

Analogously to Kleisli categories, any comonad $(D, \varepsilon, -^\dagger)$ defines a category $\mathcal{C}_D$ where $|\mathcal{C}_D| = |\mathcal{C}|$ and $\mathcal{C}_D(A, B) = \mathcal{C}(DA, B)$, $(\mathrm{id}_D)_A = \varepsilon_A$, $\ell \circ_D k = \ell \circ k^\dagger$ (*coKleisli category*) and an identity on objects functor $J : \mathcal{C} \to \mathcal{C}_D$ where $Jf = f \circ \varepsilon_A$ for $f : A \to B$.

Comonads should be fit to capture notions of "value in a context"; DA would be the type of contextually situated values of A. A context-dependent function from A to B would then be a map $A \to B$ in the coKleisli category, i.e., a map $DA \to B$ in the base category. The function $\varepsilon_A : DA \to A$ discards the context of its input whereas the coextension $k^\dagger : DA \to DB$ of a function $k : DA \to B$ essentially duplicates it (to feed it to k and still have a copy left).

Some examples of comonads are the following: each object mapping D below is a comonad:

- $DA = A$, the identity comonad,
- $DA = A \times E$, the product comonad,
- $DA = \mathsf{Str}A = \nu X.A \times X$, the streams comonad,
- $DA = \nu X.A \times FX$, the cofree comonad over F,
- $DA = \mu X.A \times FX$, the cofree recursive comonad over F [36].

Accidentally, the pragmatics of the product comonad is the same as that of the exponent monad, viz. representation of functions reading an environment. The reason is simple: the Kleisli arrows of the exponent monad are the maps $A \to (E \Rightarrow B)$ of the base category, which are of course in a natural bijection with the with the maps $A \times E \to B$ that are the coKleisli arrows of the product comonad. But in general, monads and comonads capture different notions of impure function. We defer the discussion of the pragmatics of the streams comonad until the next subsection (it is not the comonad to represent general or causal stream functions!).

For Haskell, there is no standard comonad library[2]. But of course comonads are easily defined as a type constructor class analogously to monads.

```
class Comonad d where
  counit :: d a -> a
  cobind :: (d a -> b) -> d a -> d b

cmap :: Comonad d => (a -> b) -> d a -> d b
cmap f = cobind (f . counit)
```

The identity and product comonads are defined as instances in the following fashion.

---

[2] There is, however, a contributed library by Dave Menendez, see http://www.eyrie.org/~zednenem/2004/hsce/

```
instance Comonad Id  where
  counit (Id a) = a
  cobind k d = Id (k d)

data Prod e a = a :& e

instance Comonad (Prod e) where
  counit (a :& _) = a
  cobind k d@(_ :& e) = k d :& e

askP :: Prod e a -> e
askP (_ :& e) = e

localP :: (e -> e) -> Prod e a -> Prod e a
localP g (a :& e) = (a :& g e)
```

The stream comonad is implemented as follows.

```
instance Comonad Stream  where
  counit (a :< _) = a
  cobind k d@(_ :< as) = k d :< cobind k as

nextS :: Stream a -> Stream a
nextS (a :< as) = as
```

Just as the Kleisli categories of strong monads are Freyd categories, so are the coKleisli categories of comonads.

```
newtype CoKleisli d a b = CoKleisli (d a -> b)

pair f g x = (f x, g x)

instance Comonad d => Arrow (CoKleisli d) where
  pure f = CoKleisli (f . counit)
  CoKleisli k >>> CoKleisli l = CoKleisli (l . cobind k)
  first (CoKleisli k) = CoKleisli (pair (k . cmap fst) (snd . counit))
```

5.2   Comonads for General and Causal Stream Functions

The general pragmatics of comonads introduced, we are now ready to discuss the representation of general and causal stream functions via comonads.

The first observation to make is that streams (discrete time signals) are naturally isomorphic to functions from natural numbers: $\text{Str} A = \nu X. A \times X \cong (\mu X. 1 + X) \Rightarrow A = \text{Nat} \Rightarrow A$. In Haskell, this isomorphism is implemented as follows:

```
str2fun :: Stream a -> Int -> a
str2fun (a :< as) 0 = a str2fun (a :< as) (i + 1) = str2fun as i

fun2str :: (Int -> a) -> Stream a
fun2str f = fun2str' f 0
      where fun2str' f i = f i :< fun2str' f (i + 1)
```

General stream functions $\mathsf{Str}A \to \mathsf{Str}B$ are thus in natural bijection with maps $\mathsf{Nat} \Rightarrow A \to \mathsf{Nat} \Rightarrow B$, which, in turn, are in natural bijection with maps $(\mathsf{Nat} \Rightarrow A) \times \mathsf{Nat} \to B$, i.e., $\mathsf{FunArg}\,\mathsf{Nat}\,A \to B$ where $\mathsf{FunArg}\,S\,A = (S \Rightarrow A) \times S$. Hence, for general stream functions, a value from A in context is a stream (signal) over A together with a natural number identifying a distinguished stream position (the present time). Not surprisingly, the object mapping $\mathsf{FunArg}\,S$ is a comonad (in fact, it is the "state-in-context" comonad considered by Kieburtz [23]) and, what is of crucial importance, the coKleisli identities and composition as well as the coKleisli lifting of $\mathsf{FunArg}\,\mathsf{Nat}$ agree with the identities and composition of stream functions (which are really just function identities and composition) and with the lifting of functions to stream functions. In Haskell, the parameterized comonad FunArg and the interpretation of the coKleisli arrows of $\mathsf{FunArg}\,\mathsf{Nat}$ as stream functions are implemented as follows.

```
data FunArg s a = (s -> a) :# s

instance Comonad (FunArg s) where
  counit (f :# s) = f s
  cobind k (f :# s) = (\ s' -> k (f :# s')) :# s

runFA :: (FunArg Int a -> b) -> Stream a -> Stream b
runFA k as = runFA' k (str2fun as :# 0)
     where runFA' k d@(f :# i) = k d :< runFA' k (f :# (i + 1))
```

The comonad $\mathsf{FunArg}\,\mathsf{Nat}$ can also be presented equivalently without using natural numbers to deal with positions. The idea for this alternative presentation is simple: given a stream and a distinguished stream position, the position splits the stream up into a list, a value of the base type and a stream (corresponding to the past, present and future of the signal). Put mathematically, there is a natural isomorphism $(\mathsf{Nat} \Rightarrow A) \times \mathsf{Nat} \cong \mathsf{Str}\,A \times \mathsf{Nat} \cong (\mathsf{List}\,A \times A) \times \mathsf{Str}\,A$ where $\mathsf{List}\,A = \mu X.\ 1 + (A \times X)$ is the type of lists over a given type A. This gives us an equivalent comonad LVS for representing of stream functions with the following structure (we use snoc-lists instead of cons-lists to reflect the fact that the analysis order of the past of a signal will be the reverse direction of time):

```
data List a = Nil | List a :> a            -- inductive

data LV   a = List a := a

data LVS a = LV a :| Stream a

instance Comonad LVS where
  counit (az := a :| as) = a
  cobind k d = cobindL d := k d :| cobindS d
    where cobindL (Nil      := a :| as)  = Nil
          cobindL (az' :> a' := a :| as)  = cobindL d' :> k d'
                             where d' = az' := a' :| (a :< as)
```

```
        cobindS (az := a :| (a' :< as')) = k d' :< cobindS d'
                          where d' = az :> a := a' :| as'
```

(Notice the visual purpose of our constructor naming. In values of types LVS A, both the cons constructors (:>) of the list (the past) and the cons constructors (:<) of the stream (the future) point to the present which is enclosed between the constructors (:=) and (: |).)

The interpretation of the coKleisli arrows of the comonad LVS as stream functions is implemented as follows.

```
runLVS :: (LVS a -> b) -> Stream a -> Stream b
runLVS k (a' :< as') = runLVS' k (Nil := a' :| as')
              where runLVS' k d@(az := a :| (a' :< as'))
                        = k d :< runLVS' k (az :> a := a' :| as')
```

Delay and anticipation are easily formulated in terms of both FunArg Nat and LVS.

```
fbyFA :: a -> (FunArg Int a -> a)
fbyFA a0 (f :# 0)       = a0
fbyFA _  (f :# (i + 1)) = f i

fbyLVS :: a -> (LVS a -> a)
fbyLVS a0 (Nil          := _ :| _) = a0
fbyLVS _  ((_ :> a') := _ :| _) = a'

nextFA :: FunArg Int a -> a
nextFA (f :# i) = f (i + 1)

nextLVS :: LVS a -> a
nextLVS (_ := _ :| (a :< _)) = a
```

Let us call a stream function *causal*, if the present of the output signal only depends on the past and present of the input signal and not on its future[3]. Is there a way to ban non-causal functions? Yes, the comonad LVS is easy to modify so that exactly those stream functions can be represented that are causal. All that needs to be done is to remove from the comonad LVS the factor of the future. We are left with the object mapping LV where LV $A = \text{List } A \times A = (\mu X. 1 + A \times X) \times A \cong \mu X. A \times (1 + X)$, i.e., a non-empty list type constructor. This is a comonad as well and again the counit and the coextension operation are just correct in the sense that they deliver the desirable coKleisli identities, composition and lifting. In fact, the comonad LV is the cofree recursive comonad of the functor Maybe (we refrain from giving the definition of a recursive comonad here, this can be

---

[3] The standard terminology is '*synchronous* stream functions', but want to avoid it, because 'synchrony' also refers to all signals being on the same clock and to the hypothesis on which the applications of synchronous dataflow languages are based: that in an embedded system the controller can react to an event in the plant in so little time that it can be considered instantaneous.

found in [36]). It may be useful to notice that the type constructor LV carries a
monad structure too, but the Kleisli arrows of that monad have nothing to do
with causal stream functions!

In Haskell, the non-empty list comonad LV is defined as follows.

```
instance Comonad LV where
  counit (_ := a) = a
  cobind k d@(az := _) = cobindL k az := k d
    where cobindL k Nil = Nil
          cobindL k (az :> a) = cobindL k az :> k (az := a)

runLV  :: (LV a -> b) -> Stream a -> Stream b
runLV  k (a' :< as') = runLV' k (Nil := a' :| as')
                 where runLV' k (d@(az := a) :| (a' :< as'))
                       = k d :< runLV' k (az :> a := a' :| as')
```

With the LV comonad, anticipation is no longer possible, but delay is unprob-
lematic.

```
fbyLV :: a -> (LV a -> a)
fbyLV a0 (Nil       := _) = a0
fbyLV _  ((_ :> a') := _) = a'
```

Analogously to causal stream functions, one might also consider *anticausal*
stream functions, i.e., functions for which the present value of the output signal only depends on the present and future values of the input signal. As
$A \times \text{Str}\, A \cong \text{Str}\, A$, it is not surprising now anymore that the comonad for anticausal stream functions is the comonad Str, which we introduced earlier and
which is very canonical by being the cofree comonad generated by the identity
functor. However, in real life, causality is much more relevant than anticausality!

5.3   Comonadic Semantics

Is the comonadic approach to context-dependent computation of any use? We
will now demonstrate that it is indeed by developing a generic comonadic interpreter instantiable to various specific comonads, in particular to those that
characterize general and causal stream functions. In the development, we mimic
the monadic interpreter.

As the first thing we again fix the syntax of our object language. We will
support a purely functional core and additions corresponding to various notions
of context.

```
type Var = String

data Tm = V Var | L Var Tm | Tm :@ Tm | Rec Tm
        | N Integer | Tm :+ Tm | ...
        | Tm :== Tm | ...  | TT | FF | Not Tm | ... | If Tm Tm Tm
        -- specific for both general and causal stream functions
```

```
          | Tm 'Fby' Tm
          -- specific for general stream functions only
          | Next Tm
```

The type-unaware semantic domain contains integers, booleans and functions as before, but now our functions are context-dependent (coKleisli functions). Environments are lists of variable-value pairs as usual.

```
data Val d = I Integer | B Bool | F (d (Val d) -> Val d)

type Env d = [(Var, Val d)]
```

And we are at evaluation. Of course terms must denote coKleisli arrows, so the typing of evaluation is uncontroversial.

```
class Comonad d => ComonadEv d where
    ev :: Tm -> d (Env d) -> Val d
```

But an interesting issue arises with evaluation of closed terms. In the case of a pure or a monadically interpreted language, closed terms are supposed to be evaluated in the empty environment. Now they must be evaluated in the empty environment placed in a context! What does this mean? This is easy to understand on the example of stream functions. By the types, evaluation of an expression returns a single value, not a stream. So the stream position of interest must be specified in the contextually situated environment that we provide. Very suitably, this is exactly the information that the empty environment in a context conveys. So we can define:

```
evClosedI :: Tm -> Val Id
evClosedI e = ev e (Id empty)

emptyL :: Int -> List   [(a, b)]
emptyL 0       = Nil
emptyL (i + 1) = emptyL i :> empty

emptyS :: Stream [(a, b)]
emptyS = empty :< emptyS

evClosedLVS :: Tm -> Int -> Val LVS
evClosedLVS e i = ev e (emptyL i := empty :| emptyS)

evClosedLV  :: Tm -> Int -> Val LV
evClosedLV  e i = ev e (emptyL i := empty)
```

Back to evaluation. For most of the core constructs, the types tell us what the defining clauses of their meanings must be—there is only one thing we can write and that is the right thing. In particular, everything is meaningfully pre-determined about variables, application and recursion (and, for recursion, the obvious solution works). E.g., for a variable, we must extract the environment from its context (e.g., history), and then do a lookup. For an application, we must evaluate the function wrt. the given contextually situated environment and then apply it. But since, according to the types, a function wants not just an isolated argument value, but a contextually situated one, the function has to be applied to the coextension of the denotation of the argument wrt. the given contextually situated environment.

```
_ev :: ComonadEv d => Tm -> d (Env d) -> Val d
_ev (V x)        denv = unsafeLookup x (counit denv)
_ev (e :@ e')    denv = case ev e denv of
                        F f -> f (cobind (ev e') denv)
_ev (Rec e)      denv = case ev e denv of
                        F f -> f (cobind (_ev (Rec e)) denv)
_ev (N n)        denv = I n
_ev (e0 :+ e1)   denv = case ev e0 denv of
                        I n0 -> case ev e1 denv of
                        I n1 -> I (n0 + n1)
...
_ev TT           denv = B True
_ev FF           denv = B False
_ev (Not e)      denv = case ev e denv of
                        B b -> B (not b)
...
_ev (If e e0 e1) denv = case ev e denv of
                        B b -> if b then ev e0 denv else ev e1 denv
```

There is, however, a problem with lambda-abstraction. For any potential contextually situated value of the lambda-variable, the evaluation function should recursively evaluate the body of the lambda-abstraction expression in the appropriately extended contextually situated environment. Schematically,

```
_ev (L x e)      denv = F (\ d -> ev e (extend x d denv))
```

where

```
extend :: Comonad d => Var -> d (Val d) -> d (Env d) -> d (Env d)
```

Note that we need to combine a contextually situated environment with a contextually situated value. One way to do this would be to use the strength of the comonad (we are in Haskell, so every comonad is strong), but in the case of the stream function comonads this would necessarily have the bad effect that either the history of the environment or that of the value would be lost. We would like to see that no information is lost, to have the histories zipped.

To solve the problem, we consider comonads equipped with an additional zipping operation. We define a *comonad with zipping* to be a comonad D coming with a natural transformation m with components $m_{A,B} : DA \times DB \to D(A \times B)$ that satisfies coherence conditions such as $\varepsilon_{A \times B} \circ m_{A,B} = \varepsilon_A \times \varepsilon_B$ (more mathematically, this is a symmetric semi-monoidal comonad).

In Haskell, we define a corresponding type constructor class.

```
class Comonad d => ComonadZip d where
  czip :: d a -> d b -> d (a, b)
```

The identity comonad, as well as LVS and LV are instances (and so are many other comonads).

```
instance ComonadZip Id where
  czip (Id a) (Id b) = Id (a, b)
```

```
zipL :: List a -> List b -> List (a, b)
zipL Nil       _        = Nil
zipL _         Nil      = Nil
zipL (az :> a) (bz :> b) = zipL az bz :> (a, b)
```

```
zipS :: Stream a -> Stream b -> Stream (a, b)
zipS (a :< as) (b :< bs) = (a, b) :< zipS as bs
```

```
instance ComonadZip LVS where
  czip (az := a :| as) (bz := b :| bs)
                       = zipL az bz := (a, b) :| zipS as bs
```

```
instance ComonadZip LV where
  czip (az := a) (bz := b) = zipL az bz := (a, b)
```

With the zip operation available, defining the meaning of lambda-abstractions is easy, but we must also update the typing of the evaluation function, so that zippability becomes required[4].

```
class ComonadZip d => ComonadEv d where ...
```

```
_ev (L x e) denv = F (\ d -> ev e (cmap repair (czip d denv)))
                   where repair (a, env) = update x a env
```

It remains to define the meaning of the specific constructs of our example languages. The pure language has none. The dataflow languages have Fby and Next that are interpreted using the specific operations of the corresponding comonads. Since each of Fby and Next depends on the context of the value of its main argument, we need to apply the coextension operation to the denotation of that argument to have this context available.

```
instance ComonadEv Id where
  ev e denv = _ev e denv
```

```
instance ComonadEv LVS where
  ev (e0 'Fby' e1) denv = ev e0 denv 'fbyLVS' cobind (ev e1) denv
  ev (Next e)      denv = nextLVS (cobind (ev e) denv)
  ev e             denv = _ev e denv
```

---

[4] The name 'repair' in the code below alludes both to getting a small discrepancy in the types right and to rearranging some pairings.

```
instance ComonadEv LV where
  ev (e0 'Fby' e1) denv = ev e0 denv 'fbyLV'  cobind (ev e1) denv
  ev e               denv = _ev e denv
```

In dataflow languages, the 'followed by' construct is usually defined to mean the delay of the second argument initialized by the initial value of the first argument, which may at first seem like an ad hoc decision (or so it seemed to us at least). Why give the initial position any priority? In our interpreter, we took the simplest possible solution of using the value of the first argument of Fby in the present position of the history of the environment. We did not use any explicit means to calculate the value of that argument wrt. the initial position. But the magic of the definition of fbyLVS is that it only ever uses its first argument when the second has a history with no past (which corresponds to the situation when the present actually is the initial position in the history of the environment). So our most straightforward naive design gave exactly the solution that has been adopted by the dataflow languages community, probably for entirely different reasons.

Notice also that we have obtained a generic comonads-inspired language design which supports higher-order functions and the solution was dictated by the types. This is remarkable since dataflow languages are traditionally first-order and the question of the right meaning of higher-order dataflow has been considered controversial. The key idea of our solution can be read off from the interpretation of application: the present value of a function application is the present value of the function applied to the history of the argument.

We can test the interpreter on the examples from Section 2. The following examples make sense in both the general and causal stream function settings.

```
-- pos    = 0 fby pos + 1
pos  = Rec (L "pos" (N 0 'Fby' (V "pos" :+ N 1)))
-- sum x  = x + (0 fby sum x)
sum  = L "x" (Rec (L "sumx" (V "x" :+ (N 0 'Fby' V "sumx"))))
-- diff x = x - (0 fby x)
diff = L "x" (V "x" :- (N 0 'Fby' V "x"))
-- ini  x = x fby ini x
ini  = L "x" (Rec (L "inix" (V "x" 'Fby' V "inix")))
-- fact = 1 fby (fact * (pos + 1))
fact = Rec (L "fact" (N 1 'Fby' (V "fact" :* (pos :+  N 1))))
-- fibo = 0 fby (fibo + (1 fby fibo))
fibo = Rec (L "fibo" (N 0 'Fby' (V "fibo" :+ (N 1 'Fby' V "fibo"))))
```

Testing gives expected results:

```
> runLV (ev pos) emptyS
0 :< (1 :< (2 :< (3 :< (4 :< (5 :< (6 :< (7 :< (8 :< (9 :< (10 :< ...
> runLV (ev (sum :@ pos)) emptyS
0 :< (1 :< (3 :< (6 :< (10 :< (15 :< (21 :< (28 :< (36 :< (45 :< ...
> runLV (ev (diff :@ (sum :@ pos))) emptyS
0 :< (1 :< (2 :< (3 :< (4 :< (5 :< (6 :< (7 :< (8 :< (9 :< (10 :< ...
```

The 'whenever' operator and the sieve of Eratosthenes, which use anticipation, are only allowed with general stream functions.

```
-- x wvr y = if ini y then x fby (next x wvr next y)
--                     else (next x wvr next y)
wvr = Rec (L "wvr" (L "x" (L "y" (
          If (ini :@ V "y")
              (V "x" 'Fby' (V "wvr" :@ (Next (V "x")) :@ (Next (V "y"))))
              (V "wvr" :@ (Next (V "x")) :@ (Next (V "y")))))))
```

```
-- sieve x = x fby sieve (x wvr x mod (ini x) /= 0)
sieve = Rec (L "sieve" (L "x" (
             V "x" 'Fby' (
             V "sieve" :@ (wvr :@ V "x" :@ (
                          V "x" 'Mod' (ini :@ (V "x")) :/= N 0))))))
-- eratosthenes = sieve (pos + 2)
eratosthenes = sieve :@ (pos :+ N 2)
```

Again, testing gives what one would like to get.

```
> runLVS (ev eratosthenes) emptyS
2 :< (3 :< (5 :< (7 :< (11 :< (13 :< (17 :< (19 :< (23 :< (29 :< ...
```

6   Distributive Laws

6.1   Distributive Laws: A Distributive Law for Causal Partial-Stream Functions

While the comonadic approach is quite powerful, there are natural notions of impure computation that it does not cover. One example is clocked dataflow or partial-stream based computation. The idea of clocked dataflow is that different signals may be on different clocks. Clocked dataflow signals can be represented by partial streams. A partial stream is a stream that may have empty positions to indicate the pace of the clock of a signal wrt. the base clock. The idea is to get rid of the different clocks by aligning all signals wrt. the base clock.

A very good news is that although comonads alone do not cover clocked dataflow computation, a solution is still close at hand. General and causal partial-stream functions turn out to be describable in terms of distributive combinations of a comonad and a monad considered, e.g., in [8,33]. For reasons of space, we will only discuss causal partial-stream functions as more relevant. General partial-stream functions are handled completely analogously.

Given a comonad $(D, \varepsilon, -^{\dagger})$ and a monad $(T, \eta, -^{*})$ on a category $\mathcal{C}$, a *distributive law* of the former over the latter is a natural transformation λ with components $DTA \to TDA$ subject to four coherence conditions. A distributive law of D over T defines a category $\mathcal{C}_{D,T}$ where $|\mathcal{C}_{D,T}| = |\mathcal{C}|$, $\mathcal{C}_{D,T}(A, B) = \mathcal{C}(DA, TB)$, $(\mathrm{id}_{D,T})_A = \eta_A \circ \varepsilon_A$, $\ell \circ_{D,T} k = l^{*} \circ \lambda_B \circ k^{\dagger}$ for $k : DA \to TB$, $\ell : DB \to TC$ (call it the *biKleisli category*), with inclusions to it from both the coKleisli category of D and Kleisli category of T. If the monad T is strong, the biKleisli category is a Freyd category.

In Haskell, the distributive combination is implemented as follows.

```
class (ComonadZip d, Monad t) => Dist d t where
  dist :: d (t a) -> t (d a)

newtype BiKleisli d t a b = BiKleisli (d a -> t b)

instance Dist d t => Arrow (BiKleisli d t) where
  pure f = BiKleisli (return . f . counit)
  BiKleisli k >>> BiKleisli l = BiKleisli ((>>= l) . dist . cobind k)
  first (BiKleisli k) = BiKleisli (\ d ->
                        k (cmap fst d) >>= \ b ->
                        return (b, snd (counit d)))
```

The simplest examples of distributive laws are the distributivity of the identity comonad over any monad and the distributivity of any comonad over the identity monad.

```
instance Monad t => Dist Id t where
  dist (Id c) = mmap Id c

instance ComonadZip d => Dist d Id where
  dist d = Id (cmap unId d)
```

A more interesting example is the distributive law of the product comonad over the maybe monad.

```
instance Dist Prod Maybe where
  dist (Nothing :& _) = Nothing
  dist (Just a   :& e) = Just (a :& e)
```

For causal partial-stream functions, it is appropriate to combine the causal stream functions comonad LV with the maybe monad. And this is possible, since there is a distributive law which takes a partial list and a partial value (the past and present of the signal according to the base clock) and, depending on whether the partial value is undefined or defined, gives back the undefined list-value pair (the present time does not exist according to the signal's own clock) or a defined list-value pair, where the list is obtained from the partial list by leaving out its undefined elements (the past and present of the signal according to its own clock). In Haskell, this distributive law is coded as follows.

```
filterL :: List (Maybe a) -> List a
filterL Nil                = Nil
filterL (az :> Nothing) = filterL az
filterL (az :> Just a)  = filterL az :> a

instance Dist LV Maybe where
  dist (az := Nothing) = Nothing
  dist (az := Just a)  = Just (filterL az := a)
```

The biKleisli arrows of the distributive law are interpreted as partial-stream functions as follows.

```
runLVM  :: (LV a -> Maybe b) -> Stream (Maybe a) -> Stream (Maybe b)
runLVM  k (a' :< as') = runLVM' k Nil a' as'
             where runLVM' k az Nothing  (a' :< as')
                        = Nothing       :< runLVM' k az        a' as'
                   runLVM' k az (Just a) (a' :< as')
                        = k (az := a) :< runLVM' k (az :> a) a' as'
```

6.2 Distributivity-Based Semantics

Just as with comonads, we demonstrate distributive laws in action by presenting an interpreter. This time this is an interpreter of languages featuring both context-dependence and effects.

As previously, our first step is to fix the syntax of the object language.

```
type Var = String

data Tm = V Var | L Var Tm | Tm :@ Tm | Rec Tm
        | N Integer | Tm :+ Tm | ...
        | Tm :== Tm | ... | TT | FF | Not Tm | ... | If Tm Tm Tm
        -- specific for causal stream functions
        | Tm 'Fby' Tm
        -- specific for partiality
        | Nosig | Tm 'Merge' Tm
```

In the partiality part, Nosig corresponds to a nowhere defined stream, i.e., a signal on an infinitely slow clock. The function of Merge is to combine two partial streams into one which is defined wherever at least one of the given partial streams is defined.

The semantic domains and environments are defined as before, except that functions are now biKleisli functions, i.e., they take contextually situated values to values with an effect.

```
data Val d t = I Integer | B Bool | F (d (Val d t) -> t (Val d t))

type Env d t = [(Var, Val d t)]
```

Evaluation sends terms to biKleisli arrows; closed terms are interpreted in the empty environment placed into a context of interest.

```
class Dist d t => DistEv d t where
  ev :: Tm -> d (Env d t) -> t (Val d t)

evClosedLV :: DistEv LV t => Tm -> Int -> t (Val LV t)
evClosedLV e i = ev e (emptyL i := empty)
```

The meanings of the core constructs are essentially dictated by the types.

```
_ev :: DistEv d t => Tm -> d (Env d t) -> t (Val d t)
_ev (V x)        denv = return (unsafeLookup x (counit denv))
_ev (L x e)      denv = return
                                (F (\ d -> ev e (cmap repair (czip d denv))))
                               where repair (a, env) = update x a env
_ev (e :@ e')    denv = ev e denv >>= \ (F f) ->
                               dist (cobind (ev e') denv) >>= \ d ->
                               f d
_ev (Rec e)      denv = ev e denv >>= \ (F f) ->
                               dist (cobind (_ev (Rec e)) denv) >>= \ d ->
                               f d
_ev (N n)        denv = return (I n)
_ev (e0 :+ e1)   denv = ev e0 denv >>= \ (I n0) ->
                               ev e1 denv >>= \ (I n1) ->
                               return (I (n0 + n1))
...
_ev TT           denv = return (B True )
_ev FF           denv = return (B False)
_ev (Not e)      denv = ev e denv >>= \ (B b) ->
                               return (B (not b))
_ev (If e e0 e1) denv = ev e denv >>= \ (B b) ->
                               if b then ev e0 denv else ev e1 denv
```

Similarly to the case with the monadic interpreter, the clause for of Rec in the above code this does not quite work, because recursive calls get evaluated too eagerly, but the situation can be remedied by introducing a type constructor class DistCheat of which LV with Maybe will be an instance.

```
class Dist d t => DistCheat d t where
  cobindCheat :: (d a -> t b) -> (d a -> d (t b))

instance DistCheat LV Maybe where
  cobindCheat k d@(az := _) = cobindL k az := return (unJust (k d))
               where cobindL k Nil = Nil
                     cobindL k (az :> a) = cobindL k az :> k (az := a)
```

Using the operation of the DistCheat class, the meaning of Rec can be redefined to yield a working solution.

```
class DistCheat d t => DistEv d t where ...

_ev (Rec e) denv = ev e denv >>= \ (F f) ->
                        dist (cobindCheat (_ev (Rec e)) denv) >>= \ d->
                        f d
```

The meanings of the constructs specific to the extension are also dictated by the types and here we can and must of course use the specific operations of the particular comonad and monad.

```
instance DistEv LV Maybe where
  ev (e0 'Fby' e1)   denv = ev e0 denv 'fbyLV' cobind (ev e1) denv
  ev Nosig           denv = raise
  ev (e0 'Merge' e1) denv = ev e0 denv 'handle' ev e1 denv
```

The partial, causal version of the sieve of Eratosthenes from Section 2 is defined as follows.

```
-- sieve x = if (tt fby ff) then x
--             else sieve (if (x mod ini x /= 0) then x else nosig)
sieve = Rec (L "sieve" (L "x" (
               If (TT 'Fby' FF)
                  (V "x")
                  (V "sieve" :@
                     (If ((V "x" 'Mod' (ini :@ V "x")) :/= N 0)
                         (V "x")
                         Nosig)))))
-- eratosthenes = sieve (pos + 2)
eratosthenes = sieve :@ (pos :+ N 2)
```

Indeed, testing the above program, we get exactly what we would wish.

```
> runLVM (ev eratosthenes) (cmap Just emptyS)
Just 2 :< (Just 3 :< (Nothing :< (Just 5 :< (Nothing :< (Just 7 :< (
Nothing :< (Nothing :< (Nothing :< (Just 11 :< (Nothing :< (Just 13 :< (
Nothing :< (Nothing :< (Nothing :< (Just 17 :< ...
```

7   Related Work

Semantic studies of Lucid, Lustre and Lucid Synchrone-like languages are not many and concentrate largely on the so-called clock calculus for static well-clockedness checking [10,11,14]. Relevantly for us, however, Colaço et al. [13] have very recently proposed a higher-order synchronous dataflow language extending Lucid Synchrone, with two type constructors of function spaces.

Hughes's arrows [19] have been picked up very well by the functional programming community (for overviews, see [30,20]). There exists by now not only a de facto standardized arrow library in Haskell, but even specialized syntax [29]. The main application is functional reactive programming with its specializations to animation, robotics etc. [27,18]. Functional reactive programming is of course the same as dataflow programming, except that it is done by functional programmers rather than the traditional dataflow languages community. The exact relationship between Hughes's arrows and Power and Robinson's symmetric premonoidal categories has been established recently by Jacobs and colleagues [21,22].

Uses of comonads in semantics have been very few. Brookes and Geva [8] were the first to suggest to exploit comonads in semantics. They realized that, in order for the coKleisli category of a comonad to have exponential-like objects, the comonad has to come with a zip-like operation (they called it "merge"), but did not formulate the axioms of a symmetric monoidal comonad. Kieburtz [23] made an attempt to draw the attention of functional programmers to comonads. Lewis et al. [25] must have contemplated employing the product comonad to handle implicit parameters (see the conclusion of their paper), but did not carry out the project. Comonads have also been used in the semantics of intuitionistic linear logic and modal logics [5,7], with their applications in staged computation and elsewhere, see e.g., [15], and to analyse structured recursion schemes, see e.g., [39,28,9]. In the semantics of intuitionistic linear and modal logics, comonads are strong symmetric monoidal.

Our comonadic approach to stream-based programming is, to the best of our knowledge, entirely new. This is surprising, given how elementary it is. Workers in dataflow languages have produced a number of papers exploiting the final coalgebraic structure of streams [12,24,4], but apparently nothing on stream functions and comonads. The same is true about works in universal coalgebra [34,35].

8   Conclusions and Future Work

We have shown that notions of dataflow computation can be structured by suitable comonads, thus reinforcing the old idea that one should be able to use comonads to structure notions of context-dependent computation. We have demonstrated that the approach is fruitful with generic comonadic and distributivity-based interpreters that effectively suggest designs of dataflow languages. This is thanks to the rich structure present in comonads and distributive laws which essentially forces many design decisions (compare this to the much weaker structure in arrow types). Remarkably, the language designs that these interpreters suggest either coincide with the designs known from the dataflow languages literature or improve on them (when it comes to higher-orderness or to the choice of the primitive constructs in the case of clocked dataflow). For us, this is a solid proof of the true essence and structure of dataflow computation lying in comonads.

For future work, we envisage the following directions, in each of which we have already taken the first steps. First, we wish to obtain a solid understanding of the mathematical properties of our comonadic and distributivity-based semantics. Second, we plan to look at guarded recursion schemes associated to the comonads for stream functions and at language designs based on corresponding constructs. Third, we plan to test our interpreters on other comonads (e.g., decorated tree types) and see if they yield useful computation paradigms and language designs. Fourth, we also intend to study the pragmatics of the combination of two comonads via a distributive law. We believe that this will among other things explicate the underlying enabling structure of language designs such Multidimensional Lucid [3] where flows are multidimensional arrays. Fifth, the interpreters we have provided have been designed as reference specifications of language semantics. As implementations, they are grossly inefficient because of careless use of recursion, and we plan to investigate systematic efficient implementation of the languages they specify based on interpreter transformations. Sixth, we intend to take a close look at continuous-time event-based dataflow computation.

Acknowledgments. We are grateful to Neil Ghani for his suggestion to also look into distributive laws. This work was partially supported by the Estonian Science Foundation grant No. 5567.

References

1. P. Aczel, J. Adámek, S. Milius, J. Velebil. Infinite trees and completely iterative theories: A coalgebraic view. *Theoret. Comput. Sci.*, 300 (1-3), pp. 1-45, 2003.
2. E. A. Ashcroft, W. W. Wadge. *LUCID, The Dataflow Programming Language.* Academic Press, New York, 1985.
3. E. A. Ashcroft, A. A. Faustini, R. Jagannathan, W. W. Wadge. *Multidimensional Programming.* Oxford University Press, New York, 1995.
4. B. Barbier. Solving stream equation systems. In *Actes 13mes Journées Francophones des Langages Applicatifs, JFLA 2002*, pp. 117-139. 2002.
5. N. Benton, G. Bierman, V. de Paiva, M. Hyland. Linear lambda-calculus and categorical models revisited. In E. Börger et al., eds, *Proc. of 6th Wksh. on Computer Science Logic, CSL '92*, v. 702 of *Lect. Notes in Comput. Sci.*, pp. 61-84. Springer-Verlag, Berlin, 1993.
6. N. Benton, J. Hughes, E. Moggi. Monads and effects. In G. Barthe, P. Dybjer, L. Pinto, J. Saraiva, eds., *Advanced Lectures from Int. Summer School on Applied Semantics, APPSEM 2000*, v. 2395 of *Lect. Notes in Comput. Sci.*, pp. 42-122. Springer-Verlag, Berlin, 2002.
7. G. Bierman, V. de Paiva. On an intuitionistic modal logic. *Studia Logica*, 65(3), pp. 383-416, 2000.
8. S. Brookes, S. Geva. Computational comonads and intensional semantics. In M. P. Fourman, P. T. Johnstone, and A. M. Pitts, eds., *Applications of Categories in Computer Science*, v. 177 of *London Math. Society Lecture Note Series*, pp. 1-44. Cambridge Univ. Press, Cambridge, 1992.
9. V. Capretta, T. Uustalu, V. Vene. Recursive coalgebras from comonads. *Inform. and Comput.*, 204(4), pp. 437-468, 2006.
10. P. Caspi. Clocks in dataflow languages. *Theoret. Comput. Sci.*, 94(1), pp. 125-140, 1992.
11. P. Caspi, M. Pouzet. Synchronous Kahn networks. In *Proc. of 1st ACM SIGPLAN Int. Conf. on Functional Programming, ICFP'96*, pp. 226-238. ACM Press, New York, 1996. Also in *ACM SIGPLAN Notices*, 31(6), pp. 226-238, 1996.
12. P. Caspi, M. Pouzet. A co-iterative characterization of synchronous stream functions. In B. Jacobs, L. Moss, H. Reichel, J. Rutten, eds., *Proc. of 1st Wksh. on Coalgebraic Methods in Computer Science, CMCS'98*, v. 11 of *Electron. Notes in Theoret. Comput. Sci.*. Elsevier, Amsterdam, 1998.
13. J.-L. Colaço, A. Girault, G. Hamon, M. Pouzet. Towards a higher-order synchronous data-flow language. In *Proc. of 4th ACM Int. Conf. on Embedded Software, EMSOFT'04*, pp. 230-239. ACM Press, New York, 2004.
14. J.-L. Colaço, M. Pouzet. Clocks and first class abstract types. In R. Alur, I. Lee, eds., *Proc. of 3rd Int. Conf. on Embedded Software, EMSOFT 2003*, v. 2855 of *Lect. Notes in Comput. Sci.*, pp. 134-155. Springer-Verlag, Berlin, 2003.

15. R. Davies, F. Pfenning. A modal analysis of staged computation. *J. of ACM*, 48(3), pp. 555-604, 2001.
16. L. Erkök, J. Launchbury. Monadic recursive bindings. In *Proc. of 5th ACM SIG-PLAN Int. Conf. on Functional Programming, ICFP'00*, pp. 174-185. ACM Press, New York, 2000. Also in *ACM SIGPLAN Notices*, 35(9), pp. 174-185, 2000.
17. N. Halbwachs, P. Caspi, P. Raymond, D. Pilaud. The synchronous data flow programming language LUSTRE. *Proc. of the IEEE*, 79(9), pp. 1305-1320, 1991.
18. P. Hudak, A. Courtney, H. Nilsson, J. Peterson. Arrows, robots, and functional programming. In J. Jeuring, S. Peyton Jones, eds., *Revised Lectures from 4th Int. School on Advanced Functional Programming, AFP 2002*, v. 2638 of *Lect. Notes in Comput. Sci.*, pp. 159-187. Springer-Verlag, Berlin, 2003.
19. J. Hughes. Generalising monads to arrows. *Sci. of Comput. Program.*, 37(1-3), pp. 67-111, 2000.
20. J. Hughes. Programming with arrows. In V. Vene, T. Uustalu, eds., *Revised Lectures from 5th Int. School on Advanced Functional Programming, AFP 2004*, v. 3622 of *Lect. Notes in Comput. Sci.*, pp. 73-129. Springer-Verlag, Berlin, 2005.
21. C. Heunen, B. Jacobs. Arrows, like monads, are monoids. In S. Brookes, M. Mislove, eds., *Proc. of 22nd Ann. Conf. on Mathematical Foundations of Programming Semantics, MFPS XXII*, v. 158 of *Electron. Notes in Theoret. Comput. Sci.*, pp. 219-236. Elsevier, Amsterdam, 2006.
22. B. Jacobs, I. Hasuo. Freyd is Kleisli, for arrows. In C. McBride, T. Uustalu, *Proc. of Wksh. on Mathematically Structured Programming, MSFP 2006, Electron. Wkshs. in Computing*. BCS, 2006.
23. R. B. Kieburtz. Codata and comonads in Haskell. Unpublished manuscript, 1999.
24. R. B. Kieburtz. Coalgebraic techniques for reactive functional programming, In *Actes 11mes Journées Francophones des Langages Applicatifs, JFLA 2000*, pp. 131-157. 2000.
25. J. R. Lewis, M. B. Shields, E. Meijer, J. Launchbury. Implicit parameters: Dynamic scoping with static types. In *Proc. of 27th ACM SIGPLAN-SIGACT Symp. on Principles of Programming Languages, POPL'00*, pp. 108-118. ACM Press, New York, 2000.
26. E. Moggi. Notions of computation and monads. *Inform. and Comput.*, 93(1), pp. 55-92, 1991.
27. H. Nilsson, A. Courtney, J. Peterson. Functional reactive programming, continued. In *Proc. of 2002 ACM SIGPLAN Wksh. on Haskell, Haskell'02*, pp. 51-64. ACM Press, New York, 2002.
28. A. Pardo. Generic accumulations. J. Gibbons, J. Jeuring, eds., *Proc. of IFIP TC2/WG2.1 Working Conf. on Generic Programming*, v. 243 of *IFIP Conf. Proc.*, pp. 49-78. Kluwer, Dordrecht, 2003.
29. R. Paterson. A new notation for arrows. In *Proc. of 6th ACM SIGPLAN Int. Conf. on Functional Programming, ICFP'01*, ACM Press, New York, pp. 229-240, 2001. Also in *ACM SIGPLAN Notices*, 36(10), pp. 229-240, 2001.
30. R. Paterson. Arrows and computation. In J. Gibbons, O. de Moor, eds., *The Fun of Programming, Cornerstones of Computing*, pp. 201-222. Palgrave MacMillan, Basingstoke / New York, 2003.
31. M. Pouzet. Lucid Synchrone: tutorial and reference manual. Unpublished manuscript, 2001.
32. J. Power, E. Robinson. Premonoidal categories and notions of computation. *Math. Structures in Comput. Sci.*, 7(5), pp. 453-468, 1997.
33. J. Power, H. Watanabe. Combining a monad and a comonad. *Theoret. Comput. Sci.*, 280(1-2), pp. 137-162, 2002.

34. J. J. M. M. Rutten. Universal coalgebra: a theory of systems. *Theoret. Comput. Sci.*, 249(1), pp. 3–80, 2000.
35. J. J. M. M. Rutten. Behavioural differential equations: a coinductive calculus of streams, automata, and power series. *Theoret. Comput. Sci.*, 308(1–3), pp. 1–53, 2003.
36. T. Uustalu, V. Vene. The dual of substitution is redecoration. In K. Hammond, S. Curtis (Eds.), *Trends in Functional Programming 3*, pp. 99–110. Intellect, Bristol / Portland, OR, 2002.
37. T. Uustalu, V. Vene. Signals and comonads. *J. of Univ. Comput. Sci.*, 11(7), pp. 1310-1326, 2005.
38. T. Uustalu, V. Vene. The essence of dataflow programming (short version). In K. Yi, ed., *Proc. of 3rd Asian Symp. on Programming Languages and Systems, APLAS 2005*, v. 3780 of *Lect. Notes in Comput. Sci.*, pp. 2–18. Springer-Verlag, Berlin, 2005.
39. T. Uustalu, V. Vene, A. Pardo. Recursion schemes from comonads. *Nordic J. of Computing*, 8(3), pp. 366–390, 2001.
40. P. Wadler. The essence of functional programming. In *Conf. Record of 19th Ann. ACM SIGPLAN-SIGACT Symp. on Principles of Programming Languages, POPL'92*, pp. 1–14. ACM Press, New York, 1992.
41. P. Wadler. Monads for functional programming. In M. Broy, ed., *Program Design Calculi: Proc. of Marktoberdorf Summer School 1992*, v. 118 of *NATO ASI Series F*, pp. 233–264. Springer-Verlag, Berlin, 1993. Also in J. Jeuring, E. Meijer, eds., *Tutorial Text from 1st Int. Spring School on Advanced Functional Programming Techniques AFP '95*, v. 925 of *Lect. Notes in Comput. Sci.*, pp. 24–52. Springer-Verlag, Berlin, 1995.

Temporal Properties of Clean Programs Proven in Sparkle-T*

Máté Tejfel, Zoltán Horváth, and Tamás Kozsik

Department of Programming Languages and Compilers
Eötvös Loránd University, Budapest, Hungary
{matej, hz, kto}@inf.elte.hu

Abstract. In a pure functional language a series of values computed from one another can be considered as different states of the same "abstract object". For this abstract object temporal properties (e.g. invariants) can be formulated and proved. This paper explains how to define and prove certain kinds of temporal properties of programs written in the pure functional language Clean. Sparkle, a theorem prover designed for Clean, is applied as a tool. Since Sparkle is not capable of handling temporal logical properties, its original version has been extended to support object abstraction, certain temporal properties and a new form of theorems which includes hypotheses. The resulting system is called Sparkle-T. The examples presented in this paper illustrate how object abstraction and the definition and proof of temporal properties can be carried out in Sparkle-T. Furthermore, some novel features of the Sparkle-T system are demonstrated as well.

1 Introduction

Temporal logic is a language for specifying properties of reactive and distributed systems. It is very useful for proving the correctness of (sequential or parallel) imperative programs.

When proving the correctness of functional programs, the practicability of temporal operators is not so obvious. In a pure functional programming language a variable is a value, like in mathematics, and not an object that can change its value in time, viz. during program execution. Due to referential transparency, reasoning about functional programs can be accomplished with fairly simple mathematical machinery, using, for example, classical logic and induction (see [21]). This fact is one of the basic advantages of functional programs over imperative ones.

In our opinion, however, in certain cases it is natural to express our knowledge about the behaviour of a functional program (or, we had better say, our knowledge about the values the program computes) in terms of temporal logical

---

* Supported by the Hungarian National Science Research Grant (OTKA), Grant Nr.T037742 and by the Bolyai Research Scholarship of the Hungarian Academy of Sciences.

Z. Horváth (Ed.): CEFP 2005, LNCS 4164, pp. 168–190, 2006.

operators. Moreover, in the case of parallel or distributed functional programs, temporal properties are exactly as useful as they are in the case of imperative programs. For example, those invariants which are preserved by all components of a distributed or parallel program, are also preserved by the compound program.

From this point of view, certain values computed during the evaluation of a functional program can be regarded as successive values of the same "abstract object". This corresponds directly to the view which certain object-oriented functional languages hold.

For our research Clean [23], a lazy, pure functional language was chosen. One benefit of this choice is that a theorem prover, Sparkle [21] is already built into the integrated development environment of Clean. Sparkle supports reasoning about Clean programs almost directly.

Earlier we provided correctness proofs about interactive, concurrent (interleaved) Clean programs, namely Object IO processes in [14,15]. However, these proofs were carried out by hand. We argue that the extension of the theorem prover with tools supporting temporal logical operators makes the reasoning about interactive or concurrent Clean programs easier, since temporal logical reasoning can be performed *within* the theorem prover.

In order to formulate and prove temporal properties of a Clean program, the "abstract objects" have to be determined, that is it has to be specified which functional (mathematical) values correspond to different states of the same abstract object. Therefore, Clean and correspondingly Sparkle have to be extended with some new elements. The extended Sparkle system is called *Sparkle-T*, where T stands for "temporal". The formal description of how Sparkle-T handles object abstraction and temporal logical properties was presented in [24]. This paper is more pragmatic—it focuses on examples that demonstrate the way Sparkle-T works. Furthermore, some novel features (e.g. temporal logical formulae depending on hypotheses, and support for case-expressions, patterns and guards) required in more subtle examples are introduced as well.

There are several kinds of temporal logic, e.g. Linear Temporal Logic (LTL), Computation Tree Logic (CTL) etc. This paper uses a UNITY-like special temporal logic [4]. The main operators of this logic are the *invariant, unless, always, ensures* and *leads-to* operators. All these operators can be expressed with the help of the "weakest precondition" operator [6,13]. The weakest precondition can be computed in an automated way using the concept of substitution. In our approach interleaving semantics is used for programs: this means that each legal execution of a program is equivalent to some sequential execution of its atomic statements—these statements will be referred to as state transitions.

The rest of the paper is structured as follows. First the used temporal logical operators are described briefly (Section 2). Then the object abstraction method and the way to express temporal propositions in the Sparkle-T framework is introduced through a simplistic example (Section 3). Next a more sophisticated example is provided with an *invariant* and an *unless* property (Section 4).

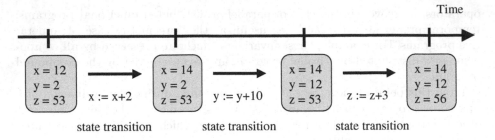

Fig. 1. Invariant property: $x > 0 \wedge y > 0 \wedge z > 0$

Finally, the discussion of related work is presented and conclusions are drawn (Section 5).

2 Temporal Logical Operators

In an imperative model of programming the execution of a program corresponds to a series of "state transitions": a state describes the actual values of the program objects (variables). The characteristic function of a certain set of states is called a "condition". A condition is a logical function over the "state space". Temporal logical operators are mathematical entities that operate on programs and conditions.

Sparkle-T currently supports the *invariant*, *unless* and *always* temporal logical operators. In the future, besides these "safety" operators some "progress" operators (*ensures* and *leads-to*) will also be added to Sparkle-T.

A condition A is an invariant with respect to a program P and an initial condition B (written as "A $\underline{\text{INV}}(P)$ B") if A "holds initially" (namely B implies A) and all the state transitions of program P preserve A. As a consequence, A holds during the whole program execution if B holds initially. Consider, for instance, the following program skeleton $P_1(dx, dy, dz)$ written in an imperative style. Let x, y and z be three objects (variables, in the imperative sense), furthermore dx, dy and dz be three values (input parameters). The program is the sequence of three atomic state transitions.

$$P_1(dx, dy, dz) = \left\{ \begin{array}{l} x := x + dx \\ y := y + dy \\ z := z + dz \end{array} \right\} \tag{1}$$

A possible execution of $P_1(2, 10, 3)$ with initial values $x = 12$, $y = 2$ and $z = 53$ is illustrated on Fig. 1. Obviously, if the input parameters dx, dy and dz are all positive, then $P_1(dx, dy, dz)$ satisfies the following *invariant* property.

$$(x > 0 \wedge y > 0 \wedge z > 0) \ \underline{\text{INV}}(P_1(dx, dy, dz)) \ (x > 0 \wedge y > 0 \wedge z > 0) \tag{2}$$

Another interesting temporal logical operator is the *unless* operator. Informally, "A $\underline{\text{UNLESS}}(P)$ B" means that during the execution of the program P, there is no state transition from $A \wedge \neg B$ to $\neg A \wedge \neg B$. Therefore, if $A \wedge \neg B$ holds in a particular state during the execution of P, then in the next state either A or B should hold. For example, if the input parameters dx, dy and dz are positive, then $P_1(dx, dy, dz)$ satisfies the following *unless* property.

$$(x > 0 \wedge y > 0 \wedge z > 0) \ \underline{\text{UNLESS}}(P_1(dx, dy, dz)) \ \text{FALSE} \tag{3}$$

This is a special kind of *unless* property, where the right-hand side is the FALSE condition. This property expresses that the left-hand side condition is preserved by all state transitions of the program—note that this is also necessary for the *invariant* property to hold.

Finally, the *always* operator indicates that a condition A holds during the execution of program P, if condition B holds initially: "$A \ \underline{\text{ALWAYS}}(P) \ B$". It is worth noting that *always* is not equivalent to *invariant*. Each *invariant* property is an *always* property, but there are *always* properties that are not *invariant* properties. For example, let dx, dy and dz be positive values and let $x \cdot y$ denote the product of x and y. Then the temporal logical assertion

$$(x \cdot y > 0) \ \underline{\text{ALWAYS}}(P_1(dx, dy, dz)) \ (x > 0 \wedge y > 0 \wedge z > 0) \tag{4}$$

is valid. However, the state transitions do not necessarily preserve condition $x \cdot y > 0$, hence $\underline{\text{ALWAYS}}$ cannot be replaced with $\underline{\text{INV}}$ here. This can be shown very easily with the formal definitions of the above temporal logical operators.

The definition of *unless* is formalized with the weakest precondition operator [6] in the following way.

$$A \ \underline{\text{UNLESS}}(P) \ B \quad \equiv \quad A \wedge \neg B \Rightarrow \text{wp}(P, \ A \vee B) \tag{5}$$

Namely, the weakest precondition $\text{wp}(t, A \vee B)$ of every state transition t of program P with respect to "$A \vee B$" must follow from "$A \wedge \neg B$".

$$\text{For all statements } t \text{ in program } P: \quad A \wedge \neg B \Rightarrow \text{wp}(t, \ A \vee B). \tag{6}$$

The weakest precondition $\text{wp}(t, X)$ of a state transition t with respect to a postcondition X is a condition—a condition that holds for a state s if and only if statement t, starting from s, always terminates in some state $s' \in t(s)$ for which the postcondition holds: $X(s') = \text{True}$. To give a formal definition, some further notations are needed. Let $t(s)$ denote the set of states that can be reached from state s by executing (the possibly non-deterministic) statement t. Moreover, let $\bot \in t(s)$ mean that the execution of t from state s may abort. (Undefined results are usually denoted by $\bot$.)

$$\text{wp}(t, X)(s) \quad = \quad \bot \notin t(s) \ \wedge \ \forall s' \in t(s) : X(s') \tag{7}$$

The weakest precondition of a statement can be computed in an automated way: the postcondition has to be rewritten according to the substitution rules defined by the state transition. This simple algorithm is illustrated in the example below. The algorithm substitutes the object y with its new value $y + 10$

in the investigated condition $x \cdot y > 0$ according the (deterministic) statement $y := y + 10$.

$$
\begin{aligned}
\mathrm{wp}(y := y + 10, \ x \cdot y > 0) \ &\equiv \ (x \cdot y > 0)[y \leftarrow y + 10] \\
&\equiv \ \big(x \cdot (y + 10) > 0\big) \tag{8}
\end{aligned}
$$

The formal definition of "$A \ \underline{\mathrm{INV}}(P) \ B$" is as follows.

$$
B \Rightarrow A \quad \text{and} \quad A \Rightarrow \mathrm{wp}(P, A) \tag{9}
$$

Note that "$A \ \underline{\mathrm{UNLESS}}(P) \ \mathrm{FALSE}$" is equivalent to the second part of this definition. Consider again property (4) and let us prove that $\underline{\mathrm{ALWAYS}}$ cannot be replaced with $\underline{\mathrm{INV}}$. According to (9), all state transitions of $P_1(dx, dy, dz)$ must preserve $x \cdot y > 0$, if dx, dy and dz are positive. In the case of, for example, the second state transition, however, this requires that $(x \cdot y > 0) \Rightarrow \big(x \cdot (y + 10) > 0\big)$ (see (8)), which does *not* hold: consider, for instance, the situation when $x = y = -1$.

Invariants characterize those states which are reachable during the execution of a program; if $A \ \underline{\mathrm{INV}}(P) \ B$ holds, $A(s) = \mathrm{False}$ and program P is started from a state s_0 such that $B(s_0) = \mathrm{True}$, then state s is not reachable during that execution of P. This yields the definition of the *always* operator: $A \ \underline{\mathrm{ALWAYS}}(P) \ B$ holds, if and only if there is a condition C such that $C \ \underline{\mathrm{INV}}(P) \ B$ and $C \Rightarrow A$. To prove (4), consider the *invariant* property in (2).

As the definitions reveal, on the one hand, the requirements for *invariants* are more strict than those for *always* properties: each *invariant* property is an *always* property. On the other hand, the example presented in (4) proved that there are *always* properties that are not *invariants*. At first glance, the concept of *always* properties might seem more sensible than that of *invariants*. However, *invariants* become extremely useful when programs are created from components. Invariant properties of components will be invariants of the compound program, but the same is not true in the case of *always* properties.

The definition of *ensures* and *leads-to* can be found in e.g. [4,13].

3   Object Abstraction

Before formulating and proving temporal properties of a functional program, "abstract objects" have to be defined. To denote them two new language constructs are needed. One of the constructs will be used to define which values (functional variables) correspond to different states of the same abstract object. The other construct will mark the state transitions of the program: in each state transition, one or more objects can change their values. State transitions will be regarded as atomic actions with respect to the temporal logical operators.

The first construct is denoted by ".|.". It has two arguments: an object identifier and a value identifier, like in " .|. object_id value_id ". This means that the value identified by value_id is associated to the abstract object identified by object_id, that is value_id identifies a state of object_id. The

```
move :: (Int, Int, Int) (Int, Int, Int) -> (Int, Int, Int)
move point3d (dx, dy, dz)
    # point3d = update1 point3d dx
    # point3d = update2 point3d dy
    # point3d = update3 point3d dz
    = point3d

update1 (x, y, z) d
    | MaxInt - d < x   = (x, y, z)
    | otherwise        = (x+d, y, z)

update2 (x, y, z) d
    | MaxInt - d < y   = (x, y, z)
    | otherwise        = (x, y+d, z)

update3 (x, y, z) d
    | MaxInt - d < z   = (x, y, z)
    | otherwise        = (x, y, z+d)
```

Fig. 2. Program P_2 = move point3d (dx,dy,dz)

second construct, used for marking steps, is similar to the let-before (#) construct of Clean, hence a similar syntax has been chosen for it: ".#.".

A function definition may introduce objects, only if the body of the function is made up of guards and let-before constructs. The objects are local to the function definition, and the same object name refers to the same object in this scope. (Defining multiple objects with the same name within the same function definition is forbidden.) Objects can only be used in "steps". In every binding within a step the same object can appear at most once on the left, and at most once on the right-hand side. Obviously, the variables constituting the states of an abstract object must be of the same type. Finally, we have to note that currently we only support objects within a single function definition: the variables that make up the states of the object must be defined in the same function.

In Fig. 2 a Clean program, which is similar to the imperative marked as (1), is shown. This program moves a point point3d in a 3D space by (dx, dy, dz). According to the Clean scoping rules this move function is equivalent to the one in Fig. 3.

Here the different point3d values are considered as different values of the same abstract object (for example point3d). Furthermore, we consider every let-before expression as a state transition. Using the two novel constructs .|. and .#., function move can be transposed to the one in Fig. 4. Note that the second argument of the move function is not considered an abstract object.

The rewritten code looks frightening, but there is no need to worry: this code is intended to be an intermediate code generated by an appropriate tool. The

```
move point3d_1 (dx, dy, dz)
    # point3d_2 = update1 point3d_1 dx
    # point3d_3 = update2 point3d_2 dy
    # point3d_4 = update3 point3d_3 dz
    = point3d_4
```

Fig. 3. P_2 with distinct variable names

```
move  (.|. point3d p1)  (dx, dy, dz)
    .#.  (.|. point3d p2)  =  update1 (.|. point3d p1) dx
    .#.  (.|. point3d p3)  =  update2 (.|. point3d p2) dy
    .#.  (.|. point3d p4)  =  update3 (.|. point3d p3) dz
    =    .|. point3d p4
```

Fig. 4. P_2 with object abstraction

tool—equipped with a graphical user interface—will make it possible to select those variables in the functional program that make up an abstract object.

Now an invariant property of P_2 is formulated. To make it shorter, an auxiliary function, allPos is introduced.

```
allPos ::  (Int, Int, Int)  -> Bool
allPos (x, y, z)  =  x>0 && y>0 && z>0
```

Similarly to the property in (2), the invariant states that if dx, dy and dz are all positive, and all coordinates of the point3d object are positive initially, then these coordinates remain invariantly positive during the execution of program P_2. Assumptions on the initial values of objects are given as pre-conditions of invariants, while assumptions on non-object values are provided as hypotheses.[1] Introduced variables and hypotheses are separated from the rest of the theorem by the $\models$ symbol.

$$point3d :: (\text{Int}, \text{Int}, \text{Int}), \quad p :: (\text{Int}, \text{Int}, \text{Int}), \quad d :: (\text{Int}, \text{Int}, \text{Int})$$

$$(\text{allPos } d)$$

$$\models \quad (\text{allPos } point3d) \; \underline{\text{INV}}(\text{move } p \; d) \; (\text{allPos } p) \tag{10}$$

---

[1] Sparkle makes it possible to use "introduced variables" and hypotheses in "goals", but not in "theorems". Sparkle-T, however, allows these two concepts to appear in theorems as well. The reason for this is that in the UNITY-based special temporal logic used in Sparkle-T the temporal logical operators can only appear in outermost positions.

p, d, $point3d\_var0$, $\_a$ :: $(\mathrm{Int}, \mathrm{Int}, \mathrm{Int})$
$(\mathrm{allPos}\ d)$, $\_a = d$, $(\mathrm{allPos}\ p)$
$\models$ $point3d\_var0 = p$ $\rightarrow$ $\mathrm{allPos}\ point3d\_var0$ (11)

p, d, $\_a$ :: $(\mathrm{Int}, \mathrm{Int}, \mathrm{Int})$
$(\mathrm{allPos}\ d)$, $\_a = d$, $(\mathrm{allPos}\ p)$
$\models$ $\neg(\_a = \bot)$ (12)

p, d, $\_a$, $point3d\_var1$, $point3d\_var1\_old$ :: $(\mathrm{Int}, \mathrm{Int}, \mathrm{Int})$
dx, dy, dz :: Int
$(\mathrm{allPos}\ d)$, $\_a = d$, $\_a = (dx, dy, dz)$
$\models$ $\mathrm{allPos}\ point3d\_var1\_old$
        $\rightarrow$ $point3d\_var1 = \mathrm{update1}\ point3d\_var1\_old\ dx$
        $\rightarrow$ $\mathrm{allPos}\ point3d\_var1$ (13)

p, d, $\_a$, $point3d\_var2$, $point3d\_var2\_old$ :: $(\mathrm{Int}, \mathrm{Int}, \mathrm{Int})$
dx, dy, dz :: Int
$(\mathrm{allPos}\ d)$, $\_a = d$, $\_a = (dx, dy, dz)$
$\models$ $\mathrm{allPos}\ point3d\_var2\_old$
        $\rightarrow$ $point3d\_var2 = \mathrm{update2}\ point3d\_var2\_old\ dy$
        $\rightarrow$ $\mathrm{allPos}\ point3d\_var2$ (14)

p, d, $\_a$, $point3d\_var3$, $point3d\_var3\_old$ :: $(\mathrm{Int}, \mathrm{Int}, \mathrm{Int})$
dx, dy, dz :: Int
$(\mathrm{allPos}\ d)$, $\_a = d$, $\_a = (dx, dy, dz)$
$\models$ $\mathrm{allPos}\ point3d\_var3\_old$
        $\rightarrow$ $point3d\_var3 = \mathrm{update3}\ point3d\_var3\_old\ dz$
        $\rightarrow$ $\mathrm{allPos}\ point3d\_var3$ (15)

Fig. 5. Subgoals from (10)

The proof of this theorem starts with the application of the INVARIANT tactic of Sparkle-T. This tactic splits the initial goal corresponding to the theorem into five subgoals, shown as (11–15) in Fig. 5.

Subgoal (11) corresponds to the first part of the definition of INV in (9): the invariant condition holds initially (viz. follows from the pre-condition). Subgoals

(13–15) correspond to the second part of the definition of INV: the three state transitions preserve the invariant condition. Finally, subgoal (12) and variable _a are required by the pattern matching that occurs at the second argument position of move. The subgoal ensures that the evaluation of this pattern expression does not yield an undefined result: if the pattern were undefined, the evaluation of move would abort.

The above subgoals can be proven in Sparkle-T in about two hundred proof steps (see Appendix A).

4   Temporal Properties of a Conditional Maximum Search

In this section a more realistic example of verifying invariant properties is presented. A well-known algorithm is analyzed—an algorithm that finds an element of the interval [low..high] for which, considering only those elements of this interval that satisfy the condition cond, function fun reaches its maximum. This algorithm can be nicely expressed in a functional language with the commonly used higher-order function while. The definition of while (in e.g. the standard libraries of Clean) looks almost like this. For the sake of simplicity, strictness and uniqueness annotations have been removed from the type declared for while.

```
while :: (a -> Bool) (a -> a) a -> a
while p f x
   | p x
     = while p f (f x)
   = x
```

The algorithm "conditional maximum search", or cms for short, can be implemented in Clean in the way shown in Fig. 6. One can make good use of the type Maybe from the standard Clean libraries as well.

Sparkle lifts local function definitions. Hence loop_condition and loop_body become global functions with the following types.

```
loop_condition ::  Int  State  ->  Bool
loop_body :: (Int -> Real) (Int -> Bool) State  ->  State
```

4.1   An *Invariant* Property

Invariants are used to describe safety requirements of systems. An important property of the concept of invariants is compositionality: if a condition is an invariant of all components of a program, then it is also an invariant of the whole program. The concept takes many forms, including, for example, type invariants, loop invariants, and synchronization invariants of parallel and distributed programs. Invariants are a powerful tool for expressing properties of parallel, distributed, event-driven and interactive *functional* programs as well. We have investigated how invariants of functional programs can be described in e.g. [16,17,24], and addressed type invariants in [18]. This section focuses on a loop invariant.

```
:: State = State Int (Maybe (Int,Real))

cms :: Int  Int  (Int -> Real)  (Int -> Bool)  ->  Maybe Int
cms low high fun cond
   = case (while loop_condition loop_body (State low Nothing)) of
           (State _ Nothing)                      -> Nothing
           (State _ (Just (maxpos,maxval)))    -> Just maxpos
   where
           loop_condition :: State -> Bool
           loop_condition (State pos _)  =  (pos <= high)

           loop_body :: State -> State
           loop_body (State pos maybeMax)
                   | not (cond pos)
                   = State (pos+1) maybeMax
           loop_body (State pos Nothing)
                   = State (pos+1) (Just (pos, fun pos))
           loop_body (State pos max=:(Just (maxpos,maxval)))
                   | curr > maxval
                   = State (pos+1) (Just (pos, curr))
                   = State (pos+1) max
                   where curr = fun pos
```

Fig. 6. Conditional maximum search

Loop invariants play an important role in the reasoning about imperative programs. An imperative implementation of the conditional maximum search algorithm contains a loop construct, and reasoning about the correctness of this imperative implementation also involves a loop invariant. How can we capture the concept of loop invariants in our approach to object abstraction? First of all, the objects should be identified by selecting and binding together those expressions occurring in the program that make up the different states of the objects. In this example there will be a single object called state of type State. The state changes of object state occur within the definition of function while. The following three expressions describe the states of this object (cf. the definition of while):

1. x
2. f x
3. while p f (f x)

Therefore there are two state transitions in the definition of while. The first one produces "f y" from some y, and the second one produces "while p f z" from some z. This is how while_, the transformed definition of while with explicit notation of objects and state transitions, is obtained. (It should be emphasised again that this kind of transformation will be supported by a software development tool, hence the programmer need not read or write code as in the one below.)

```
while_ p f (.|. state x)
  | p (.|. state x)
        .#. (.|. state x) = f (.|. state x)
        .#. (.|. state x) = while_ p f (.|. state x)
        = (.|. state x)
    = (.|. state x)
```

Some auxiliary functions are required for expressing the invariant property.

```
pos (State int _) = int
maxpos (State _ (Just mpos _) = mpos
maxval (State _ (Just _ mval) = mval
```

The invariant property of the algorithm that is addressed in this paper is the following. Consider the object **state**, an interval **[low,high]**, a function **fun** and a condition **cond**. If there is a **k** between **low** and "**pos state**" (viz. a k that was already investigated by the algorithm) for which **cond** holds, then there is a "maximum" stored in **state** (viz. the second component of **state** is not **Nothing**), and the stored maximum value is not smaller than "**fun k**".

For the sake of readability, some abbreviations ("macros") are introduced.

- $\text{DEF}(x)$ abbreviates the formula $\neg(x = \bot)$.
- $\text{DEFFUN}(f)$ abbreviates the formula
  $\forall k.((low \leq k \wedge k \leq high) \rightarrow \neg(f\ k = \bot))$.
- "A" abbreviates the introduced variables
  $state :: \text{State}, \quad low, high, k :: \text{Int}, \quad fun :: \text{Int} \rightarrow \text{Real}, \quad cond :: \text{Int} \rightarrow \text{Bool}.$
- "B" abbreviates the formula
  $\text{DEF}(low) \wedge \text{DEF}(high) \wedge \text{DEFFUN}(fun) \wedge \text{DEFFUN}(cond).$
- "C" abbreviates the formula
  $(low \leq k \wedge k < \text{pos } state \wedge cond\ k) \rightarrow (fun\ k \leq \text{maxval } state).$
- "P" abbreviates the program
  while_ (loop_condition $high$) (loop_body $fun\ cond$) (State low Nothing).

With these abbreviations, the theorem about the invariant property can be written as follows. Given the introduced variables A and hypotheses B, the formula C is an invariant of the subprogram P with respect to the pre-condition **TRUE**. Note that the abbreviations have to be expanded when the theorem is entered in Sparkle-T.

$$A,\ B\ \models\ C\ \underline{\text{INV}}(P)\ \text{TRUE} \qquad (16)$$

The proof of this theorem starts with the application of the INVARIANT tactic. This tactic replaces the theorem with the three subgoals (17–19) in Fig. 7. A formal description of the INVARIANT tactic of Sparkle-T is given in [24]. The resulting subgoals can be summarized as follows.

$state\_var0$ :: State,

f :: State $\rightarrow$ State, p :: State $\rightarrow$ Bool,

A, B,

p = loop_condition $high$, f = loop_body fun $cond$,

TRUE

$\models$ $state\_var0$ = State low Nothing

$\qquad \rightarrow$ $(low \leq k \ \wedge \ k <$ pos $state\_var0 \ \wedge \ cond\ k =$ True$)$

$\qquad \rightarrow$ $(fun\ k \leq$ maxval $state\_var0)$ $\qquad\qquad\qquad\qquad$ (17)

$state\_var1\_pat$ :: State,

f :: State $\rightarrow$ State, p :: State $\rightarrow$ Bool,

A, B,

p = loop_condition $high$, f = loop_body fun $cond$,

TRUE

$\models$ $($ $\quad(low \leq k \ \wedge \ k <$ pos $state\_var1\_pat \ \wedge \ cond\ k =$ True$)$

$\qquad\qquad \rightarrow$ $(fun\ k \leq$ maxval $state\_var1\_pat)$

$\quad) \rightarrow \neg(p\ state\_var1\_pat = \bot)$ $\qquad\qquad\qquad\qquad$ (18)

$state\_var2$, $state\_var2\_old$ :: State,

f :: State $\rightarrow$ State, p :: State $\rightarrow$ Bool,

A, B,

p = loop_condition $high$, f = loop_body fun $cond$,

$p\ state\_var2\_old$ = True

$\models$ $($ $\quad(low \leq k \ \wedge \ k <$ pos $state\_var2\_old \ \wedge \ cond\ k =$ True$)$

$\qquad\quad \rightarrow$ $(fun\ k \leq$ maxval $state\_var2\_old)$

$\quad)$

$\quad \rightarrow$ $state\_var2 = f\ state\_var2\_old$

$\quad \rightarrow$ $(low \leq k \ \wedge \ k <$ pos $state\_var2 \ \wedge \ cond\ k =$ True$)$

$\quad \rightarrow$ $(fun\ k \leq$ maxval $state\_var2)$ $\qquad\qquad\qquad\qquad$ (19)

Fig. 7. Subgoals obtained from (16)

- The invariant condition C follows from the pre-condition TRUE.
- The evaluation of `while_` starts with the evaluation of `p` on the current state of the object, namely `state_var1_pat`. The definedness of this expression has to be proven.

– Finally, the first state transition has to be analyzed. This is the case when p evaluates to **True** on the current state of the object.

There are two more cases which the INVARIANT tactic has to consider, but no subgoals are generated from these cases.

– When p is evaluated to **False** on the current state of the object: in this case no state transition happens, therefore no subgoal needs to be generated.
– When p is evaluated to **True** on the current state of the object, there are two state transitions. The first was already addressed in subgoal (19). The second state transition, the recursive application of **while** cannot violate the invariant: the same function is invoked with exactly the same arguments (values p and f, and object **state**), hence a co-inductive proof can be applied. Therefore no subgoal needs to be generated in this case.

The proof of the three subgoals can be handled in Sparkle-T in the same manner as in Sparkle.

4.2   An *Unless* Property

This section describes an *unless* property of the conditional maximum search algorithm with the same abstract object (**state**) and state transitions as seen in the previous section. (Another example of *unless* properties can be found in [24]. That example is given for the well-known dining philosophers problem.) The example presented here formulates that the "position" stored in **state** cannot change but by an increment of one.

First, an auxiliary function is required for expressing the *unless* property. The type class **eval** (from the standard library of Sparkle) is used to rule out undefined (and partially undefined) expressions. In this instance of **eval** the definedness of all components of a state is prescribed: the position, and—if present—the stored maximum position and value.

```
instance eval State
where eval (State int maybe) = eval int && eval maybe

instance eval (Maybe (Int,Real))
where eval Nothing = True
      eval (Just (mpos, mval)) = eval mpos && eval mval
```

Next an additional abbreviation is introduced, capturing legal values of a state s.

"LEGAL(s)" abbreviates the formula "*low* $\leq$ pos s $\wedge$ pos s $\leq$ *high* $\wedge$ eval s"

Furthermore, the abbreviations of the previous sections are also utilized.

Now the *unless* property can be formalized in the following way.

$$A, B \models \tag{20}$$
$$(\text{LEGAL}(state) \wedge \text{pos } state = k) \underline{\text{UNLESS}(P)} (\text{pos } state = k+1)$$

$state\_var1\_pat$ :: State,

f :: State $\rightarrow$ State, p :: State $\rightarrow$ Bool,

A, B,

$p = $ loop_condition $high$, $\quad f = $ loop_body fun $cond$,

$\models \quad \big($pos $state\_var1\_pat = k \ \land \ \text{LEGAL}(state\_var1\_pat)\big)$

$\qquad \land \ \neg($pos $state\_var1\_pat = k + 1)$

$\quad \rightarrow \ \neg(p \ state\_var1\_pat = \bot)$ $\hfill (21)$

$state\_var2$, $state\_var2\_old$ :: State,

f :: State $\rightarrow$ State, p :: State $\rightarrow$ Bool,

A, B,

$p = $ loop_condition $high$, $\quad f = $ loop_body fun $cond$,

$p \ state_var2_old = $ True

$\models \quad \big($pos $state\_var2\_old = k \ \land \ \text{LEGAL}(state\_var2\_old)\big)$

$\qquad \land \ \neg($pos $state\_var2\_old = k + 1)$

$\quad \rightarrow \ state\_var2 = f \ state\_var2\_old$

$\quad \rightarrow \ \big($pos $state\_var2 = k \ \land \ \text{LEGAL}(state\_var2)\big)$

$\qquad \lor \ ($pos $state\_var2 = k + 1)$ $\hfill (22)$

Fig. 8. Subgoals obtained from (20)

Applying the UNLESS tactic of Sparkle-T, the theorem given in (20) will be split into two subgoals: (21) and (22) in Fig. 8. The formal description of the behaviour of the UNLESS tactic can be found in [24]. The resulting subgoals can be summarized as follows.

– The evaluation of `while_` starts with the evaluation of `p` on the current state of the object, namely `state_var1_pat`. The definedness of this expression has to be proven.
– Then the first state transition has to be analyzed. This is the case when `p` evaluates to `True` on the current state of the object. Here the wp-based definition of UNLESS is used from (5).

Note that the above *unless* property (which is a safety property) could naturally be turned into a progress property, describing that a position between `low` and `high` will eventually be increased by 1 during the execution of the program. Indeed, the formal definition of the progress property *ensures* builds upon *unless* (see [4,13]).

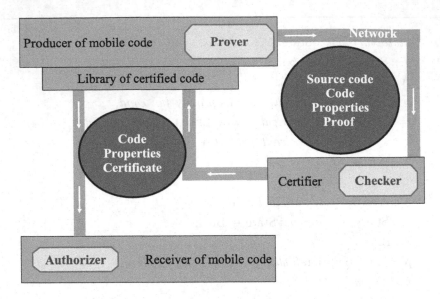

Fig. 9. CPPCC architecture

5   Conclusions

This paper introduced a method that allows the formulation and proof of invariant properties in the pure functional language Clean. The concept of object abstraction has been presented, which is based on contracting functional variables into objects which show dynamic (temporal) behaviour. Language constructs describing object abstraction have been introduced into Clean. We consider this extended Clean language as an intermediate language: programs written in this language are intended to be generated by an appropriate integrated development environment. Support for the new language constructs will thus be provided by a graphical user interface.

Programs written in the extended Clean language are processed by a theorem prover framework, Sparkle-T. This framework was obtained by enabling Sparkle, the theorem prover designed for Clean, to manage object abstraction and temporal propositions. This paper focuses on safety assertions, and presents detailed examples of *invariant* and *unless* properties.

Considering related work, a framework for reasoning about file I/O in Clean and Haskell programs is described in [3,8,9,10,11]. The semantics of file operations is defined in an explicit model of external world-state. Proofs are performed regarding the observable effect of real-world functional I/O. The Sparkle proof-assistant was used for machine-verify these proofs. Sparkle does not support Clean programs with I/O, so the proofs are meta-proofs and the properties of the I/O operations as state-transformers are not formulated in temporal logic. The state of the external world, including the file system can be regarded as an abstract object [14], of which temporal properties may be proved based on the lemmas about file-system operations presented in [9,11].

The initial results of our research on this topic were also related to functional (Clean) programs using I/O [14]. Then temporal properties of mobile code were addressed in [15]. In [16,17] the concept of object abstraction was introduced, and invariants of Clean programs were discussed. In these papers the correctness proofs were partially carried out by hand; namely, the INVARIANT tactic was not yet supported by a tool. Then [24] provided the semantical basis for Sparkle-T by extending Sparkle with a formal definition of *invariants* and *unless* properties and the corresponding tactics. Furthermore, the first implementation of the introduced concepts were described and used in some examples.

This paper enhances Sparkle-T in subtle ways. The concept of theorems is generalized to allow (classical logical) hypotheses. Hypotheses provide requirements addressing the parameters of programs. Moreover, support for programs containing case-expressions, guards and pattern matching was added to Sparkle-T. These novel features, illustrated in this paper in a number of examples, are necessary in the case of more sophisticated programs.

The advantage of our method is that the constructed proof is represented in a completely machine processable form. As a consequence, not only the program but also its proved temporal properties and the proofs themselves can be stored, transmitted or checked by a computer. This allows the transmission of the code between two remote applications in a safe manner. This transmission can be done, for example, with the Certified Proved-Property-Carrying Code (CPPCC) architecture, which contains the following three main components:

1. The producer of the mobile code adds properties of the code and their proofs.
2. The code receiver will execute the code only after all the checks have been performed.
3. The certifying authority reduces the work-load of the receiver.

Fig. 9 illustrates the CPPCC architecture. (The detailed presentation of this proof-carrying code technique can be found in [7].)

In the future the Sparkle-T framework will be made capable of handling additional temporal propositions, namely progress propositions (such as "ensures" and "leads-to" [4]). The implementation of additional tactics for the handling of these propositions is also planned. Furthermore, support for "composing specifications" [1] will be provided.

References

1. Abadi, M. – Lamport, L.: Composing specifications. *ACM Trans. Program. Lang. Syst.* 15, 1 (Jan. 1993), 73–132.
2. Achten, P., Plasmeijer, R.: Interactive Objects in Clean. *Proceedings of Implementation of Functional Languages, 9th International Workshop, IFL'97* (K. Hammond et al (eds)), St. Andrews, Scotland, UK, September 1997, LNCS 1467, pp. 304–321.
3. Butterfield, Andrew: Reasoning about I/O and Exceptions. *Proceedings of Implementation and Application of Functional Languages, IFL'04*, Lübeck, September 8–10, 2004., pp. 33–48.

4. Chandy, K. M., Misra, J.: *Parallel Program Design: a Foundation.* Addison-Wesley, 1989.
5. Dam, M., Fredlund, L., Gurov, D.: Toward Parametric Verification of Open Distributed Systems. *Compositionality: The Significant Difference* (H. Langmaack, A. Pnueli, W.-P. De Roever (eds)), Springer-Verlag 1998.
6. Dijkstra, E. W.: *A Discipline of Programming.* Prentice-Hall Inc., Englewood Cliffs (N.Y.), 1976.
7. Daxkobler K., Horváth Z., Kozsik T.: A Prototype of CPPCC - Safe Functional Mobile Code in Clean. *Proceedings of Implementation of Functional Languages'02,* Madrid, Spain, Sept. 15–19, 2002. pp. 301–310.
8. Dowse, M., Strong, G., Butterfield, A.: Proving Make Correct: I/O Proofs in Haskell and Clean. *Implementation of Functional Languages: 14th InternationalWorkshop, IFL 2002,* Madrid, Spain, September 16-18, 2002 Revised Selected Papers Springer, LNCS, Volume 2670 / 2003, pp. 68–83.
9. Dowse, M., Butterfield, A., van Eekelen, M., de Mol, M., Plasmeijer, R.: Towards Machine-Verified Proofs for I/O *Proceedings of Implementation and Application of Functional Languages, IFL'04,* Lübeck, September 8–10, 2004., pp. 469–480.
10. Dowse, M., Butterfield, A.: A Language for Reasoning about Concurrent Functional I/O (Draft) *Proceedings of Implementation and Application of Functional Languages, IFL'04,* Lübeck, September 8–10, 2004., pp. 129–141.
11. Dowse, M., Butterfield, A., van Eekelen, M.: Reasoning About Deterministic Concurrent Functional I/O *Implementation and Application of Functional Languages: 16th International Workshop, IFL 2004,* Lübeck, Germany, September 8-10, 2004 Revised Selected Papers Springer, LNCS, Volume 3474 / 2005, pp. 177–194.
12. Home of Clean. http://www.cs.kun.nl/~clean/
13. Horváth Z.: The Formal Specification of a Problem Solved by a Parallel Program— a Relational Model. *Annales Universitatis Scientiarum Budapestinensis de Rolando Eötvös Nominatae, Sectio Computatorica,* Tomus XVII. (1998) pp. 173–191.
14. Horváth Z., Achten, P., Kozsik T., Plasmeijer, R.: Proving the Temporal Properties of the Unique World. *Proceedings of the Sixth Symposium on Programming Languages and Software Tools,* Tallin, Estonia, August 1999. pp. 113–125.
15. Horváth Z., Achten, P., Kozsik T., Plasmeijer, R.: Verification of the Temporal Properties of Dynamic Clean Processes. *Proceedings of Implementation of Functional Languages, IFL'99,* Lochem, The Netherlands, Sept. 7–10, 1999. pp. 203–218.
16. Horváth Z. - Kozsik T. - Tejfel M.: Proving Invariants of Functional Programs. *Proceedings of Eighth Symposium on Programming Languages and Software Tools,* Kuopio, Finland, June 17–18, 2003., pp. 115–126
17. Horváth Z. - Kozsik T. - Tejfel M.: Verifying Invariants of Abstract Functional Objects - a case study. *6th International Conference on Applied Informatics,* Eger, Hungary January 27–31 2004.
18. Kozsik T., van Arkel, D., Plasmeijer, R.: Subtyping with Strengthening Type Invariants. *Proceedings of the 12th International Workshop on Implementation of Functional Languages* (M. Mohnen, P. Koopman (eds)), Aachener Informatik-Berichte, Aachen, Germany, September 2000. pp. 315–330.
19. Kozsik T.: Reasoning with Sparkle: a case study. *Technical Report,* Faculty of Informatics, Eötvös Loránd University, Budapest, Hungary.
20. de Mol, Maarten. PhD thesis (in preparation), Radboud University Nijmegen.
21. de Mol, M., van Eekelen, M., Plasmeijer, R.: Theorem Proving for Functional Programmers, Sparkle: A Functional Theorem Prover, Springer Verlag, LNCS 2312, p. 55 ff., 2001.

22. Peyton Jones, S., Hughes, J., et al. *Report on the Programming Language Haskell 98, A Non-strict, Purely Functional Language*, February 1999.
23. Plasmeijer, R., van Eekelen, M.: *Concurrent Clean Version 2.0 Language Report*, 2001. http://www.cs.kun.nl/~clean/Manuals/manuals.html
24. Tejfel M., Horváth Z., Kozsik T.: Extending the Sparkle Core language with object abstraction. *Acta Cybernetica* Vol. 17 (2005). pp. 419–445.

A   An Example Proof in Sparkle-T

This section describes the structure of a proof in Sparkle-T. The format used here is not exactly as the SEC file format used by Sparkle (and Sparkle-T) to export proofs: to increase readability, at certain places small modifications were made.

```
THEOREM bool_sub    : [x] ( ~(x=_|_) -> ~(x = True) -> x = False )


PROOF:
  Induction x.
  1. Definedness.
  2. Introduce H1 H2.
     Contradiction H2.
     Reflexive.
  3. Reflexive.


THEOREM point2
  : [allPos d] |=== (allPos point3d) INV(move_o p d) (allPos p)


PROOF:
  Auto_Open.
  Invariant.
  1. Introduce H4.
     Rewrite -> All H4.
     Apply H3.
  2. Contradiction.
     Rewrite <- All H2 in H1.
     Rewrite -> All H4 in H1.
     ReduceH NF All in H1 ( ).
     Definedness.
  3. Reduce NF All ( ).
     SplitCase 1.
     1. Definedness.
     2. SplitCase 1.
        1. Definedness.
        2. SplitCase 1.
           1. Definedness.
           2. Introduce H8.
```

```
SplitCase 1.
1. RefineUndefinednessH H9.
   Case Deep H9.
   1. RefineUndefinednessH H9.
      Case Deep H9.
      1. Definedness.
      2. Rewrite -> All H9 in H4.
         Rewrite -> All H4 in H2.
         Rewrite <- All H2 in H1.
         ReduceH NF All in H1 (  ).
         Definedness.
   2. Definedness.
2. Introduce H10.
   Rewrite -> All H10.
   Reduce NF All (  ).
   Rewrite -> All H6.
   Rewrite -> All H7.
   Rewrite -> All H8.
   Reduce NF All (  ).
   Reflexive.
3. Introduce H10.
   Rewrite -> All H10.
   Reduce NF All (  ).
   Rewrite -> All H7.
   Rewrite -> All H8.
   Reduce NF All (  ).
   Assume (0 < x + dx).
   1. Rewrite -> All H11.
      Reduce NF All (  ).
      Reflexive.
   2. Apply "add_right2_of_<".
      Split Deep.
      1. Apply H6.
      2. Rewrite -> All H4 in H2.
         Rewrite <- All H2 in H1.
         ReduceH NF All in H1 (  ).
         Assume (0 < dx).
         1. IntCompare.
         2. Contradiction.
            Assume (0 < dx = False).
            1. Rewrite -> All H12 in H1.
               ReduceH NF All in H1 (  ).
               AbsurdEqualityH H1.
            2. Apply "bool_sub".
               Split Deep.
```

```
                        1. Definedness.
                        2. Apply H11.
            3. Introduce H8.
               AbsurdEqualityH H8.
         3. Introduce H7.
            AbsurdEqualityH H7.
4. Reduce NF All ( ).
   SplitCase 1.
   1. Definedness.
   2. SplitCase 1.
      1. Definedness.
      2. SplitCase 1.
         1. Definedness.
         2. SplitCase 1.
            1. RefineUndefinednessH H8.
               Case Deep H8.
               1. RefineUndefinednessH H8.
                  Case Deep H8.
                  1. Definedness.
                  2. Rewrite -> All H8 in H4.
                     Rewrite -> All H4 in H2.
                     Rewrite <- All H2 in H1.
                     ReduceH NF All in H1 ( ).
                     Cut H1.
                     SplitCase 1.
                     1. Definedness.
                     2. Definedness.
                     3. Introduce H10.
                        AbsurdEqualityH H10.
            2. Definedness.
         2. Introduce H9 H10.
            Rewrite -> All H10.
            Reduce NF All ( ).
            Rewrite -> All H6.
            Rewrite -> All H7.
            Rewrite -> All H9.
            Reduce NF All ( ).
            Reflexive.
         3. Introduce H9 H10.
            Rewrite -> All H10.
            Reduce NF All ( ).
            Rewrite -> All H6.
            Rewrite -> All H9.
            Reduce NF All ( ).
            Assume (0 < y + dy).
```

```
            1. Rewrite -> All H11.
               Reduce NF All ( ).
               Reflexive.
            2. Apply "add_right2_of_<".
               Split Deep.
               1. Apply H7.
               2. Apply "bool_sub".
                  Split Deep.
                  1. Definedness.
                  2. Rewrite -> All H4 in H2.
                     Rewrite <- All H2 in H1.
                     ReduceH NF All in H1 ( ).
                     Cut H1.
                     SplitCase 1.
                     1. Definedness.
                     2. SplitCase 1.
                        1. Definedness.
                        2. Introduce H13.
                           Apply "reverse_<" to H12.
                           Rewrite -> All H14.
                           Contradiction.
                           AbsurdEqualityH H15.
                        3. Introduce H13.
                           AbsurdEqualityH H13.
                     3. Introduce H12.
                        AbsurdEqualityH H12.
         3. Introduce H8.
            AbsurdEqualityH H8.
       3. Introduce H7.
          AbsurdEqualityH H7.
5. Reduce NF All ( ).
   SplitCase 1.
   1. Definedness.
   2. SplitCase 1.
      1. Definedness.
      2. SplitCase 1.
         1. Definedness.
         2. SplitCase 1.
            1. RefineUndefinednessH H8.
               RefineUndefinednessH H8.
               Case Deep H8.
               1. Definedness.
               2. Rewrite -> All H8 in H4.
                  Rewrite -> All H4 in H2.
                  Rewrite <- All H2 in H1.
```

```
        ReduceH NF All in H1 (  ).
        Cut H1.
        SplitCase 1.
        1. Definedness.
        2. SplitCase 1.
            1. Definedness.
            2. Definedness.
            3. Introduce H11.
               AbsurdEqualityH H11.
        3. Introduce H10.
           AbsurdEqualityH H10.
     3. Definedness.
  2. Introduce H9 H10.
     Rewrite -> All H10.
     Reduce NF All (  ).
     Rewrite -> All H6.
     Rewrite -> All H7.
     Rewrite -> All H9.
     Reduce NF All (  ).
     Reflexive.
  3. Introduce H9 H10.
     Rewrite -> All H10.
     Reduce NF All (  ).
     Rewrite -> All H6.
     Rewrite -> All H7.
     Reduce NF All (  ).
     Apply "add_right2_of_<".
     Split Deep.
     1. Apply H9.
     2. Apply "bool_sub".
        Split Deep.
        1. Definedness.
        2. Rewrite <- All H2 in H1.
           Rewrite -> All H4 in H1.
           ReduceH NF All in H1 (  ).
           Cut H1.
           SplitCase 1.
           1. Definedness.
           2. SplitCase 1.
              1. Definedness.
              2. Introduce H13.
                 Apply "reverse_<" to H13.
                 Rewrite -> All H14.
                 Contradiction.
                 AbsurdEqualityH H15.
```

```
                    3. Introduce H13.
                       AbsurdEqualityH H13.
                 3. Introduce H12.
                    AbsurdEqualityH H12.
           3. Introduce H8.
              AbsurdEqualityH H8.
        3. Introduce H7.
           AbsurdEqualityH H7.
```

Tutorial on Subtype Marks*

Tamás Kozsik

Dept. Programming Languages and Compilers
Eötvös Loránd University, Budapest, Hungary
kto@elte.hu
http://kto.web.elte.hu/

1 Introduction

When developing safety critical applications, the programmer might want to be able to *prove* his or her code correct. The integration of a proof system and a programming language of industrial strength can be fairly useful in this respect, like in the case of, for instance, the B method [1], the Java Modelling Language [5] or the functional programming languages Erlang [3,7,9,24] and Clean [11,23,25]. This paper presents the concept of subtype marks, a concept that establishes still closer links between a programming language and a proof system by letting the programmer encode certain important properties of programs within the type system of the language. Subtype marks are introduced here as part of a simple functional language. This language can be regarded as a small subset of Clean.

In programming languages types play an important role with respect to safety: they can help avoid ill-behaved programs by forcing compilation-time errors (or, in case of dynamic typing, run-time type errors) for programs that use variables and operations inconsistently or possibly incorrectly. Type systems can provide a high degree of safety at low operational costs. As part of the compiler (and, in case of dynamic typing, the run-time system), they discover many semantic errors very efficiently.

There are many ways to make type systems even more powerful than usual. Among the most interesting ones is the concept of "dependent types": types that depend on values. Dependent types are, in principle, used in proof systems. However, they also appear in some programming languages, for example in Cayenne [4] and Epigram [21]. In dependently typed languages types are first class citizens, and sophisticated computations can be expressed on them. These computations are executed at compile time, during the type checking of programs. Dependent types provide significantly more information about the meaning of a program than types in traditional type systems do, hence type checking becomes more like theorem proving in dependently typed languages.

Another interesting approach to increase the expressiveness of type systems is to add *annotations* to types. The functional programming language Clean implements the "uniqueness type system" (a type system that makes destructive updates of memory and input-output operations possible without violating

---

* Supported by the Hungarian National Science Research Grant (OTKA), Grant Nr. T037742.

referential transparency) with annotations. Furthermore, annotations are used in this language to change the default lazy evaluation strategy into strict. Annotations in a type system can also carry information about concurrency [12], complexity [10,27] etc. Ownership types [6], for example, make it possible to reason about programs with respect to pointers and aliasing.

Subtype marks are annotations attached to types. They denote constraints (type invariants) imposed on the legal values of the annotated types. A type invariant, being an additional restriction on the legal values, selects a subtype of the original type: this feature justifies the terminology "subtype mark". Declaring subtype marked types for the expressions occurring in the program is a way to provide more precise information about the meaning of the program. The type system can verify that the expressions are indeed used according to their declared subtypes, hence the type invariants are never violated. In many cases the type system can infer subtypes for expressions, or check that expressions correspond to their declared subtypes; in other cases the proof system is needed to accomplish the reasoning. An advantage of subtype marks is that they reduce the need for the proof system: the programmer can let the type system invent or verify the simpler proofs.

The origins of subtype marks can be found in [13,14,15,2,19,20].

1.1   Motivating Example

Consider the function that computes the factorial of numbers. A quite natural way to code such a function (in Clean, for instance) is the following.

Example 1. *Computing the factorial of numbers: a simple solution.*

```
fac :: Int -> Int
fac 0 = 1
fac n = n * fac (n-1)
```

The problem with this function definition is that it does not behave very well when `fac` is invoked with a negative number: it starts an "infinite" computation which will finally result in a "memory full" runtime error. To get a prompt and precise description of what went wrong, a programmer defined runtime error can be used by changing the above definition to a more complex one:

Example 2. *Raising a runtime error.*

```
fac :: Int -> Int
fac n = if (n<0) (abort "Do not call fac on a negative number!")
               (f n)
    where f 0 = 1
          f n = n * f (n-1)
```

A safer solution is to prohibit the invocation of `fac` on negative numbers. One solution to achieve this is to use more precise types. Suppose that `Nat` is the type of natural (non-negative integer) numbers.

Example 3. *Using more precise types.*

```
fac :: Nat -> Nat
fac 0 = 1
fac n = n * fac (n-1)
```

When this function is called, the type system will check whether the argument belongs to type Nat. If the type system performs this check statically (during compilation time), like in Modula-2 [22,28], we have a safe solution to the problem. If the type system performs this check dynamically, like in Ada [26], we just have the prompt and precise runtime error—although with a more elegant code than the one in the previous solution.

Many languages, however, do not support the type Nat, neither does Clean. A Clean programmer might write the following code.

Example 4. *Using comments to express properties of programs.*

```
fac :: Int -> Int    // The argument should be non-negative
fac 0 = 1
fac n = n * fac (n-1)
```

The comment, the documentation can help the programmer avoid illegal uses of the function. It is, theoretically, not a safe solution at all, but in practice this technique of describing properties and forcing requirements is applied quite frequently. To achieve safety, formal reasoning about the program containing this function definition is needed; this formal reasoning can be carried out with a proof tool.

The proposed solution is a mixture of the afore-mentioned solutions. The type system will be extended with annotations, called subtype marks, which denote some properties of the values computed by the program. For instance, let the subtype mark Nat denote that an integer number is non-negative. Thus the annotated (or, as it will be called, "subtype marked") type Int{Nat} denotes the type of natural numbers. Using the Nat subtype mark, the fac function will be given in the following way.

Example 5. *Subtype marks express properties of functions.*

```
fac :: Int{Nat} -> Int{Nat}
fac 0 = 1
fac n = let n_minus_1 :: Int{Nat!} = n-1
        in  n * (fac n_minus_1)
```

The annotations will force the type system to refuse the invocations of fac with an argument not having the property Nat. Furthermore, the return value of the fac function will have the Nat property, although the type system itself cannot completely prove it—this is why the special annotation !, referred to as "believe-me mark", is necessary in the type declaration for the local variable n_minus_1.

1.2   Contents

The paper presents how to describe type invariants with subtype marks, and how the type system with subtype marks works. Although some hints on how subtype marks are mapped onto a proof system are given, this paper is not going into details about this issue. The focus will be kept on a pragmatic approach to subtype marks, and formal definitions will be avoided. A theoretical discussion of the topic, however, can be found in [16].

The rest of the article is structured in the following way. First, in Section 2, the basics of the functional programming language Enyv is presented. Some examples of type and function definitions are provided, not yet mentioning subtype marks: these examples will be used then throughout the paper. Section 3 introduces subtype marks, gives a first look at their syntax and explains the need for their two-fold semantics. Then, in Section 4, the three different ways subtype marks are used for typing functions are described. Section 5 presents believe-me marks. Believe-me marks indicate type invariants that the type system cannot prove. Subtype polymorphism implied by subtype marks is discussed in Section 6. Next, in Section 7, polymorphic subtype marks are introduced: they make it possible to provide subtype information in a fairly compact way. Section 8 addresses the types declared for data constructors. These types form the basis for the axiomatic semantics of subtype marks. Section 9 illustrates the way the typing algorithm in Enyv works through some examples. Finally, some further examples of Enyv definitions are given in Section 10.

2   The Programming Language Enyv

Now a simple functional programming language is introduced, which can be used to present the concept of subtype marks. Enyv is a lazy, pure language with a Clean-like syntax and semantics. It lacks some advanced features of modern functional languages, like modules, block structure, macros, user defined operators, many built-in types; it even lacks many features of modern type systems, like type classes, universally and existentially quantified types, bounded parametric polymorphism, dynamics, generics, strictness, uniqueness etc. Enyv is a simple language based on graph-rewriting, with algebraic types, pattern matching, higher-order functions and a restricted form of parametric polymorphism. Its type system augments the Milner-Mycroft system with subtype marks.

A program written in Enyv consists of algebraic type definitions (introducing type constructors and data constructors), function definitions, symbol type declarations, and an expression to be evaluated. (This latter is given as the right-hand side of the nullary function Start.) The expressions are made up of variables, function symbols, data constructors, applications of an expression to another, and recursive let-expressions[1]. Types in Enyv may contain *subtype marks*, which are special symbols attached to type constructors. The following example presents some Enyv definitions. They do not contain subtype marks yet, hence they are also legal in Clean. In the rest of this paper these definitions will be used for the presentation of subtype marks.

---

[1] The syntax of let-expressions of Enyv slightly differs from that of Clean.

Example 6. *Definitions written in Enyv—without subtype marks.*
First the well-known polymorphic list type is given, with some basic list manip-
ulating functions. For example, Snoc *appends an element to a list. (The name*
suggests that this function is a backwards Cons.*)*

```
:: List a = Nil | Cons a (List a)

Head :: (List a) -> a
Head (Cons x xs) = x

Tail :: (List a) -> (List a)
Tail (Cons x xs) = xs

Snoc Nil x = Cons x Nil
Snoc (Cons y ys) x = Cons y (Snoc ys x)

Reverse Nil = Nil
Reverse (Cons x xs) = Snoc (Reverse xs) x
```

The types Boolean *and* Pair *are also very common.*

```
:: Boolean = True | False

And True y = y
And x y = False

Or False y = y
Or x y = True

Not True = False
Not False = True

If True x y = x
If False x y = y

:: Pair a b = Pair a b

Fst (Pair x y) = x
Snd (Pair x y) = y
```

Now an algebraic type representing integer numbers is introduced, and some basic
arithmetic operations are implemented on this type.

```
:: Integer = Zero | Succ Integer | Pred Integer
Add Zero y = y
Add (Succ x) y = Add x (Succ y)
Add (Pred x) y = Add x (Pred y)
```

```
Minus Zero = Zero
Minus (Succ x) = Pred (Minus x)
Minus (Pred x) = Succ (Minus x)

Substract x y = Add x (Minus y)

Multiply Zero y = Zero
Multiply (Succ x) y = Add (Multiply x y) y
Multiply (Pred x) y = Substract (Multiply x y) y
```

This representation of integer numbers is a total function (in the sense that every value of type Integer *represents exactly one integer number), which is surjective (all integer numbers can be represented by values of type* Integer*), but not injective: the same integer number can be represented by different* Integer *values. For example,* Zero *and* Succ (Pred Zero) *both represent the integer number 0. There is, however, a "canonical representation" for every integer number: the* Integer *value built up of either* Zero *and* Succ*, or* Zero *and* Pred*, but not a mixture of all three data constructors. The function* Canonical *can be used to find the canonical representation of an integer number.*

```
Canonical :: Integer -> Integer
Canonical x = let pair = CollectSuccPred x Zero Zero
              in  Simplify (Fst pair) (Snd pair)

CollectSuccPred :: Integer -> Integer -> Integer
                                      -> Pair Integer Integer
CollectSuccPred Zero pos neg = Pair pos neg
CollectSuccPred (Succ x) pos neg =
                        CollectSuccPred x (Succ pos) neg
CollectSuccPred (Pred x) pos neg =
                        CollectSuccPred x pos (Pred neg)

Simplify Zero neg = neg
Simplify pos Zero = pos
Simplify (Succ x) (Pred y) = Simplify x y
```

Next some further operations on type Integer *are provided.*

```
Factorial x = FactorialC (Canonical x)

FactorialC Zero = Succ Zero
FactorialC (Succ x) = Multiply (Succ x) (FactorialC x)

Abs x = AbsC (Canonical x)
AbsC (Pred x) = Succ (AbsC x)
AbsC x = x
```

Finally, two functions implementing an insertion sort algorithm are defined. To make writing programs easier, Enyv provides some built-in types (like Int *or* Real*) and the usual operators on them. The functions below operate on lists over the built-in type* Int.

```
Insert :: List Int -> Int -> List Int
Insert Nil e = Cons e Nil
Insert (Cons x xs) e = If (x<e) (Cons x (Insert xs e))
                               (Cons e (Cons x xs))
Sort Nil = Nil
Sort (Cons x xs) = Insert (Sort xs) x
```

3   Syntax and Semantics of Subtype Marks

Subtype marks are annotations attached to types. More precisely, they are attached to type constructors, either to algebraic type constructors, or to the predefined "function space" type constructor (->). Curly braces are used to delimit the possibly multiple subtype marks attached to a type constructor, like in the type "List{C,S} Int{Nat}". The order of subtype marks attached to the same type constructor is irrelevant. Hence the previous type can also be written as "List{S,C} Int{Nat}".

A subtype mark denotes a property that should hold for every value belonging to the annotated type. Let C denote that a list is non-empty (it is created by a Cons data constructor) and S denote that the list is sorted (in an ascending order). Then the meaning of the type "List{C,S} Int{Nat}" is "the set of non-empty, sorted lists containing non-negative integer numbers". The properties can be expressed by logical formulas.

Example 7. *Logical formula defining subtype mark* C. *Let* $\mathbb{L}$ *denote the set of the truth values* **t** *and* **f**.

$$C : \text{List } a \longmapsto \mathbb{L}$$
$$C(xs) = (\exists y, ys : xs = \text{Cons } y \ ys)$$

However, this definition is not used by the type system. The type system works with annotations, not with logical formulas. The meaning of a subtype mark is provided for the type system by declaring the type of data constructors. These type declarations can be regarded as axioms: they are used by the type system to derive subtype information for expressions and functions.

Example 8. *Axioms: types declared for data constructors.*

```
Nil   :>:  List a
Cons  :>:  a  ->  List a  ->  List{C} a
```

The above types declared for the data constructors of List express that lists constructed with the Cons data constructor are always non-empty, while lists constructed with the `Nil` data constructor are not necessarily non-empty. Therefore, the presence of a subtype mark expresses that a value is *known to have* the corresponding property, while the absence of the subtype mark expresses that the value is *not known to have* the property.

The type system cannot make use of the logical formulas describing the meaning of subtype marks—but these logical formulas can be the input for a proof system. Thus the correctness of a program can be proved by using the type system and the proof system together.

One may say that subtype marks are given two semantics: the denotational semantics, provided by logical formulas are used by the proof system, while the axiomatic semantics provided by the type declarations for data constructors are used by the type system. The proof system should be used to prove that the axiomatic semantics is sound with respect to the denotational. For example, the axiom connecting the subtype mark `C` and the data constructor `Cons` is obviously sound with respect to the formula given for `C`. In order to see this, the following theorem has to be proven. For any type "a",

$$\forall x \in a, \ \forall xs \in \textbf{List} \ a : \ \text{Cons} \ x \ xs \ \in \ \textbf{List}\{\text{C}\} \ a.$$

Using the logical formula given for `C`, this can be unfolded in the following way. For any type "a",

$$\forall x \in a, \ \forall xs \in \textbf{List} \ a, \ \exists y \in a, \ \exists ys \in \textbf{List} \ a : \ \text{Cons} \ x \ xs \ = \ \text{Cons} \ y \ ys.$$

The proof of this theorem is fairly simple; x is a witness for y and xs is a witness for ys.

The forthcoming sections will focus on the axiomatic semantics of subtype marks, and they will investigate how the type system manages to derive properties of Enyv programs.

4   The Type of Functions

Subtype marks provide a way to express properties of functions. The type system checks these properties by analyzing the function definitions. Starting from Example 6, three ways to encode properties of functions with subtype marked types will be shown: preconditions, postconditions, and, finally, subtype propagation will be described.

4.1   Preconditions

Preconditions for a function can be expressed by restricting the type of its arguments by subtype marks. This is illustrated in Example 5 with the function `fac`: we want to prohibit invocations of this function with negative numbers, so we make a restriction on its argument by adding the subtype mark `Nat` to the argument type `Int`. Let us see another simple example. Functions `Head` and `Tail` are only partially defined on lists. They are undefined for the empty list, `Nil`. The evaluation of the expression `Head Nil` results in a runtime error. To make sure that these two functions are never invoked on empty lists in our program, not even by accident, a precondition can be introduced by adding a subtype mark to their declared types.

Example 9. *Precondition for functions* `Head` *and* `Tail`.

```
Head  ::  List{C} a  ->  a
Tail  ::  List{C} a  ->  List a
```

Now, if either of these two functions is invoked on an expression whose type is not guaranteed to have the C subtype mark, the type system emits a compilation error.

Example 10. *Violating the precondition for functions* `Head` *and* `Tail`.

```
BadGuy  ::  List a  ->  List a
BadGuy xs = Snoc (Tail xs) (Head xs)
```

This function does not compile: its argument, `xs` *is of type* `List a`, *thus it is a type error to pass this value to either* `Head` *or* `Tail`.

Besides making the use of partial functions safer, preconditions can express further useful restrictions on function arguments. Consider the type `Integer` and the function `AbsC`.

The definition of the function `AbsC` assumes that it will only be called on canonical values of type `Integer` (hence the letter C is in its name). This function is not a partial one; it is defined for all `Integer` values—it simply fails to do what it should do, namely computing the absolute value of a number, if it is called on a non-canonical value, e.g. on `Succ (Pred Zero)`. Let us introduce the subtype mark `Can` to denote that an `Integer` value is a canonical representation of an integer number. A type declaration for `AbsC` can help the programmer to avoid unintended uses of this function.

Example 11. *Precondition for function* `AbsC`.

```
AbsC  ::  Integer{Can}  ->  Integer
```

Based on the subtype mark `Can`, the type system refuses the invocations of `AbsC` on non-canonical values. Obviously, the invocation of `AbsC` in `Abs` is correct, since the function `Canonical` returns a value in canonical form. The same technique is applied in function `Factorial`, which computes the factorial of an `Integer`. The argument of `FactorialC`, however, has to fulfill two requirements: it should be a canonical value, and it should be non-negative. Let us denote this latter subtype invariant with the subtype mark `Nat`. This example shows how to attach more than one subtype marks to a single type constructor.

Example 12. *Two preconditions for function* `FactorialC`.

```
FactorialC  ::  Integer{Can,Nat}  ->  Integer
```

In the last two examples some requirements on the argument of the `AbsC` and `FactorialC` functions have been expressed, but it is clear that subtype information about the *result* of these functions could have also been provided. This issue is discussed next.

4.2 Postconditions

When the return type of a function contains a subtype mark, it can express a postcondition of the function: the returned value satisfies a certain subtype invariant. It is straightforward, for instance, that the return values of the functions AbsC and FactorialC satisfy the subtype invariant Nat.

Example 13. *Pre- and postconditions for function* FactorialC.

```
FactorialC  ::  Integer{Can,Nat}  ->  Integer{Nat}
```

An even more obvious example can be given with function Snoc. The result of this function is a non-empty list, hence it satisfies the subtype invariant C.

Example 14. *A postcondition for function* Snoc.

```
Snoc  ::  List a  ->  a  ->  List{C} a
```

Indeed, the type system can verify very easily that the postcondition holds: the right-hand side of both alternatives in the definition of Snoc is a list constructed with Cons, hence the second axiom given in Example 8 can be applied.

4.3 Subtype Propagation

Subtype marks are often used to express the propagation of subtype information. A function is *subtype-propagating*, if its result satisfies a subtype invariant whenever its argument satisfies the same or a different subtype invariant. For instance, if you give a non-empty list to the function Reverse, the result will be a non-empty list. This is not simply a pair of a precondition and a postcondition: Reverse can be applied on a possibly empty list as well. If you can guarantee the non-emptiness of the argument, the type system guarantees the non-emptiness of the result. If you cannot guarantee the non-emptiness of the argument, there will be no guarantee for the non-emptiness of the result, either. Hence Reverse propagates the non-emptiness property from its argument to its result.

Propagation can be expressed by declaring two (or more) alternative types for the same function. It is the task of the type system to find out which of those types suits best whenever the function is used in an expression.

Example 15. *Two alternative types declared for function* Reverse.

```
Reverse  ::  List a       ->  List a
Reverse  ::  List{C} a  ->  List{C} a
```

When typing the expression Reverse (Cons x xs) the second declared type can be used, while the first one is useful for typing the expression Reverse(Tail xs).

Another example of subtype propagation can be given with the Tail function and the sortedness property, denoted by the subtype mark S. The Tail function can be invoked both on sorted and on not necessarily sorted lists; if the argument is sorted, the result is sorted as well. The type of Tail from Example 9 can be refined in this way.

Example 16. *Two alternative types for function* `Tail`.

```
Tail  ::  List{C} a    -> List a
Tail  ::  List{C,S} a  -> List{S} a
```

It would be rather inconvenient to declare more than one type for a single function. Therefore, Section 7 will introduce the concept of polymorphic subtype marks, which helps provide several alternative function types with a single type declaration.

5   Believe-Me Marks

Reasoning about programs, in the present approach, is accomplished with the use of the type system and a theorem prover *in collaboration*. The theorem prover is required in such cases when the type system itself cannot prove a property of the program. Consider, for example, the subtype mark `Can`, which denotes that a value of type `Integer` is a canonical representation of an integer number. Function `Canonical` is used to compute the canonical representation of an integer from a possibly non-canonical one. The type system is not required to try to prove that the result of `Canonical` is a canonical representation, nor that this function propagates non-negativeness.

Example 17. *Believe-me marked types for* `Canonical`.

```
Canonical  ::  Integer       -> Integer{Can!}
Canonical  ::  Integer{Nat}  -> Integer{Can!,Nat!}
```

However, the type system *is* required to use this information and establish type correctness of the function `Factorial` (cf. Example 6).

Example 18. *Pre- and postcondition for function* `Factorial`.

```
Factorial  ::  Integer{Nat} -> Integer{Nat}
Factorial x = FactorialC (Canonical x)
```

Function `Factorial` expects a non-negative `Integer`. It computes a canonical representation of this non-negative `Integer` (see the second type of `Canonical` from Example 17), which is a legal value for `FactorialC` (see Example 13). The result of `Factorial` is just the result of `FactorialC`, that is a non-negative integer (see again Example 13).

Believe-me marks are used to identify the points in the program text where the proof of correctness cannot be obtained by the type system, but a theorem prover is also required. In the above example, we asked the type system to "believe" that the result of function `Canonical` satisfies the subtype invariant `Can` and that the function propagates the subtype invariant `Nat`. These properties can be proven with a theorem prover, given the logical formulas describing the denotational semantics of subtype marks `Can` and `Nat`.

Functions `Abs` and `AbsC` can be type-checked in a similar way. The argument of `AbsC` must be in canonical form, and its result is non-negative.[2] However, note that this latter subtype invariant is annotated with a believe-me mark: reasoning about the second alternative of the function definition requires the denotational semantics of the subtype marks and the help of a theorem prover.

Example 19. *Typing functions* `Abs` *and* `AbsC`.

```
Abs   ::  Integer  ->  Integer{Nat}
Abs x = AbsC (Canonical x)


AbsC  ::  Integer{Can}  ->  Integer{Nat!}
AbsC (Pred x) = Succ (AbsC x)
AbsC x = x
```

Why does the type system fail to type-check the second alternative of `AbsC` without the believe-me mark? To prove that the right-hand side of this alternative is non-negative, we have to show that the argument, namely variable `x`, is non-negative. This alternative is selected only when the first alternative failed, that is if `x` does not start with a `Pred`, but rather with a `Succ` or a `Zero`. Since `x` is in canonical form and does not start with a `Pred`, it cannot contain any `Pred` data constructors, only `Succ` and `Zero`. Thus `x` is indeed non-negative. This reasoning made use of the logical formulas describing the denotational semantics of the subtype marks. Since the type system has no access to the denotational semantics, the type system cannot carry out this reasoning in this way. Hence a believe-me mark was added to subtype mark `Nat` in the type of `AbsC`. An alternative, semancically equivalent, but longer and less efficient definition for `AbsC` could be used to get rid of the believe-me mark: see section 9.4.

The next example of believe-me marks revisits Example 5. When writing the definition for function `fac`, the local variable `n_minus_1` was declared to be of type `Int{Nat!}`: given the information that `n` is a non-negative integer, the type system cannot prove the non-negativeness of `n-1`. Again, the reason is that the denotational semantics of `Nat` is needed to find out that in the second alternative of `fac` the variable `n` refers to a positive value, hence `n-1` is indeed non-negative, and the recursive call to `fac` is type correct.

Finally, consider the sortedness property with respect to the `Insert` and the `Sort` functions, which implement an *insertion sort* algorithm for lists of integer numbers.

Example 20. *Typing functions* `Insert` *and* `Sort`.

```
Insert  ::  List{S} Int  ->  Int  ->  List{S!,C} Int


Sort    ::  List Int     ->  List{S} Int
Sort    ::  List{C} Int  ->  List{S,C} Int
```

---

[2] Moreover, it is also possible to prove that the result of both `AbsC` and `Abs` is in canonical form. The proof, which is similar to the one in Section 9.3, is left to the Reader.

Insert takes a sorted list and inserts a number in a way that sortedness is preserved. The believe-me mark in the postcondition shows that the type system cannot prove this property. In the postcondition of Sort, however, no believe-me mark is needed, since, using the postcondition of Insert, the type system can prove that the result of Sort is sorted.

6   Subtype Polymorphism

Examples 14, 15, 16 and 20 have provided types for the list manipulating functions. According to these types, if xs is a list of integers and x is an integer, is the following expression type correct?

Reverse (Tail (Sort (Snoc xs x)))

Example 14 reveals that "Snoc xs x" is of type "List{C} Int". The second type of Sort in Example 20 is applicable, so "Sort (Snoc xs x)" is of type "List{S,C} Int". From Example 16, the second type of Tail can now be applied, giving type "List{S} Int" for "Tail (Sort (Snoc xs x))". The problem is that, according to Example 15, Reverse expects an argument either of type "List Int" or "List{C} Int". These types do not deal with sortedness. However, for typing the outermost function application in the expression "Reverse (Tail (Sort (Snoc xs x)))", subtype polymorphism allows the type system to discard the sortedness subtype invariant of the subexpression "Tail (Sort (Snoc xs x))", to use the first type for Reverse and to accept type "List Int" for the whole expression.

Subtype (or, with another name, inclusion) polymorphism, which can be found in most object-oriented languages, is based on the *substitution principle*, which says that in any expression a value of the supertype can always be replaced with a value of the subtype. In our context this means that if an expression (e.g. Tail (Sort (Snoc xs x))) can be typed with a subtype (e.g. List{S} Int), then it can also be typed with a supertype (e.g. List Int). The subtype relation is a weak partial order, that is a reflexive, antisymmetric and transitive binary relation on types.

In the type system of Enyv, subtypes are expressed with the subtype marks. The types that are in subtype relation differ only in the subtype marks attached to the type constructors. When defining the subtype relation, extra care must be taken with respect to the function space type constructor. According to the substitution principle, the result type of a function is "*co-variant*", but the argument type is "*contra-variant*". This means e.g. that Integer -> Integer{Nat} is a subtype of both Integer -> Integer and Integer{Nat} -> Integer{Nat}, and that all three function types are subtypes of Integer{Nat} -> Integer. The type Integer -> Integer is a subtype of Integer{Nat} -> Integer, because whenever a function from natural numbers to integer numbers is required, we can also use a function from integers to integers.

Due to subtype polymorphism, functions and expressions can have more types than we have declared for them. In Example 15, for instance, two types for function Reverse are declared; the two types express subtype propagation. However, subtype polymorphism provides further types for this function: all the supertypes of the two declared types.

Example 21. *Two alternative types declared for function* Reverse, *and some further supertypes.*

```
Reverse  ::  List a       ->  List a
Reverse  ::  List{C} a    ->  List{C} a

Reverse  ::  List{C} a    ->  List a
Reverse  ::  List{S} a    ->  List a
Reverse  ::  List{C,S} a  ->  List a
Reverse  ::  List{C,S} a  ->  List{C} a
```

Note that the two types declared for Reverse are not in subtype relation with each other. One cannot be obtained from the other by means of subtype polymorphism, and this is exactly why both of them had to be declared.

The contra- and co-variant behaviour of subtypes can be observed not only for the function space type constructor, but also for the algebraic type constructors. When there is a function space on the right-hand side of the definition of a parametric algebraic type, the parameter of the algebraic type constructor might become contra-variant.

Example 22. *Co- and contra-variant arguments of an algebraic type constructor.*

```
:: ListFun a b  =  ListFun [a] -> [b]
```

Values of type ListFun a b, *for arbitrary types* a *and* b, *are functions that take a list of* a-s *and produce a list of* b-s. *The first argument of the type constructor* ListFun *is contra-variant, and the second argument is co-variant. Therefore,* ListFun Integer Integer{Nat} *is a subtype of* ListFun Integer{Nat} Integer.

An argument of an algebraic type constructor is *non-variant*, if it is contra- and co-variant at the same time. (Some people use the word *invariant* instead of non-variant.)

Example 23. *Non-variant argument of an algebraic type constructor.*

```
:: BinaryOperator a  =  BinOp a -> a -> a
```

A binary operator on an arbitrary type a *takes two values of type* a, *and produces a third one. The argument of the type constructor* BinaryOperator *is non-variant, because it appears both on the left- and the right-hand side of a function space type constructor. Notice that the types* BinaryOperator Integer *and* BinaryOperator Integer{Nat} *are not in subtype relation.*

In the case of recursive or mutually recursive algebraic type definitions, due to the contra-, co- and non-variance of the arguments, deciding whether two types are in subtype relation might become non-trivial: it requires a fixed-point computation.

7   Polymorphic Subtype Marks

One can express subtype propagation by declaring multiple types for the same symbol. In Examples 15–17 two alternative types for each of the function symbols Reverse, Tail and Canonical have been provided. Declaring more than one type to a symbol is rather cumbersome. Furthermore, the type checking and type inferencing algorithms become computationally more complex if symbols are given more than one type. To avoid these problems, another level of abstraction is introduced by parameterizing subtype marks. This leads us to the concept of *"polymorphic subtype marks"*. A single type with polymorphic subtype marks stands for a number of types with non-polymorphic (also called *"monomorphic"*) subtype marks.

Polymorphic subtype marks may contain *subtype mark variables*. During typing, each such variable may take one of two values: YES and DUBIOUS. The value YES corresponds to the presence of the subtype mark, and the value DUBIOUS corresponds to its absence. The types with polymorphic subtype marks of Reverse, Tail and Canonical follow the same pattern.

Example 24. *Types with polymorphic subtype marks.*

```
Reverse    ::  List{p:C} a      -> List{p:C} a
Tail       ::  List{C,p:S} a    -> List{p:S} a
Canonical  ::  Integer{p:Nat}   -> Integer{Can!,p:Nat!}
```

Substituting the subtype mark variable "p" with values YES and DUBIOUS gives us the types with monomorphic subtype marks, two for each function, as seen in Examples 15, 16 and 17.

A type can contain more than one subtype mark variable. Let us introduce two subtype marks for describing the parity of integer numbers: the subtype marks Odd and Even. The type of the data constructor Succ can be declared with respect to these two subtype marks.

Example 25. *Two subtype mark variables in one type.*

```
Succ  :>:  Integer{p:Odd, q:Even}  -> Integer{q:Odd, p:Even}
```

The two subtype mark variables can take the values YES and DUBIOUS independently. Hence four types with monomorphic subtype marks can be obtained from the one with polymorphic subtype marks.

```
Succ  :>:  Integer{Odd,Even}  -> Integer{Odd,Even}
Succ  :>:  Integer            -> Integer
Succ  :>:  Integer{Odd}       -> Integer{Even}
Succ  :>:  Integer{Even}      -> Integer{Odd}
```

However, this is only the axiomatic view, used by the type system. If we take the denotational semantics of parity into account, it turns out that the first of the four types in senseless: a value can never be odd and even at the same time.

7.1 Inequalities

The expressive power of polymorphic subtype marks can be significantly increased with the introduction of inequalities (similarly to the inequalities present, e.g. in the uniqueness type system of Clean). Inequalities impose restrictions on how the subtype mark variables can be substituted with YES and DUBIOUS. An inequality relates two subtype mark variables, like p and q in the inequality (p,q). Such an inequality should be read as p≤q, that is "p can only take the value YES when q also takes the value YES". (The two possible values for subtype mark variables are ordered in this way: DUBIOUS ≤ YES.)

Example 26. *Type with inequalities.*

```
Add  ::  Integer{c:Can,n:Nat}  ->  Integer{c:Can,n:Nat}
                                 ->  Integer{x:Can!,n:Nat!}
                                  |  (x,c)  (x,n)
```

The type declared for Add *contains two inequalities (written after the* | *sign). The inequalities tell us that* x *can only be substituted with* YES *when both* c *and* n *are substituted with* YES. *Therefore, the five possible types with monomorphic subtype marks obtained from the type above are the following.*

```
Add :: Integer{Can,Nat} -> Integer{Can,Nat} -> Integer{Can!,Nat!}
Add :: Integer{Can,Nat} -> Integer{Can,Nat} -> Integer{Nat!}
Add :: Integer{Nat}     -> Integer{Nat}     -> Integer{Nat!}
Add :: Integer{Can}     -> Integer{Can}     -> Integer
Add :: Integer          -> Integer          -> Integer
```

The two inequalities specify that the result of Add *is guaranteed to be a canonical representation of an integer number if the two arguments are both canonical representations of non-negative integer numbers.*

Remember that, due to subtype polymorphism, Add *has further types, namely all the supertypes of the types above. For instance, this is also a legal type for* Add.

```
Add :: Integer{Can} -> Integer -> Integer
```

Furthermore, notice that there is some redundancy in the five types derived from the type with inequalities: the second is a supertype of the first, and the fourth is a supertype of the fifth. Hence the legal types for Add *can be described, modulo subtype polymorphism, by the following three types with monomorphic subtype marks.*

```
Add :: Integer{Can,Nat} -> Integer{Can,Nat} -> Integer{Can!,Nat!}
Add :: Integer{Nat}     -> Integer{Nat}     -> Integer{Nat!}
Add :: Integer          -> Integer          -> Integer
```

Inequalities play an important role in many type systems with subtyping. In the present case it would be more straightforward to use the logical connectives ∧ and ∨ of propositional logic than inequalities, but, in contrast to inequalities, logical connectives would significantly increase the computational complexity of the type checking and type inferencing algorithms.

8   Type of Data Constructors

From the point of view of the type system, the types declared for the data constructors are axioms, used for typing functions. Example 8 gave the axiomatic semantics of subtype mark C by declaring the type for Nil and Cons, the data constructors of List.

Sortedness, denoted by subtype mark S, was used in Examples 16, 20 and 24. Let us provide the axiomatic semantics of this subtype invariant. Obviously, empty lists are sorted. But what about non-empty lists—lists that are constructed with the data constructor Cons? If we take an element and a list, and put them together with Cons, no guarantee can be given about the sortedness of the resulting list. However, if we take a sorted list constructed with Cons, and decompose it to an element and a tail, then the sortedness of the tail can be guaranteed. Hence Cons behaves differently with respect to S, when used in an expression (used to compose a list from some components), and when used in a pattern (used to decompose a list into its components). Due to this duality, two types are needed for each data constructor: a *composition type*, denoted by ":>:", and a *decomposition type*, denoted by ":<:". The arrowheads in the notation indicate the direction of the operations corresponding to the two types.

Example 27. *Composition and decomposition types.*

```
:: List a  =  Nil  |  Cons a (List a)

Nil  :>:  List{S} a
Nil  :<:  List{S} a

Cons :>:  a  ->  List a        ->  List{C} a
Cons :<:  a  ->  List{s:S} a  ->  List{C,s:S} a
```

These types add information about subtype mark S *to the types given in Example 8.*

The above example explains the types declared for Tail in Examples 16 and 24. These types express the propagation of the subtype mark S: if the argument is a sorted list then the result is sorted as well. The definition of Tail (see Example 6) contains a single alternative.

```
Tail (Cons x xs) = xs
```

According to Example 24, the argument of Tail, namely Cons x xs is supposed to be of type List{C,p:S} a. Applying the decomposition type of Cons (from Example 27), variables x and xs will be of type a and List{p:S} a, respectively. (Note that in this step the decomposition type of Cons has been instantiated to match the type of Tail. This required the substitution of the subtype mark variable s with the subtype mark variable p.) Since Tail returns xs, the return type of this function is indeed List{p:S} a, as stated in the type given in Example 24.

Now let us take a more sophisticated example of composition and decomposition types. Consider the algebraic type constructor `Integer` and the subtype marks `Can` and `Nat`.

Example 28. *Composition and decomposition types for the data constructors of* `Integer`.

```
Zero :>: Integer{Can,Nat}
Zero :<: Integer{Can,Nat}
Succ :>: Integer{c:Can,n:Nat} -> Integer{x:Can,n:Nat} | (x,c)(x,n)
Succ :<: Integer{c:Can,c:Nat} -> Integer{c:Can,n:Nat}
Pred :>: Integer               -> Integer
Pred :<: Integer{c:Can,n:Nat} -> Integer{c:Can,n:Nat}
```

Among the six types above, the most interesting ones are the types for `Succ`. Its composition type contains two inequalities, which constrain the `Can` property of the result: `Succ X` is in canonical form if (and, in fact, only if) `X` is a canonical representation of a non-negative integer.

The decomposition type of `Succ` is even trickier. If `Succ X` is in canonical form, then so is `X`. Furthermore, in that case `X` is also non-negative. But what about the `Nat` property of `Succ X`? Why was the subtype mark variable `n` used for this subtype mark? Because it expresses that `Succ X` *might* have the `Nat` property. In the expression `Succ Zero` the subtype invariant holds, but in the expression `Succ (Pred (Pred Zero))` it does not. Compare this to the C property of lists— see Example 27. `Nil` *cannot* be a non-empty list, hence its decomposition type does not contain the subtype mark `C`. On the other hand, a list constructed with `Cons` is *always* a non-empty list, thus the decomposition type of `Cons` contains the subtype mark `C` without a subtype mark variable. In the case of decomposition types, the absence of a subtype mark from the return type—in contrast to any other uses of subtype marks—does not mean dubiety, but rather impossibility. Dubiety in this case is expressed, as in the decomposition type of `Succ`, with a "fresh" subtype mark variable: a subtype mark variable which is not used elsewhere in the type. This anomaly in the meaning of the absence of subtype marks turns out fairly useful when typing function definitions with multiple alternatives.

9 Typing Functions

So far all the fundamental rules on the use of subtype marks have been explained. Now let us apply these rules on some function definitions and explore how the typing algorithm of Enyv works. The formal description of this algorithm will not be given here (for such a description refer to [16]), but rather an illustration of how typing in Enyv is done with some examples.

9.1 Typing Snoc

According to Examples 6 and 14, the type and the definition of function `Snoc` is the following.

```
Snoc  :: List a  -> a  -> List{C} a
Snoc Nil x = Cons x Nil
Snoc (Cons y ys) x = Cons y (Snoc ys x)
```

To verify that the function definition is type correct and corresponds to the declared type, the two function alternatives have to be checked separately.

The left-hand side of the first alternative introduces variable x with type a. Let us take the composition type List{S} a of Nil from Example 27. Due to subtype polymorphism, this type can be weakened to List a. Applying the composition type of Cons (again from Example 27) gives the required type List{C} a for the right-hand side of this alternative.

The second alternative contains three variables: y, ys and x, with x having again type a. To find out the type for y and ys, the decomposition type of Cons from Example 27 has to be applied. Since the type of the first argument of Snoc is List a, the subtype mark variable s in the decomposition type of Cons is substituted with DUBIOUS, and the subtype mark C is ignored. This gives types a and List a for variables y and ys, respectively. According to the declared type of Snoc, the expression Snoc ys x is type correct, and it is of type List{C} a. This type has to be weakened to List a, and then the composition type of Cons has to be applied. This gives the required type List{C} a for the right-hand side of the second alternative as well.

9.2 Typing Reverse

According to Examples 6 and 24, the type and the definition of function Reverse is the following.

```
Reverse  :: List{c:C} a  -> List{c:C} a
Reverse Nil = Nil
Reverse (Cons x xs) = Snoc (Reverse xs) x
```

Again, the two alternatives have to be type-checked separately. Furthermore, since the declared type of Reverse contains polymorphic subtype marks, the types with monomorphic subtype marks are generated from it by substituting the subtype mark variable c with YES and DUBIOUS.

```
Reverse  :: List a  -> List a
Reverse  :: List{C} a  -> List{C} a
```

Now let us verify that Reverse is typeable with both of these types.

The left-hand side of the first alternative contains the pattern Nil. From Example 27, the decomposition type of this data constructor is List{S} a. To match the left-hand side of the first type with monomorphic subtype marks, the irrelevant subtype information that the empty list is sorted must be ignored. The right-hand side of this alternative is Nil again. Its composition type is also List{S} a. Subtype polymorphism allows the weakening of this type to List a, which is the type required for this case.

The argument type of the second type with monomorphic subtype marks is List{C} a. The pattern of the first alternative, Nil, simply does not match this type: as explained in Section 8, the absence of subtype mark C from the result type of the decomposition type of Nil means that Nil cannot have this subtype invariant. Hence, when the argument of Reverse is of type List{C} a, the first alternative will not be selected. This is why the first alternative with the second type of Reverse does not have to be type-checked.

Type checking the second alternative is simpler by far. For both types with monomorphic subtype marks, the decomposition type of Cons (from Example 27) can be applied by substituting the subtype mark variable s with DUBIOUS. (In the case of the first type of Reverse the unused subtype mark C has to be ignored from the decomposition type as well.) The application of the decomposition type ensures that the pattern variables x and xs are given the types a and List a, respectively. To type the expression Reverse xs the value DUBIOUS can be substituted into the subtype mark variable c of the declared type of Reverse. Thus the type List a is obtained for this expression, which, together with a, the type of xs, matches the type of Snoc (from Example 14). Applying the type of Snoc gives type List{C} a for the right-hand side of the second alternative. It is exactly what is needed to match the second type with monomorphic subtype marks of Reverse, and it has to be weakened by subtype polymorphism to match the first one. In both cases, however, the type-checking succeeds. This completes the type-checking of function Reverse.

It is possible to formulate the typing algorithm in such a way that it can work with polymorphic subtype marks, hence generating the types with monomorphic subtype marks and verifying conformance with these generated types separately is not necessary. This more sophisticated typing algorithm is computationally less complex, so it is chosen to be implemented in the compiler of Enyv. For the sake of simplicity, however, the presentation of this algorithm is omitted from this paper.

9.3   Typing FactorialC

Let us show that function FactorialC (introduced in Example 6) can be typed with the following type (cf. Example 13).

```
FactorialC  ::   Integer{Can,Nat}  ->   Integer{Can,Nat}
FactorialC Zero = Succ Zero
FactorialC (Succ x) = Multiply (Succ x) (FactorialC x)
```

Typing the first alternative is fairly straightforward. The decomposition type of Zero (see Example 28) matches the argument type of FactorialC. Furthermore, its composition type, Integer{Can,Nat} allows us to use the type Integer{Can,Nat} -> Integer{Can,Nat} for Succ (obtained by substituting all three subtype mark variables in the composition type of Succ with YES), thus the right-hand side of this alternative receives the type Integer{Can,Nat} as required.

The pattern of the second alternative is a value constructed with Succ. According to the declared type of FactorialC, it is of type Integer{Can,Nat}. The subtype mark variable c can be substituted in the decomposition type of Succ with YES; the other subtype mark variable, n can be substituted with either YES or DUBIOUS, but in the latter case the unused subtype mark Nat in the argument type of FactorialC should be ignored. In both cases the pattern variable x will be typed with Integer{Can,Nat}. The subexpression FactorialC x is therefore type correct, and it is also of type Integer{Can,Nat}, and so is subexpression Succ x (again, the subtype mark variables of the composition type of Succ have been substituted by YES). It is left to the Reader to prove that functions Add and Multiply can be typed with the following type:

```
Integer{c:Can,n:Nat}  ->  Integer{c:Can,n:Nat}
                               ->  Integer{x:Can!,n:Nat!}
                                |  (x,c)  (x,n)
```

Substituting YES into all three subtype mark variables of the type of Multiply gives the required type Integer{Can,Nat} for the right-hand side of the alternative. Note that the typing algorithm used the Nat subtype mark with believe-me mark from the return type of Multiply.

The type just proven for FactorialC ensures the following type for function Factorial (cf. Example 18).

```
Factorial  ::  Integer{Nat}  ->  Integer{Can,Nat}
```

9.4 Typing AbsC

Example 19 explained why a believe-me mark in the declared type of AbsC is required. It is possible, however, to give an alternative definition for AbsC which provides more information to the type system about the behaviour of this function, and hence eliminates the need for the believe-me mark. This alternative definition is longer and less efficient than the one appearing in examples 6 and 19, but it lets the progammer reduce the use of a proof system, or, when Enyv is intended to be used without a proof system, enables the type system to provide a safety guarantee.

Example 29. *Gain safety at the expense of reduced compactness and efficiency.*

```
AbsC  ::  Integer{Can}  ->  Integer{Can,Nat}
AbsC Zero = Zero
AbsC (Pred x) = Succ (AbsC x)
AbsC (Succ x) = Succ x
```

In the third, critical alternative of this definition the type system gains additional subtype information from the decomposition type of the data constructor Succ: it figures out that x is of type Integer{Can,Nat}.

Consider now the following definition for AbsC. This definition is even more readable than the one in examples 6 and 19. Unfortunately, this definition requires a believe-me mark not only for Nat, but also for Can.

Example 30. *Gain readability at the expense of introducing believe-me marks.*

```
AbsC  ::  Integer{Can}  ->  Integer{Can!,Nat!}
AbsC (Pred x) = Minus (Pred x)
AbsC x = x
```

Here the problem is that in the first alternative the subtype information Can is known for the pattern Pred x on the left-hand side, but it is lost for the expression Pred x in the right-hand side. Note that extending Enyv with named patterns (patterns identified by variables) would be very helpful in such situations.

Example 31. *The use of named patterns in a possible extention to Enyv. The syntax of Clean is applied in this example.*

```
AbsC  ::  Integer{Can}  ->  Integer{Can,Nat!}
AbsC x=:(Pred y) = Minus x
AbsC x = x
```

9.5   Typing Sort and Insert

This section reveals that the following function definitions (from Examples 6 and 20) are type correct.

```
Insert  ::  List{S} Int  ->  Int  ->  List{S!,C} Int
Insert Nil e = Cons e Nil
Insert (Cons x xs) e = If (x<e) (Cons x (Insert xs e))
                                (Cons e (Cons x xs))


Sort  ::  List{c:C} Int  ->  List{S,c:C} Int
Sort Nil = Nil
Sort (Cons x xs) = Insert (Sort xs) x
```

The declared type of Insert contains a believe-me mark for the subtype mark S. Therefore, the type system has only to prove that the definition of Insert can be typed with the following type:

```
Insert  ::  List{S} Int  ->  Int  ->  List{C} Int
```

Typing the first alternative is straightforward. However, the second alternative is more involved. The decomposition type of Cons tells that the variable xs is of type List{S} Int—the type variable a was substituted with Int, the subtype mark variable s with YES, and the unused subtype mark C was ignored. This type of xs (and the declared type of e) makes the recursive call to Insert type correct. The subtype mark S in the declared return type of Insert is allowed to be used to type the expression Insert xs, which thus has the type List{S,C} Int. These two subtype marks will be discarded when typing Cons x (Insert xs e); the type of this expression, similarly to that of Cons e (Cons x xs) is List{C} Int. Now the following type for If is needed:

```
If  ::  Boolean  ->  a  ->  a  ->  a
```

The type variable a in this type has to be instantiated with List{C} Int, which also becomes the type of the right-hand side of the alternative.

Typing Sort proceeds in the following way. The pattern of the first alternative is Nil. The decomposition type of this data constructor tells that this value cannot hold subtype mark C. Hence the subtype mark variable c in the declared type of Sort can be substituted with DUBIOUS, and the type to check for this alternative becomes

```
Sort  ::  List Int  ->  List{S} Int.
```

This type is fairly simple to check: only the type variable a in the composition type of Nil needs to be instantiated with Int.

The second alternative contains a Cons pattern. The decomposition type of Cons reveals that this pattern always has the subtype mark C. This is why the subtype mark variable c in the declared type of Sort can be substituted with YES, and the type to check for this alternative becomes

```
Sort  ::  List{C} Int  ->  List{S,C} Int.
```

The decomposition type of Cons gives type Int and List Int to variables x and xs, respectively (note that the subtype mark variable s in the decomposition type of Cons had to be substituted with DUBIOUS to match the argument type List{C} Int of Sort). The recursive call to Sort will use the declared type of Sort with subtype mark variable c substituted with DUBIOUS. Hence the type of Sort xs becomes List{S} Int. Applying the declared type of Insert gives the required type List{S,C} Int to the right-hand side of the alternative.

The fact that we use the declared type of a function (e.g. that of Sort) to prove that the function can be typed with that declared type might at first sight seem erroneous—but it is not. Since we are proving safety properties (invariants), we have to show that nothing can violate the property. In the case of recursive functions it might happen that the value returned by the recursive call is undefined (either giving a run-time error or initiating an infinite computation), but, if nothing else violates the invariant, neither will the recursive call.

Finally, it is worth devoting some words to the believe-me mark in the type of Insert. This believe-me mark indicates that the proof of the postcondition S is not the responsibility of the type system, but rather that of a theorem prover. We should be able to generate automatically a theorem from such a believe-me marked type. There is no space here to go into details about how this can be done. As a hint, however, the theorem corresponding to Insert is provided for use in Sparkle, the dedicated theorem prover of the Clean system. First, the predicate Sorted has to be defined in Clean.

```
Sorted Nil = True
Sorted (Cons x Nil) = True
Sorted (Cons x xs=:(Cons y ys))  =  x <= y  &&  Sorted xs
```

Then the theorem can be formulated.

$$\forall xs \in \text{List Int},\ \forall e \in \text{Int}:$$
$$\neg(\text{Sorted } xs = \text{False})\ \rightarrow\ \neg\big(\text{Sorted (Insert } xs\ e) = \text{False}\big)$$

In this theorem "not false" means "true or undefined". Using the syntax for Sparkle, the theorem reads like this.

```
[xs::List Int] [e::Int]
~(Sorted xs = False)   ->   ~(Sorted (Insert xs e) = False)
```

It is possible to prove this theorem in about 300 proof steps [18].

10   Further Examples

In this section some further examples on Enyv definitions are presented. Only some brief remarks on the main ideas behind the examples will be provided: it is left to the Reader as an exercise to verify that the examples are indeed type correct.

First an implementation of the insertion sort algorithm on lists of Integers (rather than on lists of Ints) is given. Then two, slightly different definitions of complex numbers are introduced. The examples on complex numbers make use of the predefined type Real of floating point numbers and the common arithmetic and trigonometric operations on this type.

10.1   Implementing Insertion Sort on Lists of Integers

Since sorting requires many comparisons, and comparing non-canonical Integer values is much less efficient than comparing canonical ones, it is worth turning the elements of the list into canonical representation before sorting. Therefore, the comparison function Less will work on Integers in canonical form.

```
Less ::  Integer{Can} ->  Integer{Can}  ->  Boolean
Less (Pred x) (Pred y) = Less x y
Less (Pred x) y = True
Less (Succ x) (Succ y) = Less x y
Less (Succ x) y = False
Less Zero (Succ y) = True
Less Zero y = False
```

Now let us see how sorting lists of Integers in canonical form is done. The functions InsertC and SortC below directly correspond to the functions Insert and Sort from Example 6. Besides prescribing the Can property for the elements of the lists as a pre- and postcondition, it is also indicated that these functions propagate the non-negativeness of the list elements.

```
InsertC  ::   List{S} Integer{Can,n:Nat}  ->  Integer{Can,n:Nat}
                              -> List{S!,C} Integer{Can,n:Nat}
InsertC Nil e = Cons e Nil
InsertC (Cons x xs) e = If (Less x e ) (Cons x (InsertC xs e))
                                       (Cons e (Cons x xs))
```

```
SortC  ::  List{c:C} Integer{Can,n:Nat} ->
               List{S,c:C} Integer{Can,n:Nat}
SortC Nil = Nil
SortC (Cons x xs) = InsertC (SortC xs) x
```

Finally, the sorting function on lists of possibly non-canonical Integers is provided. Before invoking SortC, this function applies Canonical to each element of the list. This is best done with the help of the well-known higher-order function Map.

```
Map  ::  (a->b)  ->  List{c:C} a  ->  List{c:C} b
Map f Nil = Nil
Map f (Cons x xs) = Cons (f x) (Map f xs)


Sort  ::  List{c:C} Integer{n:Nat} ->
              List{S,c:C} Integer{Can,n:Nat}
Sort xs = SortC (Map Canonical xs)
```

This example illustrates that subtype marks can be attached not only to the top-level type constructors in a type (e.g. to List), but also to inner ones (e.g. to Integer).

10.2   Two-Fold Representation of Complex Numbers

There are two common representations for complex numbers: the Cartesian and the polar representation. Here a type that allows a mixed representation of complex numbers is defined. The two data constructors are Cart and Polar. According to the two-fold representation, the type value set of Complex is divided into two subtypes by introducing two, mutually exclusive subtype marks, which are also called Cart and Polar.

```
::  Complex  =  Cart Real Real  |  Polar Real Real
Cart  :>:  Real -> Real -> Complex{Cart}
Cart  :<:  Real -> Real -> Complex{Cart}
Polar :>:  Real -> Real -> Complex{Polar}
Polar :<:  Real -> Real -> Complex{Polar}
```

One can convert values from one representation to the other with the following functions.

```
cart :: Complex -> Complex{Cart}
cart (Polar r phi) = Cart (r * (cos phi)) (r * (sin phi))
cart (Cart re im) = Cart re im

polar :: Complex -> Complex{Polar}
polar (Cart re im) = let delta :: Real = if (im<0.0) 1.0 0.0
   in Polar (sqrt (re*re + im*im)) ((atan (im/re)) + delta*Pi)
polar (Polar r phi) = Polar r phi
```

The idea behind supporting both Cartesian and polar representation is that certain operations on complex numbers can be more efficiently implemented on Cartesian, while others on polar representation. First let us consider some operations requiring Cartesian representation. The requirement is expressed with pre- and postconditions.

```
addCC :: Complex{Cart} -> Complex{Cart} -> Complex{Cart}
addCC (Cart re1 im1) (Cart re2 im2) = Cart (re1+re2) (im1+im2)

subCC :: Complex{Cart} -> Complex{Cart} -> Complex{Cart}
subCC (Cart re1 im1) (Cart re2 im2) = Cart (re1-re2) (im1-im2)

mulCC :: Complex{Cart} -> Complex{Cart} -> Complex{Cart}
mulCC (Cart re1 im1) (Cart re2 im2) =
     Cart (re1*re2-im1*im2) (im1*re2+im2*re1)

divCC :: Complex{Cart} -> Complex{Cart} -> Complex{Cart}
divCC (Cart re1 im1) (Cart re2 im2) =
    let a :: Real = (re2*re2 + im2*im2)
    in  Cart  ((re1*re2+im1*im2) / a)  ((im1*re2-im2*re1) / a)

conjugate :: Complex{Cart} -> Complex{Cart}
conjugate (Cart re im) = Cart re (0.0-im)
```

Some operations on polar representation come next.

```
mulCP :: Complex{Polar} -> Complex{Polar} -> Complex{Polar}
mulCP (Polar r1 phi1) (Polar r2 phi2) = Polar (r1*r2) (phi1+phi2)

divCP :: Complex{Polar} -> Complex{Polar} -> Complex{Polar}
divCP (Polar r1 phi1) (Polar r2 phi2) = Polar (r1/r2) (phi1-phi2)

absCP :: Complex{Polar} -> Real
absCP (Polar r phi) = r

powCP :: Complex{Polar} -> Real -> Complex(Polar)
powCP (Polar r phi) x = Polar (r^x) (x*phi)
```

The operations defined only on subtypes of Complex can help the programmer keep better control on efficiency. However, in certain cases it is useful to have operations that accept complex numbers in either representations.

```
addC :: Complex -> Complex -> Complex{Cart}
addC c1 c2 = addCC (cart c1) (cart c2)

subC :: Complex -> Complex -> Complex{Cart}
subC c1 c2 = subCC (cart c1) (cart c2)
```

```
mulC :: Complex{p:Polar,c:Cart} -> Complex{p:Polar,c:Cart} ->
                                   Complex{p:Polar,c:Cart!}
mulC (Cart re1 im1) (Cart re2 im2) = mulCC (Cart re1 im1)
                                           (Cart re2 im2)
mulC c1 c2 = mulCP (polar c1) (polar c2)


divC :: Complex{p:Polar,c:Cart} -> Complex{p:Polar,c:Cart} ->
                                   Complex{p:Polar,c:Cart!}
divC (Cart re1 im1) (Cart re2 im2) = divCC (Cart re1 im1)
                                           (Cart re2 im2)
divC c1 c2 = divCP (polar c1) (polar c2)


absC :: Complex -> Real
absC (Polar r phi) = r
absC (Cart re im) = sqrt (re*re + im*im)


powC :: Complex -> Real -> Complex(Polar)
powC c x = powCP (polar c) x
```

10.3   Three-Fold Representation of Complex Numbers

If the same complex number is passed many times to many different operations,
it might be worth caching its value in both Cartesian and polar representation.
The following type definition makes this possible. For this reason a third data
constructor, Both is introduced, which is used to construct Complex values that
belong to both subtypes Complex{Cart} and Complex{Polar}.

```
:: Complex = Cart  Real Real
           | Polar Real Real
           | Both  Real Real Real Real
Cart  :>:  Real -> Real -> Complex{Cart}
Cart  :<:  Real -> Real -> Complex{Cart}
Polar :>:  Real -> Real -> Complex{Polar}
Polar :<:  Real -> Real -> Complex{Polar}
Both  :>:  Real -> Real -> Real -> Real -> Complex{Cart,Polar}
Both  :<:  Real -> Real -> Real -> Real -> Complex{Cart,Polar}
```

When using this type, one must be careful to keep Both-values consistent,
preserving the type invariant that the first two real numbers represent the same
value in Cartesian than the second two real numbers in polar representation.
Therefore, it is a good idea to hide the representation of this type from its
clients. Unfortunately this is not possible in Enyv, because, due to its simplicity,
Enyv does not support modules and type abstraction. However, one can provide the constructors and selectors that could be used in the case of a hidden
representation.

```
createCart :: Real -> Real -> Complex{Cart}
createCart re im = Cart re im

createPolar :: Real -> Real -> Complex{Polar}
createPolar r phi = Polar r phi

re_part :: Complex{Cart} -> Real
re_part (Cart re im) = re
re_part (Both re im r phi) = re

im_part :: Complex{Cart} -> Real
im_part (Cart re im) = im
im_part (Both re im r phi) = im

absCP :: Complex{Polar} -> Real
absCP (Polar r phi) = r
absCP (Both re im r phi) = r

argCP :: Complex{Polar} -> Real
argCP (Polar r phi) = phi
argCP (Both re im r phi) = phi
```

The conversion operations cart and polar are syntactically the same as the ones in Section 10.2, but semantically they are different. For example, the second alternative of cart can receive arguments constructed not only with Cart, but also with Both. Due to subtype polymorphism, cart can return values constructed with Both unchanged.

```
cart ::  Complex  ->  Complex{Cart!}
cart (Polar r phi) =  Cart  (r * (cos phi))  (r * (sin phi))
cart c = c

polar ::  Complex  ->  Complex{Polar!}
polar (Cart re im) =  let delta :: Real = if (im<0.0) 1.0 0.0
                      in  Polar  (sqrt (re*re + im*im))
                                 ((atan (im/re)) + delta*Pi)
polar c = c

both :: Complex -> Complex{Cart,Polar}
both (Cart re im)  = let p :: Complex{Polar} = polar (Cart re im)
                     in Both re im (absCP p) (argCP p)
both (Polar r phi) = let c :: Complex{Cart} = cart (Polar r phi)
                     in Both (re_part c) (im_part c) r phi
both (Both re im r phi) = Both re im r phi
```

The selector operators make it easy to define the usual arithmetic operations. Some of these are for the Cartesian representation (for values constructed with `Cart` and with `Both`), others are for the polar representation (for values constructed with `Polar` and with `Both`). As an illustration, two operations are shown here; it is left to the Reader to develop the rest.

```
conjugate :: Complex{Cart} -> Complex{Cart}
conjugate c = Cart (re_part c) (0.0-(im_part c))

powCP :: Complex{Polar} -> Real -> Complex(Polar)
powCP c x = Polar ((absCP c)^x) (x*(argCP c))
```

Multiplication on complex numbers of matching subtypes are made available by `mulCC` and `mulCP`. These operations do not forget to behave correctly with respect to the data constructor `Both`.

```
mulCC :: Complex{Cart} -> Complex{Cart} -> Complex{Cart}
mulCC c1 c2 = let re1 :: Real = re_part c1,
                  re2 :: Real = re_part c2,
                  im1 :: Real = im_part c1,
                  im2 :: Real = im_part c2
              in Cart (re1*re2-im1*im2) (im1*re2+im2*re1)

mulCP :: Complex{Polar} -> Complex{Polar} -> Complex{Polar}
mulCP c1 c2 = let r1   :: Real = absCP c1,
                  r2   :: Real = absCP c2,
                  phi1 :: Real = argCP c1,
                  phi2 :: Real = argCP c2
              in Polar (r1*r2) (phi1+phi2)
```

Finally, the multiplication operator that accepts complex numbers in either representations is presented. Function `mulH` is an auxiliary function needed by the implementation. Since Enyv supports neither modules nor block-structure, there is, unfortunately, no way in Enyv to reduce the scope of this function.

```
mulC :: Complex{p:Polar,c:Cart} -> Complex{p:Polar,c:Cart}
                                -> Complex{p:Polar,c:Cart}
mulC (Both re im r phi) c = mulH c (Both re im r phi)
mulC (Polar r phi) c = mulCP (Polar r phi) (polar c)
mulC c (Polar r phi) = mulCP (polar c) (Polar r phi)
mulC (Cart re im) c2 = let cc2 :: Complex{Cart!} = c2
                       in mulCC (Cart re im) cc2

mulH :: Complex{p:Polar,c:Cart} -> Complex{Polar,Cart}
                                -> Complex{p:Polar,c:Cart}
mulH (Both re im r phi) c =
        let prodP :: Complex{Polar} = mulCP (Polar r phi) c,
            prodC :: Complex{Cart} = mulCC (Cart re im) c
        in Both (re_part prodC) (im_part prodC)
```

```
                    (absCP prodP) (argCP prodP)
mulH (Polar r phi) c = mulCP (Polar r phi) c
mulH (Cart re im) c = mulCC (Cart re im) c
```

11   Conclusions

This paper has presented subtype marks as part of a simple functional programming language, Enyv. The type system of Enyv augments the classical Milner-Mycroft system with subtype marks. Subtype marks:

- are annotations attached to (algebraic or function space) type constructors;
- express "subtype invariants", which are constraints that restrict the set of legal values of types;
- introduce subtype (inclusion) polymorphism in the type system;
- are used in three major ways: expressing preconditions, postconditions, and propagation of subtype invariants;
- make it possible to provide more precise types for the expressions occurring in our programs;
- although less expressive, are much easier to use than dependent types;
- are useful for reasoning about the correctness of the code, because they link the type system to a theorem prover. When a type system with subtype marks is linked to a proof system, reasoning about the correctness of programs becomes less tedious and time-consuming, since many (less complicated) proofs can be automatically performed by the type system.

The semantics of subtype marks is two-fold. From the point of view of the theorem prover, each subtype mark corresponds to a logical predicate; a predicate on the types whose top-most type constructor is annotated by the subtype mark. From the point of view of the type system, however, the meaning of a subtype mark is provided by the types declared for the data constructors. The data constructors have different types when used in left- or right-hand sides of function definitions: in patterns the decomposition types are used, while in right-hand sides the composition types.

Believe-me marks provide further input to the type system. They are used to annotate subtype marks. When the type system cannot prove a subtype invariant, the corresponding subtype mark should be annotated with a believe-me mark. This indicates that the proof of the subtype invariant has to be accomplished with a theorem prover.

Often more than one type with subtype marks is necessary to properly describe the properties of a function or a data constructor—especially when propagation of subtype invariants should be expressed. Types with polymorphic subtype marks contain subtype mark variables and inequalities. Such a type corresponds to a set of types with monomorphic subtype marks. Therefore polymorphic subtype marks enable a new dimension of polymorphism with respect to subtype polymorphism. Although types with polymorphic subtype marks are less expressive than sets of types with monomorphic subtype marks [17], in practice their expressive power is sufficient in most cases. The type system of Enyv is based on types with polymorphic subtype marks, hence the programmer can declare a single type for each function, and two types (a composition and a decomposition type) for data constructors.

There are many properties of programs that are possible to express with subtype marks, and many others that are not. Even those properties that can be expressed might require special care when constructing the program text. Sometimes semantics preserving changes in the definition of a function can help the type system prove a property—a property that was beyond the proving capabilities of the type system before the changes. The programmer has to tolerate this anomaly: if (s)he wants to produce code that should be proven correct, the code should be written in a way (or style) that the type system prefers. Consider e.g. section 9.4, or compare the definitions for `cart` and `polar` given in sections 10.2 and 10.3: the use of "redundant" patterns, like in example 29 or in section 10.2, usually (but not always) increase the chances of the type system in proving a property, and hence decrease the need for believe-me marks (and for proofs to be carried out in a proof system).

It is possible to enhance the type system of Enyv with respect to subtype marks in a number of ways. One possibility is to take the evaluation strategy into account. Many functional languages, including Enyv, applies the functional strategy, which means that pattern matching considers the alternatives of a function definition from top to bottom. When typing a function alternative, the type system could gain further subtype information from the fact that the previous alternatives did not match [16]. This approach could solve, for instance, the problem with the definition of `fac` (Example 5), which, as explained in section 5, requires a believe-me mark. Although this enhancement to the type system is safe, it makes the typing rules much more complex: the type correctness of a function alternative becomes dependent on the previous alternatives. For this reason this feature was omitted from Enyv.

Enyv is a research language. While focusing on the use of subtype marks, it neglects many important design issues of programming languages, such as modularity, local definitions etc. However, it is worth to devote a few words to modularizing subtype marks. When developing a library, the programmer cannot predict all future uses of that library, hence (s)he is unable to anticipate all the properties, all the subtype marks that might be relevant to the functions in that library. The possibility to add subtype information to functions defined long ago and/or in another module would be extremely helpful. A language that is applicable in the software industry, and has a type system with subtype marks could benefit from an aspect-oriented approach [8].

References

1. Abrial, J-R.: *The B-Book*. Cambridge University Press, 1996.
2. van Arkel, D. F. R.: *Annotated Types*. M.Sc. thesis, Rijksuniversiteit te Leiden, Vakgroep Informatica, 1998.
3. Armstrong, J. – Virding, R. – Williams, M. – Wikstrom, C.: *Concurrent Programming in Erlang*, Prentice Hall, 1996

4. Augustsson, L.: Cayenne—a language with dependent types. In *ACM International Conference on Functional Programming '98*. ACM, 1998.
5. Burdy, L. – Cheon, Y. – Cok, D. – Ernst, M. – Kiniry, J. – Leavens, G. T. – Rustan K. – Leino, M. – Poll, E.: An overview of JML tools and applications. *International Journal on Software Tools for Technology Transfer*, 7(3), 2005. pp. 212–232.
6. Clarke D. G. – Potter, J. M. – Noble, J.: Ownership types for flexible alias protection. In *Object-Oriented Programming, Systems, Languages, and Applications (OOPSLA)*, October 1998.
7. *Erlang Verification Tool—Version 2.0 (01) of April 9, 2001*. August 2005. http://www.sics.se/fdt/vericode/evt.html
8. Filman, R. E. – Elrad, T. – Clarke, S. – Akşit, M. (eds): *Aspect-Oriented Software Development*. Addison-Wesley, 2005. ISBN 0-321-21976-7.
9. Fredlund, L-Å.: *A Framework for Reasoning about* ERLANG *Code*. PhD. thesis, Royal Institute of Technology, Sweden, August 2001.
10. Hammond, K.: Hume. *Proceedings of the Central-European Functional Programming School (CEFP)*, Budapest, Hungary, 2005.
11. *Home of Clean*. August 2005. http://www.cs.ru.nl/~clean/
12. Kesseler, M. H. G.: *The Implementation of Functional Languages on Parallel machines with Distributed Memory*. Ph.D. thesis, University of Nijmegen. 1996.
13. Koopman, P.: *Constrained data types*. Technical Report 96-36., Computer Science, Leiden University, The Netherlands, 1996.
14. Koopman, P.: *Language Support to Enforce Constraints on Data Types*. Technical Report 96-37., Computer Science, Leiden University, The Netherlands, 1996.
15. Koopman, P.: Constrained data types. In *Dagstuhl Seminar Report, No. 156*, 1996.
16. Kozsik T.: *Altípusjeles típusok*. PhD thesis (in Hungarian). Eötvös Loránd University, Budapest, Hungary. Under preparation.
17. Kozsik T.: The expressive power of inequalities. Abstract in: *Proceedings of 5th Joint Conference on Mathematics and Computer Science (5th MaCS)*, Debrecen, Hungary, 2004.
18. Kozsik T .: *Reasoning with Sparkle: a case study*. Technical Report, University Eötvös Loránd, Faculty of Informatics, Budapest, Hungary, 2004.
19. Kozsik T .: *Subtyping with subtype marks*. Technical Report 2003-P05, University Eötvös Loránd, Faculty of Informatics, Budapest, Hungary, 2003.
20. Kozsik T. – van Arkel, D. – Plasmeijer, R.: Subtyping with Strengthening Type Invariants. In *Proceedings of the 12th International Workshop on Implementation of Functional Languages* (Mohnen, M. – Koopman, P. (eds)), Aachener Informatic-Berichte, Aachen, Germany, September 2000. pp. 315–330.
21. McBride, C.: Epigram: practical programming with dependent types. *5th International Summer School on Advanced Functional Programming (AFP 2004)*, Tartu, Estonia, 2004. In preparation. Available at http://www.dur.ac.uk/CARG/epigram/epigram-afpnotes.pdf
22. *MODULA-2*. August 2005. http://www.modula2.org/
23. de Mol, M. – van Eekelen, M. – Plasmeijer, R.: Theorem proving for Functional Programmers, Sparkle: A Functional Theorem Prover. In *LNCS 2312*, p. 55 ff., Springer Verlag, 2001.
24. *Open Source Erlang*. August 2005. http://www.erlang.org/
25. Plasmeijer, R. – van Eekelen, M.: *Functional Programming and Parallel Graph Rewriting*, Addison-Wesley, 1993, ISBN 0-201-41663-8.
26. *The Ada 95 Reference Manual*. Available at e.g. http://lgl.epfl.ch/ada/
27. *The Hume Page*. August 2005. http://www-fp.dcs.st-and.ac.uk/hume/
28. Wirth, N.: *Programming in Modula-2*. Springer-Verlag, 1983.

Designing Distributed Computational Skeletons in D-Clean and D-Box*

Viktória Zsók[1], Zoltán Hernyák[2], and Zoltán Horváth[1]

[1] Eötvös Loránd University, Faculty of Informatics
Department of Programming Languages and Compilers
H-1117 Budapest, Pázmány Péter sétány 1/C
{zsv, hz}@inf.elte.hu
[2] Eszterházy Károly College
Department of Information Technology
H-3300 Eger, Eszterházy tér 1
aroan@ektf.hu

Abstract. Functional programming has inherent parallel features. This situation can be exploited by building different language constructs for parallel and distributed programming. Earlier we designed two languages for skeleton based distributed functional programming on a cluster. The two languages have different expressive power and abstraction levels. Our distributed functional computation is based on a multiparadigm-oriented environment with several different layers. On the highest level D-Clean coordination language primitives are applied in order to define the distribution of the pure functional computation subtasks over a PC cluster. This distribution is made according to a predefined computational scheme, which is an algorithmic skeleton, parameterized by functions, types and data. The D-Clean programs are transformed into D-Box, a lower level description language including the computational nodes implemented in the lazy functional language Clean. The computational nodes are distributed over the cluster and they communicate using the middleware services. This paper presents skeleton based functional and distributed programming using the D-Clean and D-Box languages. The main goal is to illustrate the appropriateness and applicability of the previously introduced languages for distributed evaluation of the functional programs on clusters. Here, therefore, we design distributed functional computational skeletons and we have provided a set of known algorithmic skeletons implemented as D-Clean schemes and a set of D-Box programs.

1 Introduction

Parallel functional programming already has a history spanning several years. Parallel programming in the lazy functional programming language Clean had several development phases. At the very beginning there was a transputer version

---

* Supported by OTKA T037742, by GVOP-3.2.2.-2004-07-0005/3.0 ELTE IKKK and by Bolyai Scholarship of the Hungarian Academy of Sciences.

of the language [13]. The annotations [20] were introduced in order to specify which parts of a function should be evaluated in parallel. The parallel strategies [11] were based on annotations and we were able to define the evaluation order according to the structure of the results.

In a previously developed environment [9,21] Clean programs could be interconnected via the direct call of middleware services, making possible the asynchronous communication between the distributed functional components. It was recognized that the distributed evaluation of functions and the communication between Clean programs needed a higher level process description and control mechanism. For this reason a control language, the D-Clean language and an intermediate level language, the D-Box language and their informal semantics were introduced in [10]. The paper describes in details the D-Clean primitives and the structure of the D-Box language elements. D-Clean contains high-level language elements for the coordination of the purely functional computational nodes in our distributed environment on a cluster. The D-Clean primitives offer the advantage of writing distributed and functional applications without knowing the details of the application environment and middleware services. Therefore the programs can be written on a high level, abstracting from the technical aspects.

The paper aims to present a set of D-Clean and D-Box programs from very simple examples tending later towards more complex ones. D-Clean is a Clean-like language for distributed computations on clusters, and it consists of a relatively small number of coordination language primitives. The appendix summarizes the introduced coordination structures (see Section A.1).

The keyword for computational skeletons is SCHEME. This describes the structure of the distributed computations. Here we define some algorithmic skeletons of parallel programming as D-Clean schemes. The implemented D-Clean programs are using these defined schemes.[1]

In functional programming skeletons are higher order functions. In D-Clean a SCHEME is an high level, abstract definition of the distributed computation and it is parameterized by functions, type and data.

A scheme is actually identified and described by compositions of coordination primitives. The coordination primitives have the role of manipulating and controlling the pure functional components written in Clean, which however express the pure computational aspects. The middleware services enable the distributed communication between the computational nodes.

A coordination primitive uses channels for receiving the input data required for the arguments of their function expressions. The results of the function expression are sent to the output channels. Every channel is capable of carrying data elements of a specified base type from one computational node to another one. We use the unary algebraic type constructor Ch a to construct channel types, where the base type a is a transmissible type.

A coordination primitive usually has two parameters: a function expression (or a list of function expressions) and a sequence of input channels. The coordination

---

[1] The term skeleton is used also at the middleware level computation. The D-Clean schemes are used for describing parallel algorithmic skeletons.

primitives return a sequence of output channels. The signature of the coordination primitive, i.e. the types of the input and output channels are inferred according to the type of the embedded Clean expressions. In the appendix aCh denotes a channel type, while aCh* denotes a finite sequence of channel types (see the appendix A.1).

2   Skeletons Implemented in D-Clean

This section presents the D-Clean implementation of some skeletons of parallel functional programming [18,7]. The examples use the introduced coordination primitives [10], which are also described here briefly for clarifying the examples. In the figure of a coordination primitive below, F denotes the function expression embedded into it.

The figures in this section illustrate in an intuitive way the computational skeletons. The primitives coordinate the whole distributed computation process at a higher level. The coordination primitives can be composed similarly to functions in a functional programming style.

The examples of this section use an input generator function to provide the input data in a simple way, usually a list of integers. The generator can easily be extended to any other data structure.

The task of the DStart primitive is to start the distributed computation by producing the input data for the dataflow graph. It has no input channels, only output channels (see Figure 1). The DStart primitive will take the input given by the generator function and it then starts the computation. The results of the generator are sent to the output channels. Each D-Clean program contains at least one DStart primitive. The primitive can be used as in the following example.

```
DStart generator

generator :: [Int]
generator = [1, 2, 3, 4, 5]
```

Fig. 1. DStart node

The other coordination primitive which must be included in any D-Clean program is the DStop primitive. If a function expression embedded into a DStop primitive has k arguments, then the computation node evaluating the expression needs k input channels. Each input channel carries one argument for the function expression (see Figure 2).

The task of this primitive is to receive and save the result of the computation. It has as many input channels as the function expression requires, but it has no output channels. DStop closes the computational process. Each D-Clean program contains at least one DStop primitive. The primitive can be used as in the following example.

```
DStop terminate
where
    terminate = saveToFile "result.dat"
```

DStop is a final element of the D-Clean composition, a last element of the process network. In some cases when the dataflow contains forks, the distributed computation has multiple DStop primitives.

Fig. 2. DStop node

In the examples the **terminate** function parameter will be used as the parameter of the DStop. It collects the subresults arriving through the input channels and saves the final result. The **saveToFile** function is used for saving the final result into a file. At the end of each example we mention the result in a comment, i.e. the content of the saved file. The applications of the schemes are illustrated by figures.

2.1 Schemes Using Map Operations

Our first simple example illustrates how to use the distributed version of the well known standard **map** library function. The D-Clean variant of the **map** function is a simple computational scheme and it applies the primitive designed for this purpose:

```
SCHEME XMap f = DMap f
```

The scheme modifies the incoming data elements, processing them one by one. The parameter function of a DMap must be an elementwise processable function [11].

Fig. 3. DMap nodes

The XMap scheme can, for example, be applied in the distributed computation of the squares of the elements of a list of integers.

```
DistrStart = (DStop terminate)(XMap square)(DStart generator)
where
    terminate = saveToFile "resultmap.dat"

generator :: [Int]
generator = [1, 2, 5, 7, 12, 14, 17, 25, 30, 45]

square :: Int -> Int
square x = x^2

// resultmap.dat: 1 4 25 49 144 196 289 625 900 2025
```

The parameter function of the XMap scheme can be any function that operates on lists. A valid function argument for XMap can be a function either of type a->b or of type [a]->[b]. Suppose we have a list of n sublists as input data, then the qsort::[!a]->[a] sorting function[2] is a valid function argument for XMap. It takes every sublist element of the input list and applies the parameter function argument, i.e. the qsort function to it. The result will be the list of the n sorted sub-lists.

Since the coordination primitives can be composed, a D-Clean SCHEME can be written as compositions of D-Clean language primitives.

Suppose we compose three DMap elements, then the D-Clean SCHEME is as follows:

```
SCHEME Map3 f1 f2 f3 = (DMap f3)(DMap f2)(DMap f1)
```

The computation scheme can be visualized as in the Figure 4.

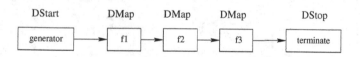

DStart　　　DMap　　　DMap　　　DMap　　　DStop

| generator | → | f1 | → | f2 | → | f3 | → | terminate |

Fig. 4. An application of the Map3 scheme

The Map3 scheme using three pure Clean functions can be applied very easily.

```
DistrStart = (DStop terminate)(Map3 fm1 fm2 fm3)(DStart generator)
where
    terminate = saveToFile "resultmap3.dat"

generator :: [Int]
generator = [1, 2, 3, 5, 1, 4, 3, 6, 3, 5]

fm1 :: Int -> Int
fm1 x = ((^) 2) x
```

---

[2] ! denotes strict evaluation of the argument.

```
fm2 :: Int -> Int
fm2 x = x*x
fm3 :: Int -> Int
fm3 x = ((+) 1) x
```

```
// resultmap3.dat: 5 17 65 1025 5 257 65 4097 65 1025
```

2.2 Using the DApply Primitive

Similar schemes can be written in a more general way, using the DApply coordination primitive.

The first variant of DApply applies the same function expression n times (see Figure 5.a) on $n * k$ channels. When the function expression has k arguments of types $t_1, t_2, ..., t_k$, the number of input channels is $n * k$. The types of the arguments periodically match the type of the channels.

If the expression produces a tuple with m elements of the type $(p_1, p_2, ..., p_m)$, then the output channel sequence will contain $m * n$ elements, repeating the m type-sequences n times. It can be observed that DMap is a special case of DApply.

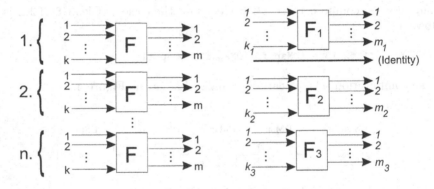

Fig. 5. DApply variant a) and variant b)

For example by using the **total** function, which computes the sum of the elements of a sublist, the DApply primitive can be used as follows.

```
DistrStart = (DStop terminate)(DApply mfold)(DStart generator)
where
    terminate = saveToFile "resultgenmap.dat"

mfold :: [[Int]]->[Int]
mfold data = map total data

generator :: [[Int]]
generator = [[11, 223, 445, 21, 5], [5, 88, 7, 6, 3]]
```

```
total :: [Int] -> Int
total x = foldr (+) 0 x
```

```
// resultgenmap.dat: 705 109
```

The second variant of `DApply` may apply different function expressions, which are given in a function sequence. The types and the number of the arguments of the function expressions can also be different. If the function sequence contains an identity function, then the data received via the corresponding channel is forwarded directly to the output channel and afterwards to the next node.

The sequence of the input channels is constructed according to the types required by the function expressions of the sequence. The output sequence of channels is built up according to the results obtained by applying the function expressions. For example, `DApply` $[F_1, id, F_2, F_3]$ yields the structure presented in Figure 5.b.

Analogously to the `Map3` scheme, a composition of `DApply` primitives can be written.

```
SCHEME Apply3 f1 f2 f3 = (DApply f3)(DApply f2)(DApply f1)
```

```
DistrStart = (DStop terminate)(Apply3 f1 f2 f3)(DStart generator)
where
    terminate = saveToFile "resultapply3.dat"
```

```
generator :: [Int]
generator = [1, 2, 3, 6, 4, 5, 7, 6, 8]
```

```
f1 :: [Int] -> [Int]
f1 x = map ((^) 2) x
f2 :: [Int] -> [Int]
f2 x = map f x
f3 :: [Int] -> [Int]
f3 x = map ((+) 1) x
```

```
f x = x * x
```

```
// resultapply3.dat: 5 17 65 4097 257 1025 16385 4097 65537
```

Figure 6 illustrates the above example similarly to Figure 4.

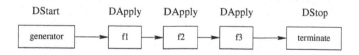

Fig. 6. An application of the `Apply3` scheme

2.3 The Pipeline Scheme

The pipeline computational skeleton is an often used skeleton. It takes a list of functions and applies the composition of these functions to every element of the input.

In our implementation, the pipeline skeleton is based on the `DLinear` primitive.

```
SCHEME Pipeline fl = DLinear fl
```

The `DLinear` coordination primitive is specially designed for pipeline computations. It simplifies the definition of the pipeline computation graph, where the nodes are connected to each other in a linear way (see Figure 7). `DLinear` has a list of functions as parameter.

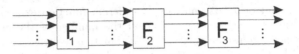

Fig. 7. `DLinear` nodes

An instantiation of the scheme will use three functions as subtask of the computation nodes, each one of type `[Int] -> [Int]` (see Figure 8).

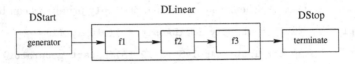

Fig. 8. The application of the `Pipeline` scheme

The functions can for example be the ones defined in the previous section at the composition of three `DApply` primitives.

```
DistrStart = (DStop terminate)(Pipeline function_list)(DStart generator)
where
    terminate = saveToFile "resultpipeline.dat"
    function_list = [f1, f2, f3]

generator :: [Int]
generator = [1, 2, 3, 6, 5, 4, 1, 7]

f1 :: [Int] -> [Int]
f1 x = map ((^) 2) x
f2 :: [Int] -> [Int]
f2 x = map f x
f3 :: [Int] -> [Int]
f3 x = map ((+) 1) x

f x = x * x

// resultpipeline.dat:  5 17 65 4097 1025 257 5 16385
```

Similarities between the previous examples can be observed. Some computational skeletons have similar functionality, i.e compute the same result, but using different coordination primitives and function parameters. Since the `DMap` coordination primitive is a special case of the `DApply` primitive, the `Map3` can be also considered a special case of the `Apply3` scheme. Choosing carefully the function parameters, the same computational skeleton can be expressed by different compositions of basic primitives.

2.4   The Farm Computational Skeleton

The farm skeleton divides the original task into subtasks, computes the subresults and builds up the final results from the subresults (see Figure 9).

```
SCHEME Farm c f d N = (DMerge c)(DApply f)(DDivideS d N)
```

The skeleton uses two more D-Clean primitives: `DDivideS` for dividing the input into parts and `DMerge` for merging inputs. Here they are presented in more detail.

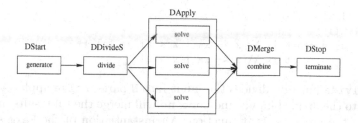

Fig. 9. An application of the `Farm` scheme

`DDivideS` is a static divider (see Figure 10). The expression splits the input data list into n parts and broadcasts them to n computational nodes. This primitive is called a static divider since the value of n must be known at pre-compile time.

The base type of the sublists has to be the same type as the type of the original list. Therefore, the output channels have the same type as the input channels. Consequently, there will be n output channels.

Fig. 10. DDivideS node

The farm skeleton also uses the `DMerge` primitive. `DMerge` collects the input sublists from channels and builds up the output data lists. All the input channels must have the same type (see Figure 11).

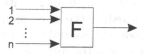

Fig. 11. DMerge node

The farm computational skeleton uses the following Clean function arguments for the dividing and combining phases.

```
combine_lists :: [[Int]] -> [Int]
combine_lists [] = []
combine_lists [x:xs] = merge x (combine_lists xs)

divide :: Int [Int] -> [[Int]]
divide n xs = [split n (drop i xs) \\ i<-[0..n-1]]
where
    split n [] = []
    split n [x:xs] = [x : split n (drop (n-1) xs)]

qsort :: [Int] -> [Int]
qsort [] = []
qsort [a:xs] = qsort [x \\ x <- xs | x < a] ++ [a] ++
               qsort [x \\ x <- xs | x > a]
```

The `divide` function divides the input into N parts, `solve` applies the `qsort` function to the divided inputs and `combine` will merge the subresults into a final one using the `combine_list` function. An instantiation of the `Farm` scheme is given in the following:

```
DistrStart = (DStop terminate)(Farm combine solve divider N)
             (DStart generator)
where
    combine = combine_lists
    solve = qsort
    divider = divide N
    N = 3
    terminate = saveToFile "resultfarm.dat"

generator :: [Int]
generator = [1, 9, 4, 6, 2, 8, 5, 3, 10, 7]

// resultfarm.dat: 1 2 3 4 5 6 7 8 9 10
```

Another version of the farm skeleton may use the `DReduce` primitive instead of `DApply` (see Figure 12).

```
SCHEME FarmReduce c f d N = (DMerge c)(DReduce f)(DDivideS d N)
```

`DReduce` is another special case of `DApply` with some restrictions. A valid expression for `DReduce` has to reduce the dimension of the input channel type[3], i.e. has the type of form `[a]->b`. For example, the `sum::[a]->a` function - which computes the sum of the elements of the input list - is a valid function parameter for `DReduce`.

A modified farm skeleton can be used with the same `divide` function and with the `sum` function as below.

---

[3] For example: list of lists → list.

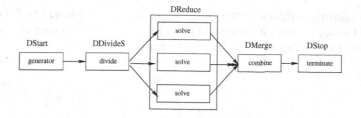

Fig. 12. An other version of farm skeleton

```
DistrStart = (DStop terminate)(FarmReduce combine solve divider N)
             (DStart generator)
where
    combine = sum
    solve = sum
    divider = divide N
    N = 3
    terminate = saveToFile "resultfarmreduce.dat"

generator :: [Int]
generator = [1, 9, 4, 6, 2, 8, 5, 3, 10, 7]

// resultfarmreduce.dat: 19
```

The opposite of the DReduce is the DProduce primitive, which is another special case of DApply. The expression has to increase the dimension of the channel type[4]. A valid expression must be of the form a->[b]. For example, the divisors :: Int->[Int] function - which generates all the divisors for an integer number - is a valid expression for a DProduce.

2.5 Composed Schemes

The following example uses the same farm computation skeleton but here the subtasks are pipeline schemes. The example shows the compositionality of the introduced distributed computational skeletons (see Figure 13).

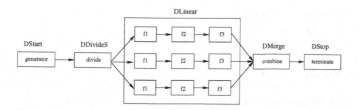

Fig. 13. A farm and pipeline skeleton combination

---

[4] For example: list → list of lists.

The square root values of the elements given by the **generate** function are computed using Newton iterations. The approximate square root of the value a is calculated according to the following formula:

$$x_0 = \frac{a}{2}$$

$$x_{i+1} = \frac{1}{2} * \left(\frac{a}{x_i} + x_i \right)$$

The generated real numbers are first converted into a record containing the proper value and the first iteration (the half of the value). The **Farm** scheme is used for distributing the values among three **Pipeline** computation skeletons. Each **Pipeline** makes a number of iterations according to the list of parameter functions.

```
SCHEME FarmLinear c fl d N = (DMerge c)(Pipeline fl)(DDivideS d N)
```

After dividing the input, each branch applies the pipeline scheme. When every pipeline finishes the iterations, the combine function collects the subresults into a final list. At the end the final result is saved into a file.

```
:: Pair = { d :: Real
          , a :: Real
          }

DistrStart = (DStop terminate)(FarmLinear combine f_list divider N)
             (DStart generate)
where
    generate = transform generator
    divider = divide N
    f_list = [f, f, f, f, f, f, f]
    f = iteration
    combine = combine_lists
    terminate = saveToFile "resultsquareroots.dat"
    N = 3

generator :: [Real]
generator = [1.0, 9.0, 4.0, 6.0, 2.0, 8.0, 5.0, 3.0, 10.0, 7.0]

transform :: [Real] -> [Pair]
transform x = map t x

t :: Real -> Pair
t x = {d = x/2.0, a = x}

divide :: Int [Pair] -> [[Pair]]
divide n xs = [split n (drop i xs) \\ i<-[0..n-1]]
where
    split n [] = []
    split n [x:xs] = [x : split n (drop (n-1) xs)]
```

```
combine_lists :: [[Pair]] -> [Pair]
combine_lists x = flatten x

step :: Pair -> Pair
step x = {d = 0.5*((x.a/x.d)+x.d), a = x.a}

iteration :: [Pair] -> [Pair]
iteration x = map step x


// resultsquareroots.dat: 1 2.44948974278318 2.23606797749979
// 2.64575131106459 3 1.4142135623731 1.73205080756888
// 2 2.82842712474619 3.16227766016838
```

2.6 Other Type of Schemes

The fork skeleton divides the input and starts several computation nodes and terminates each node individually (see Figure 14).

```
SCHEME Fork fl d N = (DApply fl)(DDivideS d N)
```

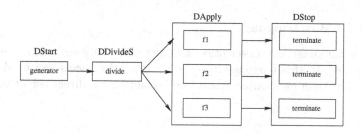

Fig. 14. An application of the fork skeleton

```
DistrStart = (DStop [terminate, terminate, terminate])
             (Fork function_list divider N)(DStart generator)
where
    divider = divide N
    N = 3
    function_list = [f1, f2, f3]
    terminate = saveToFile "resultfork.dat"


f1 :: [Int] -> [Int]
f1 x = map ((^) 2) x
f2 :: [Int] -> [Int]
f2 x = map f x
f3 :: [Int] -> [Int]
f3 x = map ((+) 1) x

f x = x * x
```

```
divide :: Int [Int] -> [[Int]]
divide n xs = [split n (drop i xs) \\ i<-[0..n-1]]
where
    split n [] = []
    split n [x:xs] = [x : split n (drop (n-1) xs)]

generator :: [Int]
generator = [1, 4, 6, 2, 4, 5, 3, 2, 7]

// resultfork.dat:  7 6 8
```

3 Introduction to D-Box

D-Clean is compiled to an intermediate level language called D-Box. The D-Clean generic constructs are instantiated into D-Box expressions. D-Box is designed for the description of the computational nodes, which define a computational graph (see Figure 15). D-Box expressions hide implementation details and enable direct control over the process-network. The asynchronous communication is based on language-independent middleware services.

3.1 The D-Box Language

The D-Box language is a description language for the source codes of computational nodes. In this language input and output protocols can be defined. A graphical developer environment was built to support a direct use of the D-Box language.

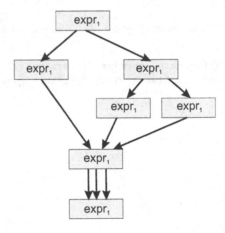

Fig. 15. A computational graph

To describe this kind of graph, the nodes and the edges (connections) must be defined.

A computational node may use more than one input channel. At this level a channel identification mechanism is used. An input channel is described by its type and by the unique ID of the channel. Notation $[T]$ is used in the type description of a channel, which is used to transfer a single list of elements of the base type T. Whenever a list of lists is sent via a channel, type $[[T]]$ is associated to it.

The input protocol also determines the synchronization mode of the input channels. There are three modes: `memory`, `join1` and `joink` (see [10], and see A.2). The input is completely defined when the list of the input channels (`<INPUT_CHANNEL_LIST>`) and the input protocol (`INPUT_PROC_MODE`) is given.

The number and/or the base types of the input channels can be different from the types of arguments of the expression (`<ARGUMENT_TYPE_LIST>`). The matching of channel types to argument types is completed at code generation time according to the actual protocol. The same holds for the `<RESULT_TYPE_LIST>` too.

The output protocol definition has the same structure as the input definition (see [10] and A.2). A complete D-Box definition has the following parts:

```
BOX <BOXID>
  {   <SubGraphID>,
  { (<INPUT_CHANNEL_LIST>), INPUT_PROC_MODE },
  { (<ARGUMENT_TYPE_LIST>), <EXPRESSION>, (<RESULT_TYPE_LIST>) },
  { (<OUTPUT_CHANNEL_LIST>), OUTPUT_PROC_MODE } }
```

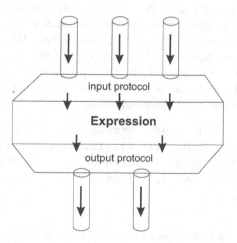

Fig. 16. A general structure of a D-Box with channels

The `BoxID_00` definition describes a computational node, which generates the data. Because it requires no input there are no input channels, and the input protocol is the `memory` protocol. It produces a tuple of a list of integers and a list of characters. These lists are sent to two different channels #1002 and

#1004. The `split1` protocol (see Figure 17) means a one-to-one mapping of the components of the result tuple to the output channels.

```
BOX BoxID_00  // in Clean:  "generator:: ([Int],[Char])"
{1,   { ( null ), memory }, // INP CHNS and PROT
      { ( null ), generator, ( [Int],[Char] ) }, // EXPR
      { ((([Int],1002),([Char],1004)) , split1 } // OUTP
}
```

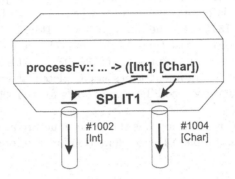

Fig. 17. The mapping of `split1`

The `BoxID_01` definition receives **integer** elements from channel #1001, and **real** elements from channel #1002. The `join1` protocol (see Figure 18) reads these input channels and passes the data elements to the expression as arguments. The expression applies the function `processFv` to them.

The result of the *processFv* is a list of lists of **Int**. When it consists of two sub-lists, it can be decomposed and sent into two different channels (#1002 and #1003). This is done automatically by the `splitk` protocol (see Figure 19). It is important that there should be exactly two sublists. Other cases (a lower or higher number of sublists will cause run-time error).

```
BOX BoxID_01  // in Clean: "processFv:: [Int] [Real]-> [[Int]]"
{1,    { ( ([Int],1001), ([Real],1002) ),  join1 }, // INPUT
       { ( [Int], [Real] ), processFv, ( [[Int]] ) }, // EXPR
       { ( ([Int], 1003 ), ( [Int], 1004 ) ), splitk } // OUTPUT
}
```

The `BoxID_02` definition implements a data-saving task. It receives two lists of integers from channel #1001 and from #1002. As the expression does not need the two sublists but rather the joined list of lists, the `joink` (see Figure 20) protocol is used (otherwise, the `join1` should have been used). The unique parameter (*World) cannot be transported through channels, so it is not collected by the input protocol.

As the result of the expression is the modified unique *World alone, no output channel is needed, so the the output protocol is **memory**.

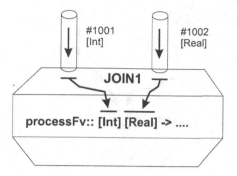

Fig. 18. The mapping of `join1`

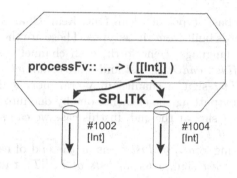

Fig. 19. The mapping of `splitk`

```
// in Clean: "saveToFile::String [[Int]] *World -> *World"
BOX BoxID_02
{1, { ( ([Int],1001), ([Int],1002)) , joink },
    { ( [[Int]],*World ), saveToFile "s:\\result.dat", (*World)},
    { ( null ), memory }
}
```

A detailed description of the D-Box language (syntax and semantics) are presented in [10].

3.2 Transmissible Types

At this point the types of the channels should be mentioned. A type determines the type of the data elements transported by the channel from one node to another. A channel acts as a buffered queue between the two nodes. We use a middleware to implement the two most important operations of the channel: the put (store) and the get (receive) operation. Because of the limitation of the middleware, we cannot transport every kind of data from one node to another, so we must define the *transmissible* types (marked by $\mathcal{T}$).

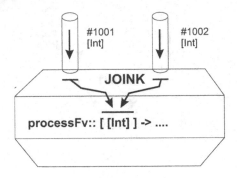

Fig. 20. The mapping of `joink`

At this time, the basic types of Clean (Int, Real, Char, Bool) can be transported, and the records built from these types. These are the basic transmissible types of the D-Box language. Henceforth, each channel can transport special signs, such as *endOfList*, *endOfSubList* and *endOfChannel*.

Using the *endOfList* sign, a channel may transport a list of transmissible type data elements by putting the elements one by one into the channel and by putting the *endOfList* sign at the end. In this case we can say that the type of this channel is a *list of* $\mathcal{T}$, $[\mathcal{T}]$.

Similarly, by putting *endOfSubList* signs at the end of each sub-list, and by putting a final *endOfList* sign, a *list of lists of* $\mathcal{T}$, $[[\mathcal{T}]]$ can be transported as well.

The last sign (*endOfChannel*) can be put into the channel indicating that all the data have been given: the sender node finished its job, so no other data will ever arrive on this channel.

A channel is a queue with limited storage capacity. When the channel is empty and a node tries to get (receive) an element from it, the channel will **block** the node until the element is ready **or** a specified **time-out** is reached.

When the channel is full and the node tries to put (store) an element into it, the same thing will happen - the node will be blocked until a successful get (receive) frees a slot for the item, or time-out is reached.

4   Examples in D-Box

4.1   Saving to File

Let us consider the smallest, simplest graph (with only two nodes) which works. The first graph generates a simple list of integer values and sends them to the next node, which writes them to a file.

The D-Clean expression is the following:

```
DistrStart = DStop (saveToFile "s:\\intlist.dat) DStart generator
```

This example shows the two most important tasks of the graph: there is at least one node which generates the data to the graph, and at least one node which collects the final results and saves them to file. Usually it is not possible to write the results to the console because in the distributed environment on a cluster this final node will be started on *a randomly-selected* machine, and usually it is difficult to locate its screen.

The D-Box version of this expression is:

```
BOX BoxID_1001 { 1, { (null), memory},
      { (null) , generator ,([Int]) },
      { ((([Int],1)), split1} }
```

```
BOX BoxID_1002 { 1, { ((([Int],1)), join1},
      { ([Int], *World) , saveToFile "s:\\intlist.dat",(*World) },
      { (null), memory} }
```

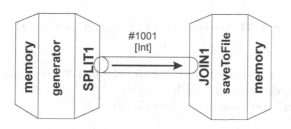

Fig. 21. The structure of *saving to file*

4.2 Picking up the Even Numbers

Let us complete the previous exercise: picking up only the even numbers from the generated list of integers. First, write the necessary Clean function:

```
pickUpEvens::[Int]->[Int]
pickUpEvens [] = []
pickUpEvens [n:xs]
    | isEven n  = [n:pickUpEvens xs]
    | otherwise = pickUpEvens xs
```

Then insert a computational node between the two nodes:

```
DistrStart = DStop (saveToFile "s:\\evens.dat")
            DApply pickUpEvens DStart generator
```

```
BOX BoxID_1001 { 1, { (null), memory },
      { (null) , generator ,([Int])  },
      { ((([Int],1)), split1 }  }
```

```
BOX BoxID_1002 { 1, { (([Int],1)), join1 },
     { ([Int]) , pickUpEvens ,([Int])  },
     { (([Int],2), split1 }  }

BOX BoxID_1003 { 1, { (([Int],2)), join1 },
     { ([Int], *World) , saveToFile "s:\\evens.dat",(*World)  },
     { (null), memory }  }
```

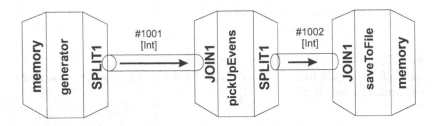

Fig. 22. The structure of *picking up even numbers*

The insertion is done by redirecting the channel **#1** to this new node and its output must be directed into the last node.

The D-Clean expression which does the same is:

```
DistrStart = DStop (saveToFile "s:\\evens.dat")
     DApply pickUpEvens DStart generator
```

4.3   Picking up Prime Numbers on Two Threads

The problem is the same as in the previous case but this time we suppose that the list of numbers is very long - so we will use two different *threads* to speed the process up.

The generated list will be cut into two parts, elements at odd positions go to the first list, elements at even positions to the second list. The following cutting technique is not useful when the original order of the elements is important.

```
cutter::[Int]->[[Int]]
cutter data = [data1,data2]
     where
          (data1,data2) = cutter2 data

cutter2 [] = ([],[])
cutter2 [a] = ([a],[])
cutter2 [a:b:xs] = ([a:fxs],[ b:sxs])
     where
          (fxs,sxs) = cutter2 xs
```

We can then use a merger function to merge the numbers again:

```
merger:: [[Int]]->[Int]
merger [] = []
merger [[],[]] = []
merger [[],[b:xs2]] = [b:merger [[],xs2]]
merger [[b:xs2],[]] = [b:merger [xs2,[]]]
merger [[a:xs1],[b:xs2]] = [a:b:merger [xs1,xs2]]
```

We can separate all the functions into different boxes:

```
DistrStart = DStop (saveToFile "s:\\evens.dat") DMerge merger
    DApply pickUpEvens
    DDivideS cutter 2 DStart generator
```

Let us observe that the DDivideS sends the two sub-lists (generated by the cutter) into different channels and because the pickUpEvens processes only one channel, the DApply will apply this process twice to cover both channels. It behaves in the same way:

```
DistrStart = DStop (saveToFile "s:\\evens.dat") DMerge merger
    DApply [pickUpEvens,pickUpEvens]
    DDivideS cutter 2 DStart generator
```

The generated boxes are the following:

```
BOX BoxID_1000  // DStart
{ 1, { ( null ), memory},
      { ( null ), generator ,([Int]) },
      { (([Int],1001)), split1}}

BOX BoxID_1001  // DDivideS
{ 1, { (([Int],1001)), join1},
      { ([Int]), cutter ,([[Int]]) },
      { (([Int],1002),([Int],1003)), splitk} }

BOX BoxID_1002  // DApply
{ 1, { (([Int],1002)), join1},
      { ([Int]), pickUpEvens ,([Int]) },
      { (([Int],1004)), split1} }

BOX BoxID_1003  // DApply
{ 1, { (([Int],1003)), join1},
      { ([Int]), pickUpEvens ,([Int]) },
      { (([Int],1005)), split1} }

BOX BoxID_1004  // DMerge
{ 1, { (([Int],1004),([Int],1005)), joink},
```

```
    { ([[Int]]), merger ,([Int]) },
    { (([Int],1006)), split1} }

BOX BoxID_1005   // DStop
{ 1, { (([Int],1006)), join1},
      { ([Int],*World), saveToFile "s:\\evens.dat",(*World) },
      { ( null ), memory} }
```

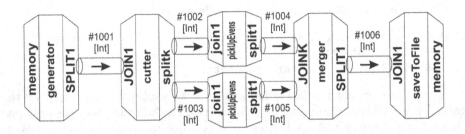

Fig. 23. The structure of *picking up even numbers on two threads*

This time on `BoxID_1001` we use the `splitk` protocol to send the sub-lists into different channels (into #1002 and #1003 channels) because the `cutter` function generated a list of lists.

Let us suppose that we want to use the `cutter2` directly. In this case we cannot use the `splitk` protocol, if we do so, that will cause a type error (compile time):

```
BOX BoxID_1001
{ 1, { (([Int],1001)), join1},
      { ([Int]), cutter2 ,([Int],[Int]) },
      { (([Int],1002),([Int],1003)), splitk} }
```

The solution is to use the SPLIT1 :

```
BOX BoxID_1001
{ 1, { (([Int],1001)), join1},
      { ([Int]), cutter2 ,([Int],[Int]) },
      { (([Int],1002),([Int],1003)), split1} }
```

The suitable D-Clean expression for this case is the following:

```
DistrStart = DStop (saveToFile "s:\\sorted.dat") DMerge merger
    DApply [pickUpEvens,pickUpEvens]
    DApply cutter2 DStart generator
```

Unfortunately this is not a valid D-Clean expression because the pre-compiler tries to find a `DDivideS` pair of the `DMerge` keyword and refuses to interpret the expression, but this is valid in the D-Box language.

4.4   Farm

The D-Clean example mentioned in section 2.4 can be written in D-Box language directly.

```
DistrStart = (DStop terminate) (DMerge combine) (DApply solve)
             (DDivideS divider N) (DStart generator)
where
    divider = divide N
    solve = qsort
    combine = combine_lists
    terminate = saveToFile "s:\\sorted.dat"
    N = 2
```

In this example N equals 2. This means, that the divider function will generate two sublists. In this case, two solver boxes are needed (on two threads). They are BoxID_02 and BoxID_03 boxes.

```
// for the "DStart generator"
// in Clean: "generator :: [Int]"
BOX BoxID_00
{1,  { ( null ), memory },
     { ( null ), generator, ( [Int] ) },
     { ( ( [Int], 1 ) ), split1 }
}

// for the "DDivideS divide N"
// in Clean: "divide :: Int [Int] -> [[Int]]"
BOX BoxID_01
{1,   { ( ( [Int], 1 ) ), join1 },
      { ( [Int] ), divide N, ( [[Int]] ) },
      { ( ( [Int], 2 ), ( [Int], 3 ) ), splitk }
}

// for the "DMap qsort"
// in Clean: "qsort:: [!Int]->[Int]"
BOX BoxID_02
{1,   { ( ( [Int], 2 ) ), join1  },
      { ( ![Int] ), qsort, ( [Int] ) },
      { ( ( [Int], 4 ) ), split1 } }

// for the "DMap qsort"
BOX BoxID_03
{1,   { ( ( [Int], 3 ) ), join1  },
      { ( ![Int] ), qsort, ( [Int] ) },
      { ( ( [Int], 5 ) ), split1 } }

// for the "DMerge (mergeSort lessThan)"
// in Clean: "mergeSort::(Int Int->Bool) [[Int]]"
// and also: "lessThan::Int Int->Bool"
```

```
BOX BoxID_04
{1,  { ( ( [Int], 4 ), ( [Int], 5 ) ), joink },
     { ( ( [[Int]] ), mergeSort lessThan, ( [Int] ) ) },
     { ( ( [Int], 6 )), split1 }}


// for the "DStop (saveToFile "s:\\sorted.dat")"
// in Clean: "saveToFile:: String *World [Int] -> *World
BOX BoxID_05 //
{1,  { ( ( [Int], 6 )), join1 },
     { ( *World, [Int] ), saveToFile "s:\\sorted.dat",  (*World) },
     { ( null ), memory } }
```

5   The D-Clean and D-Box Package

To compile a `DistrStart` expression, a D-Clean pre-compiler (see Appendix A.3) is needed. It reads the Clean source file, which contains this expression, and the user defined functions. After analyizing them it makes some type deduction and generates the final computational graph.

Programming at a lower abstraction level, the D-Box pre-compiler (see Appendix A.3) can read and analyze D-Box definitions. At this level the computational graph is described directly.

The pre-compilers generate the source code for the computational nodes, and the source code for the channels one-by-one. The source code patterns come from a skeleton library shipped with the pre-compiler, which parameterize them with the actual types and expressions. To compile these source codes a Clean compiler, a C++ compiler and a C# compiler (and the linkers) are required.

Every distributed application needs a distributed environment to work within. To store, start, and support a complete D-Clean project, a special environment was build (see Appendix A.4).

The package can be downloaded and installed from the project homepage, from `http://dragon.ektf.hu/dclean`.

6   Related Works

- PMLS and GpH are implicit parallel extensions of ML and Haskell respectively [15], but instead, D-Clean uses explicit coordination structures.

    Opposed to skeleton based languages, D-Clean is designed to implement skeletons of distributed functional computations in the language itself.
- Eden [16,14] extends Haskell to explicitly define parallel computation. An Eden program consists of processes and uses communication channels, and the programmer has explicit control over the communication topology. The execution is based on the GHC implementation of concurrency, the runtime system controls sending and receiving messages, process placements and data distribution. On the other hand, the middleware supporting the implementation of D-Clean and D-Box languages is not language specific,

components developed using other languages can be integrated into easily distributed applications.
- Nimo [3] is a visual functional dataflow language, supporting process networks. Nimo allows totally graphic programming only, while D-Clean and D-Box programs can also be expressed in textual code form. Nodes in Nimo are restricted to a fixed set of primitive operations of the Haskell prelude while in D-Clean nodes Clean expressions are allowed in order to achieve the full power of functional programming at node level. Nimo does not support distributed computing, only concurrent execution is supported.
- JoCaml is an extension of Objective Caml with primitives for network-transparent distributed and mobile programming [6] based on the join-calculus model instead of a pure data flow approach. Advanced discussion and survey of the dataflow languages can be found in [12]. Data oriented skeletons (like the farm skeleton) can be implemented using primitives which are quite similar to the primitives of dataflow languages.

7   Conclusion

The examples of this paper provide a set of distributed algorithmic skeletons. They are implemented as D-Clean schemes based on coordination primitives. They describe in a general way common algorithmic skeletons parameterized by functions and data. The computational skeletons are identified and described by compositions of coordination primitives. The computation is distributed over a network of computation nodes according to the description provided by the coordination primitives. The coordination constructs have the role of manipulating and controlling the components written in the functional language Clean, which however express the pure computational aspects. The D-Clean code is compiled into D-Box expressions. Here we have provided several examples of the application of D-Box expressions.

The presented set of schemes implemented in D-Clean and in D-Box illustrates the applicability and composibility of the previously introduced language elements. The set of schemes are suitable for the designing of complex distributed computational skeletons.

References

1. Berthold, J., Klusik, U., Loogen, R., Priebe, S., Weskamp, N.: High-level Process Control in Eden, In: Kosch, H., Böszörményi L., Hellwagner, H. (Eds.): *Parallel Processing, 9th International Euro-Par Conference, Euro-Par 2003*, Proceedings, Klagenfurt, Austria, August 26-29, 2003, Springer Verlag, LNCS Vol. 2790, pp. 732-741.
2. Best, E., Hopkins, R. P.: B(PN)^2 - a Basic Petri Net Programming Notation, In: Bode, A., Reeve, M., Wolf, G. (Eds.): *Parallel Architectures and Languages Europe, 5th International PARLE Conference, PARLE'93*, Proceedings, Munich, Germany, June 14-17, 1993, Springer Verlag, LNCS Vol. 694, pp. 379-390.
3. Clerici, S., Zoltan, C.: A Graphic Functional-Dataflow Language, In: Loidl, H.W. (Ed.): *Proceedings of the Fifth Symposium on Trends in Functional Programming*, München, 25-26 November, 2004, pp. 345-359.

4. Danelutto, M., Di Cosmo, R., Leroy, X., Pelagatti, S.: Parallel Functional Programming with Skeletons: the OCAMLP3L experiment, *Proceedings of the ACM Sigplan Workshop on ML*, Baltimore, USA, September 1998, pp. 31-39.
5. Dezső B.: *D-Box Developer Environment*, Project work documentation, Department of Programming Languages and Compilers, University Eötvös L., Budapest, Hungary, 2005.
6. Fournet, C., Le Fessant, F., Maranget, L., Schmitt, A.: JoCaml: A Language for Concurrent Distributed and Mobile Programming, In: Johan Jeuring, Simon Peyton Jones (Eds): *Advanced Functional Programming*, 4th International School, AFP 2002, Oxford, Revised Lectures, , 2003, Springer, LNCS 2638, pp. 129-158.
7. Hammond, K., Michaelson, G. (Eds.): *Research Directions in Parallel Functional Programming*, Springer Verlag, 1999.
8. Hammond, K., Portillo, A. J. R.: Haskel: Algorithmic Skeletons in Haskell, In: Koopman, P.; Clack, C. (Eds.): *Implementation of Functional Languages 11th International Workshop IFL'99*, Lochem, The Netherlands, September 7-10, 1999, Selected Papers, 2000, Springer Verlag, LNCS Vol. 1868, pp. 181-198.
9. Hernyák Z., Horváth Z., Zsók V.: Clean-CORBA Interface Supporting Skeletons, In: *Proceedings of the 6th International Conference on Applied Informatics*, Eger, Hungary, January 27-31, 2004, Vol. 1, pp. 191-200.
10. Horváth Z., Hernyák Z, Zsók V.: Coordination Language for Distributed Clean, *Acta Cybernetica* 17 (2005), 247-271.
11. Horváth Z., Zsók V., Serrarens, P., Plasmeijer, R.: Parallel Elementwise Processable Functions in Concurrent Clean, *Mathematical and Computer Modelling* 38, Pergamon, 2003, pp. 865-875.
12. Johnston, W.M., Hanna, J.R.P., Millar, R.J.: Advances in dataflow programming languages, *ACM Computing Surveys* 36 (1), ACM Press, March 2004, pp. 1-34.
13. Kesseler, M.H.G.: *The Implementation of Functional Languages on Parallel Machines with Distributed Memory*, PhD Thesis, Catholic University of Nijmegen, 1996.
14. Loidl, H-W., Klusik, U., Hammond, K., Loogen, R., Trinder, P.W.: GpH and Eden: Comparing Two Parallel Functional Languages on a Beowulf Cluster, In: Gilmore, S. (Ed.): *Trends in Functional Programming*, Vol. 2, Intellect, 2001, pp. 39-52.
15. Loidl, H-W., Rubio, F., Scaife, N., Hammond, K., Horiguchi, S., Klusik, U., Loogen, R., Michaelson, G.J., Peña, R., Priebe, S. , Rebón Portillo, Á.J., Trinder, P.W.: Comparing Parallel Functional Languages: Programming and Performance, *Higher-Order and Symbolic Computation* 16 (3), Kluwer Academic Publisher, September 2003, pp. 203-251.
16. Peña, R, Rubio, F., Segura, C.: Deriving Non-Hierarchical Process Topologies, In: Hammond, K., Curtis, S.: *Trends in Functional Programming*, Vol 3., Intellect, 2002, pp. 51-62.
17. Plasmeijer, R., van Eekelen, M.: *Concurrent Clean Version 2.0 Language Report*, 2001, http://www.cs.kun.nl/~clean/Manuals/manuals.html.
18. Rabhi, F.A., Gorlatch, S. (Eds.): *Patterns and Skeletons for Parallel and Distributed Computing*, Springer Verlag, 2002.
19. Rauber Du Bois, A., Tinder, P., Loidl, H.W.: *Towards Mobility Skeletons*, 2004
20. Serrarens, P.R.: *Communication Issues in Distributed Functional Computing*, PhD Thesis, Catholic University of Nijmegen, January 2001.
21. Zsók V., Horváth Z., Varga Z.: Functional Programs on Clusters In: Striegnitz, Jörg; Davis, Kei (Eds.): *Proceedings of the Workshop on Parallel/High-Performance Object-Oriented Scientific Computing (POOSC'03)*, Interner Bericht FZJ-ZAM-IB-2003-09, July 2003, pp. 93-100.

A Appendix

A.1 The D-Clean Language Reference

- DStart fun_expr :: aCh* starts the distributed computation.
- DStop fun_expr :: aCh* -> <> receives and saves the result of the computation.
- DApply fun_expr :: aCh* -> aCh* applies the same function expression n times on $n * k$ channels.
- DApply [fun_expr] :: aCh* -> aCh* applies different function expressions on the input channel list.
- DFilter fun_expr :: aCh* -> aCh* filters the elements of the input channels using a boolean function.
- DFilter [fun_expr] :: aCh* -> aCh* filters the elements of the input channels using boolean functions.
- DMap fun_expr :: aCh* -> aCh* applies an elementwise processable function of type a->b on channels.
- DMap [fun_expr] :: aCh* -> aCh* applies a list of elementwise processable function of type [a]->[b].
- DReduce fun_expr :: aCh* -> aCh* applies a function of type [a]->b.
- DReduce [fun_expr] :: aCh* -> aCh* applies a list of functions of type [a]->b.
- DProduce fun_expr :: aCh* -> aCh* applies a function of type a->[b].
- DProduce [fun_expr] :: aCh* -> aCh* applies a list of functions of type a->[b].
- DDivideS fun_expr n :: aCh* -> aCh* splits the input data list into n parts and broadcasts them to n computational nodes.
- DMerge fun_expr :: aCh* -> aCh* collects the input sublists from channels and builds up the output input data list.
- DLinear [fun_expr] :: aCh* -> aCh* simplifies the definition of the pipeline computation graph where the nodes are connected in a linear way.
- DDivideN fun_expr :: aCh* -> aCh* is the dynamic version of the previously introduced DDivideS, where the number of the threads N is calculated at run-time.

A.2 The Pseudo-code of the Protocols

The Pseudo-code of JOIN

The two input protocols are based on the Join function which collects all the data of the given input data streams into one list of lists.

```
Join   :: [ChannelID] -> [Transmissible]
Join [] = []
Join [ch:chs] = [data:remains]
    where
        data    = collectStream ch
        remains = Join chs
```

The `collectStream` collects all the data from one channel. This pseudo code does not deal with the various types of data coming from the different channels, but collects them into one list of lists. The `Join` does nothing special, but collects them into a list of lists.

The Pseudo-code of the Input Protocols

The protocol `join1` is implemented in the following way:

```
data     = Join channel_list
data_1st = data !! 0
data_2nd = data !! 1
result   = expression data_1st data_2nd
```

This shows that after reconstructing the input data elements the list is separated into sub-lists and delivers these to the expression separately. When the protocol is `joink`, this step is not needed because the expression requires the list merged:

```
data     = Join channel_list
result   = expression data
```

The Pseudo-code of SPLIT

The `split` protocol sends a T-type element (see section 3.2) of the list into different channels. The ID-s of the channels are given in a channel-list:

```
Split [Transmissible] [ChannelID] *World -> *World

Split [] _ w = w
Split [data:xs] [c:cs] env = Split xs cs env2
  where env2 = sendStream data c env
```

`sendStream` sends a T-type element into the given channel.

The Pseudo-code of the Output Protocols

Both output protocols (`split1` and `splitk`) are based on the same `Split` function.

Let us suppose the expression produces a tuple of T-type elements. First, a list is constructed containing these elements:

```
(res_0, res_1, ..., res_k) = expression data
result                     = [res_0, res_1, ..., res_k]
w                          = Split result outp_channels w
```

As can be seen, one element of the tuple is sent to one channel of the channel-list. Naturally, the number of elements of the tuple must be the same as the number of the elements of the channel-list.

The `splitk` protocol is almost the same. The difference is that in this case the expression does not yield a tuple but immediately a list of T-type elements:

```
result = expression data // 'result' a list of lists
w      = Split result outp_channels w
```

Then the same happens as in the case of `split`, the elements of `result` go into different channels described by the channel-list.

A.3   The D-Clean and D-Box Pre-compiler

The two compilers are integrated into one executable file called `DCleanComp.exe`. It is a command-line pre-compiler, which must be parameterized by giving arguments in the command-line. `DCleanCom /?` writes the possible command-line parameters.

Normally, the D-Clean compiler generates the source codes for the computational nodes and the channels and generates the `makefile`-s to compile them. These `makefiles` contain the used command line compiler names, paths and parameters. To compile the final executable codes the following will be needed:

- `CleanCompiler.exe` is the command line Clean compiler and is used to compile the computational node source code to the `.abc` form.
- `CodeGenerator.exe` is used to compile the `.abc` form to `.obj` form.
- `cl.exe` a C++ compiler to compile the additional `.CPP` codes (which provides the middleware interface routines to Clean).
- `link.exe` a C++ linker to link these files together.
- `slice2cpp.exe` is part of the I.C.E. middleware system and is used to generate the C++ helper classes from the `.ICE` interface definition (just like CORBA IDL2CPP utility).
- `slice2cs.exe` is part of the I.C.E. middleware system and is used to generate the C# helper classes from the `.ICE` interface definition.
- `csc.exe` is the C# command line compiler and is used to compile the channel's source code to an executable code. The channels are written in C#. This compiler is part of the Microsoft.NET system.

These compilers and linkers use several **include files** and **library files** to complete their job. The names of these files and directories are included in the `LocalSett.xml` file, which must be updated according to the local settings.

The I.C.E. middleware is under the GPL and can be downloaded from http://www.zeroc.com/the Microsoft.NET framework is free and can be downloaded from the Microsoft web page. Clean is also free and can be downloaded from http://www.cs.ru.nl/~clean/ site. Currently, the D-Clean code generator is tested with the C++ compiler and linker shipped into the Microsoft Visual Studio.NET 2003.

Actually, in D-Clean the schemes can be used to describe communication patterns. The scheme files can be put into a scheme library, which is a directory containing the scheme definition files. The path for this directory can be set in this `LocalSett.xml` file as well.

The D-Clean pre-compiler generates a lot of source codes for the computational nodes, the channels, the middleware interfaces and so on. These codes are mainly pre-written and are called skeletons. These skeletons must be actualized according to the actual types and other parameters. These skeleton files come with the D-Clean pre-compiler and are stored in a directory. The path of this directory must also be set in the `LocalSett.xml` file.

The second configuration file `DCleanConf.xml` is shipped into the skeleton package, containing the description of file types, file names and the role of the file. This file usually does not need to be updated because the file paths are relative to the skeleton directories given in the `LocalSett.xml` file.

These setting files are usually stored beside the `DCleanComp.exe`. If you want to use other setting files or if these files are not in the same directory, you may specify these file names.

The -L option is used to define the `LocalSett.XML` file path and name:

```
DCLeanComp -L C:\mySettings\MyLocalSett.XML
```

The -C is used to define the skeleton package settings:

```
DCLeanComp -C C:\mySettings\MySkelPackages.XML
```

The Project Name

Multiple computational graphs can be run on a cluster at the same time with the same box ID's and channel ID's, and another parameter is needed to indicate the difference between them. The project name must be unique and is coded into the source codes, so it must be set during the compilation with the -P option:

```
DCLeanComp -P myProject
```

If a project name is not defined, a random generated list of characters is used.

The D-Clean Pre-compiler

When a D-Clean expression is to be compiled, all the user-defined functions and types have to be written into an .icl file. This .icl file is a standard main .icl file, containing an `import` list as well, but instead of a `Start` expression, it must contain a `DistrStart` expression.

```
DCLeanComp myProg.icl
```

This will read this .icl file and will generate the necessary source code files into the `.\GENERATED` directory. If you want to put them into another directory you must specify the target directory after the -T option:

```
DCLeanComp myProg.icl -T c:\myTarget
```

If you want to see the D-Box definitions, you must set the file name where they are written. This file name must have the `.box` filename-extension:

```
DCLeanComp myProg.icl myProg.box
```

If you do not want to generate the source codes but just the D-Box definition, you must specify the -BOX option:

```
DCLeanComp myProg.icl myProg.box -BOX
```

The D-Box Pre-compiler

To use the pre-compiler to work from the D-Box definition directly instead of the `DistrStart` expression you must specify the input D-Box file, the input .icl file with the user defined functions and types. The required additional parameter is the `WDBOX` command-line parameter.

```
DCLeanComp myProg.box myProg.icl -WDBOX
```

In this case the `myProg.icl` may contain a `DistrStart` expression but will be ignored.

Compiling the Generated Project

The source code is generated into the `.\GENERATED` directory or the specified target directory. This directory contains a platform directory (actually it is `WIN_ICE`), which means that the generated code will run on Microsoft Windows operating system using the I.C.E. middleware. According to the skeleton packages other platforms may be developed and used later.

This platform directory contains other subdirectories. The computational nodes (boxes) are generated into the `BoxID_nnn` directories, which are the same as the box IDs were. The code of the channels is reusable and universal, so there are not so many channel directories as channel IDs. There are as many channel codes as different channel types. These channel codes are in the `Chn_Server_mmm` directories, where `mmm` is the name of the type.

The Middleware-C-Clean interfaces are stored in `Chn_mmm` directories, where `mmm` is the name of the channel type.

The other directories constain code that is shared between the channel servers, the channel interfaces and the computational nodes. To compile a specified code, you must follow this order:

- `Chn_Shared` the shared code between the channel interfaces
- `Chn_mmm` the channel interfaces for all types
- `Box_Shared` the shared code between the computational nodes
- `Box_nnnn` the comp.node codes
- `Chn_Srv_Shared` the shared codes between the channel servers
- `Chn_Srv_mmm` the channel servers for all types

Each directory contains a separate `Makefile` to compile the source codes and generate the object or executable codes. You may modify the codes by hand before compiling them.

If you want to compile all the codes you may use the general `Makefile`, which is located in the root directory of the platform directory.

A.4 The Application Environment

The executable codes must be deployed and started on the computers of the cluster. This requires a kind of application environment. This environment supports the following operations:

- (1) A local part of the environment which provides the minimal operations so that the computer can become part of the cluster environment.
- (2) Storing the executable files for a specified project. This is needed because by default there is no network file system on the Windows platform. This facility acts as a kind of FTP server allowing the system to upload and download files automatically, identified by their project name, by the subGraphID, BoxID, channel type and by other parameters.
- (3) Name servicing to find the components already started.
- (4) A scheduler to find an appropriate idle node to start a new component of the project.
- (5) An optional component for monitoring the events of the environment.

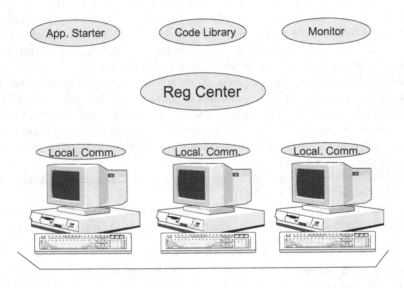

Fig. 24. The structure of the application environment

The special environment is still under development but the basic functionality is ready to test the D-Clean projects on a cluster. This environment consists of several executable files developed in C# using the Microsoft.NET environment and I.C.E. middleware. The components of the environment broadcast messages on the local network to find the other components on other nodes. The used ports are configurable through an attached `config` file, which is a simple text file.

Each component uses the `icecs.DLL` and a `DBroadcasting.dll` file and the `config` file.

The first component called *Local Communicator* must be started on each computer of the cluster to make it capable of downloading and starting a component of a project. This is the `DLocalCommServer.exe`.

The second component is a *Code Library Server*, which is the FTP-like service mentioned before. This functionality is coded into DCodeLibServer.exe.

The third component is the *Name Servicing*, which serves as a registration center. All components send their location to it and can query the others' location. It is coded into DRegCenterServer.exe.

The fourth component is the *Scheduler* which finds the idle nodes through the naming service, asks them for their capacity and then decides where to start the next component (a channel or a computational node). This is coded into the executable DAppStarterServer.exe.

The fifth component is the *Monitoring* service, which acts as a shared console to write the events and other messages of the services and the project components. This component is usually started on the administrator node to see the notes and it also writes all the messages into a log file to analyze the events later. This is coded into DMonitor.exe.

Uploading a Project
Before starting the project on the cluster the components of the application environment must be started. After that, the XAppEnv.exe utility helps to give commands to the environment.

The first step is to upload the generated and compiled executable files to the *Code Library Server*. To automatize this event you can use the generated uploads file, which contains the suitable command line arguments of the XAppEnv utility to finish this step. This can be done by giving this file as a command line parameter to the utility with the following syntax: XAppEnv @uploads. This can also be done by make upload because this is also in the root Makefile.

Starting a Project
After the successful upload the project can be started with the XAppEnv -P <projectname> -START command, where the *projectname* must be given. This step also can be completed by the make start command, because it is also in the root Makefile.

Terminating a Project
The project will stop itself when all the nodes and channels have finished. But when something goes wrong a termination signal must be sent to all the nodes of the cluster.

The command XAppEnv -P <projectname> -KILL sends this signal to stop the project components. This step also can be completed by the make stop command because it is also in the root Makefile.

Result Data Filenames
If the last node saves the data into a disk file, make sure you define this filename. This is because the run-time environment selects the computer to start this last node - the file that will be created on which computers of the cluster. It is not determined which computer this will be on. A shared volume is helpful, which has (for example) the S: label and which can be accessed by all the nodes of the

cluster. If the last node saves the data into this shared volume it is easy to find this file.

If more than one project is running at the same time the names of the result files must be different. The *name of the project* can be used in creating the result file name because each generated computational node source code contains a `projectID` constant function.

```
(openok,outf,tfs) = fopen "S:\\result" +++ projectID +++
    ".txt" FWriteText fs
```

When more than one node saves data files the `boxID` constant function may help to create different file names:

```
(openok,outf,tfs) = fopen "S:\\result_" +++ projectID +++
    "_" +++ boxID +++ ".txt" FWriteText fs
```

A.5   D-Box Graphical Environment

It is possible to design the computational graph by using the D-Box Graphical Environment, which is a Java application. This is a visual development kit. The expressions can be inserted into the boxes and the protocols can be selected from a drop-down list. By adding ports to the boxes the channels can be defined easily.

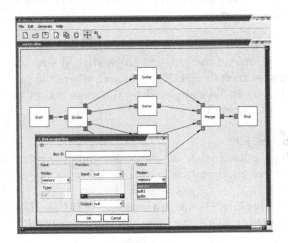

Fig. 25. Using the D-Box Graphical Environment

Author Index

Lecture Notes in Computer Science

For information about Vols. 1–4154

please contact your bookseller or Springer

Vol. 4199: O. Nierstrasz, J. Whittle, D. Harel, G. Reggio (Eds.), Model Driven Engineering Languages and Systems. XVI, 798 pages. 2006.

Vol. 4198: O. Nasraoui, O. Zaiane, M. Spiliopoulou, B. Mobasher, B. Masand, P. Yu (Eds.), Web Minding and Web Usage Analysis. IX, 177 pages. 2006. (Sublibrary LNAI).

Vol. 4197: M. Raubal, H.J. Miller, A.U. Frank, M.F. Goodchild (Eds.), Geographic, Information Science. XIII, 419 pages. 2006.

Vol. 4196: K. Fischer, I.J. Timm, E. André, N. Zhong (Eds.), Multiagent System Technologies. X, 185 pages. 2006. (Sublibrary LNAI).

Vol. 4195: D. Gaiti, G. Pujolle, E. Al-Shaer, K. Calvert, S. Dobson, G. Leduc, O. Martikainen (Eds.), Autonomic Networking. IX, 316 pages. 2006.

Vol. 4194: V.G. Ganzha, E.W. Mayr, E.V. Vorozhtsov (Eds.), Computer Algebra in Scientific Computing. XI, 313 pages. 2006.

Vol. 4193: T.P. Runarsson, H.-G. Beyer, E. Burke, J.J. Merelo-Guervós, L. D. Whitley, X. Yao (Eds.), Parallel Problem Solving from Nature - PPSN IX. XIX, 1061 pages. 2006.

Vol. 4192: B. Mohr, J.L. Träff, J. Worringen, J. Dongarra (Eds.), Recent Advances in Parallel Virtual Machine and Message Passing Interface. XVI, 414 pages. 2006.

Vol. 4191: R. Larsen, M. Nielsen, J. Sporring (Eds.), Medical Image Computing and Computer-Assisted Intervention – MICCAI 2006, Part II. XXXVIII, 981 pages. 2006.

Vol. 4190: R. Larsen, M. Nielsen, J. Sporring (Eds.), Medical Image Computing and Computer-Assisted Intervention – MICCAI 2006, Part I. XXXVVIII, 949 pages. 2006.

Vol. 4189: D. Gollmann, J. Meier, A. Sabelfeld (Eds.), Computer Security – ESORICS 2006. XI, 548 pages. 2006.

Vol. 4188: P. Sojka, I. Kopeček, K. Pala (Eds.), Text, Speech and Dialogue. XIV, 721 pages. 2006. (Sublibrary LNAI).

Vol. 4187: J.J. Alferes, J. Bailey, W. May, U. Schwertel (Eds.), Principles and Practice of Semantic Web Reasoning. XI, 277 pages. 2006.

Vol. 4186: C. Jesshope, C. Egan (Eds.), Advances in Computer Systems Architecture. XIV, 605 pages. 2006.

Vol. 4185: R. Mizoguchi, Z. Shi, F. Giunchiglia (Eds.), The Semantic Web – ASWC 2006. XX, 778 pages. 2006.

Vol. 4184: M. Bravetti, M. Núñez, G. Zavattaro (Eds.), Web Services and Formal Methods. X, 289 pages. 2006.

Vol. 4183: J. Euzenat, J. Domingue (Eds.), Artificial Intelligence: Methodology, Systems, and Applications. XIII, 291 pages. 2006. (Sublibrary LNAI).

Vol. 4182: H.T. Ng, M.-K. Leong, M.-Y. Kan, D. Ji (Eds.), Information Retrieval Technology. XVI, 684 pages. 2006.

Vol. 4180: M. Kohlhase, OMDoc – An Open Markup Format for Mathematical Documents [version 1.2]. XIX, 428 pages. 2006. (Sublibrary LNAI).

Vol. 4179: J. Blanc-Talon, W. Philips, D. Popescu, P. Scheunders (Eds.), Advanced Concepts for Intelligent Vision Systems. XXIV, 1224 pages. 2006.

Vol. 4178: A. Corradini, H. Ehrig, U. Montanari, L. Ribeiro, G. Rozenberg (Eds.), Graph Transformations. XII, 473 pages. 2006.

Vol. 4177: R. Marín, E. Onaindía, A. Bugarín, J. Santos (Eds.), Current Topics in Artificial Intelligence. XV, 482 pages. 2006. (Sublibrary LNAI).

Vol. 4176: S.K. Katsikas, J. Lopez, M. Backes, S. Gritzalis, B. Preneel (Eds.), Information Security. XIV, 548 pages. 2006.

Vol. 4175: P. Bücher, B.M.E. Moret (Eds.), Algorithms in Bioinformatics. XII, 402 pages. 2006. (Sublibrary LNBI).

Vol. 4174: K. Franke, K.-R. Müller, B. Nickolay, R. Schäfer (Eds.), Pattern Recognition. XX, 773 pages. 2006.

Vol. 4173: S. El Yacoubi, B. Chopard, S. Bandini (Eds.), Cellular Automata. XV, 734 pages. 2006.

Vol. 4172: J. Gonzalo, C. Thanos, M. F. Verdejo, R.C. Carrasco (Eds.), Research and Advanced Technology for Digital Libraries. XVII, 569 pages. 2006.

Vol. 4169: H.L. Bodlaender, M.A. Langston (Eds.), Parameterized and Exact Computation. XI, 279 pages. 2006.

Vol. 4168: Y. Azar, T. Erlebach (Eds.), Algorithms – ESA 2006. XVIII, 843 pages. 2006.

Vol. 4167: S. Dolev (Ed.), Distributed Computing. XV, 576 pages. 2006.

Vol. 4166: J. Górski (Ed.), Computer Safety, Reliability, and Security. XIV, 440 pages. 2006.

Vol. 4165: W. Jonker, M. Petković (Eds.), Secure, Data Management. X, 185 pages. 2006.

Vol. 4164: Z. Horváth (Ed.), Central European Functional Programming School. VII, 257 pages. 2006.

Vol. 4163: H. Bersini, J. Carneiro (Eds.), Artificial Immune Systems. XII, 460 pages. 2006.

Vol. 4162: R. Královič, P. Urzyczyn (Eds.), Mathematical Foundations of Computer Science 2006. XV, 814 pages. 2006.

Vol. 4161: R. Harper, M. Rauterberg, M. Combetto (Eds.), Entertainment Computing - ICEC 2006. XXVII, 417 pages. 2006.

Vol. 4160: M. Fisher, W.v.d. Hoek, B. Konev, A. Lisitsa (Eds.), Logics in Artificial Intelligence. XII, 516 pages. 2006. (Sublibrary LNAI).

Vol. 4159: J. Ma, H. Jin, L.T. Yang, J.J.-P. Tsai (Eds.), Ubiquitous Intelligence and Computing. XXII, 1190 pages. 2006.

Vol. 4158: L.T. Yang, H. Jin, J. Ma, T. Ungerer (Eds.), Autonomic and Trusted Computing. XIV, 613 pages. 2006.

Vol. 4156: S. Amer-Yahia, Z. Bellahsène, E. Hunt, R. Unland, J.X. Yu (Eds.), Database and XML Technologies. IX, 123 pages. 2006.

Vol. 4155: O. Stock, M. Schaerf (Eds.), Reasoning, Action and Interaction in AI Theories and Systems. XVIII, 343 pages. 2006. (Sublibrary LNAI).